DRAFT COMPREHENSIVE CONSERVATION PLAN
AND ENVIRONMENTAL ASSESSMENT

BAYOU SAUVAGE NATIONAL WILDLIFE REFUGE

ORLEANS PARISH, LOUISIANA

U.S. Department of the Interior
Fish and Wildlife Service

Southeast Region
Atlanta, Georgia

March 2009

TABLE OF CONTENTS

SECTION A. DRAFT COMPREHENSIVE CONSERVATION PLAN

I. BACKGROUND 1

    Introduction 1
    Purpose And Need For The Plan 1
    Fish and Wildlife Service 1
    National Wildlife Refuge System 2
    Legal and Policy Context 4
    National and International Conservation Plans and Initiatives 5
    Relationship To State Wildlife Agency 6
    Relationship to the Louisiana Department of Wildlife and Fisheries 6

II. REFUGE OVERVIEW 9

    Introduction 9
    Refuge History and Purpose 9
    Special Designations 11
    Ecosystem Context 11
    Regional Conservation Plans and Initiatives 12
    Ecological Threats and Problems 14
        Alterations to Hydrology 14
        Climate Change 14
        Urbanization 15
        Proliferation of Invasive Plants and Animals 15
    Physical Resources 15
        Climate 15
        Geology and Topography 17
        Soils 18
        Hydrology and Water Quality and Quantity 18
        Air Quality 19
    Biological Resources 20
        Habitat 20
        Wildlife 23
    Cultural Resources 27
    Socioeconomic Environment 28
    Refuge Administration and Management 30
        Land Protection and Conservation 30
        Visitor Services 30
        Personnel, Operations, and Maintenance 35

III. PLAN DEVELOPMENT 37

    Summary of Issues, Concerns, and Opportunities 37
        Fish and Wildlife Population Management 37
        Habitat Management 38
        Resource Protection 40
        Visitor Services 41
        Refuge Administration 42

IV. MANAGEMENT DIRECTION 43

Introduction 43
Vision 43
Goals, Objectives, and Strategies 44
    Fish and Wildlife Population Management 44
    Habitat Management 46
    Visitor Services 49
    Refuge Administration 54

V. PLAN IMPLEMENTATION 57

Introduction 57
Proposed Projects 57
    Fish And Wildlife Population Management 57
    Habitat Management 58
    Resource Protection and Refuge Administration 63
    Visitor Services 64
Funding and Personnel 67
Partnership/Volunteer Opportunities 71
Step-Down Management Plans 72
Monitoring and Adaptive Management 72
Plan Review and Revision 73

SECTION B. ENVIRONMENTAL ASSESSMENT

I. BACKGROUND 75

Introduction 75
Purpose and Need for Action 75
Decision Framework 76
Planning Study Area 76
Authority, Legal Compliance, and Compatibility 76
    Compatibility 76
Public Involvement and the Planning Process 77

II. AFFECTED ENVIRONMENT 79

III. DESCRIPTION OF ALTERNATIVES 81

Formulation of Alternatives 81
Description of Alternatives 81
    Alternative A: Current Management (No Action) 81
    Alternative B: Restore and Improve Ecological diversity and Augment Visitor Services
    (Proposed Alternative) 82
    Alternative C: Custodial Management, While Maximizing Visitor Services 83
Features Common to all Alternatives 84
Comparison of the Alternatives by Issue 85
Alternatives Considered But Eliminated From Further Analysis 107

IV. ENVIRONMENTAL CONSEQUENCES 109

Overview 109
Effects Common to All Alternatives 109
    Environmental Justice 109

Climate Change 109
Other Management 110
Land Acquisition..110
Cultural Resources..110
Refuge Revenue-Sharing..111
Other Effects 111
Summary of Effects by Alternative 111
Alternative A (Current management--No Action) 111
Alternative B (Proposed Action – Restore and Improve Ecological Diversity and Augment
Visitor Services) 112
Alternative C (Custodial Management, While Maximizing Visitor Services) 112
Unavoidable Impacts and Mitigation Measures...119
Water Quality Impacts from Soil Disturbance and use of herbicides 119
Wildlife Disturbance 119
Vegetation Disturbance 120
User Group Conflicts 120
Effects on Adjacent Landowners...120
Cumulative Impacts 120
Direct and Indirect Effects or Impacts...121
Short-term Impacts Versus Long-term Productivity 121

V. CONSULTATION AND COORDINATION..123
Overview..123

SECTION C. APPENDICES

APPENDIX A. GLOSSARY...125

APPENDIX B. REFERENCES AND LITERATURE CITATIONS...135

APPENDIX C. RELEVANT LEGAL MANDATES AND EXECUTIVE ORDERS 139

APPENDIX D. PUBLIC INVOLVEMENT 153
Summary Of Public Scoping Comments 153

APPENDIX E. APPROPRIATE USE DETERMINATIONS 155

APPENDIX F. COMPATIBILITY DETERMINATIONS 165

APPENDIX G. INTRA-SERVICE SECTION 7 BIOLOGICAL EVALUATION................................181

APPENDIX H. WILDERNESS REVIEW 185

APPENDIX I. REFUGE BIOTA..187

APPENDIX J. BUDGET REQUESTS 189
Refuge Operating Needs System (RONS) 189
Maintenance Management System Needs...190

APPENDIX K. LIST OF PREPARERS...191

LIST OF FIGURES

Figure 1. Location of Bayou Sauvage NWR in relation to regional conservation area 7
Figure 2. Current and acquisition boundaries of Bayou Sauvage NWR 10
Figure 3. General habitat types on Bayou Sauvage NWR 22
Figure 4. Impacts of Hurricane Katrina on Bayou Sauvage NWR 24
Figure 5. Location of public use areas on Bayou Sauvage NWR 34
Figure 6. Current staffing chart for Bayou Sauvage NWR and Southeast Louisiana
NWR Complex 68
Figure 7. Proposed staffing chart for Bayou Sauvage NWR 69

LIST OF TABLES

Table 1. Air quality statistics around Bayou Sauvage NWR 20
Table 2. Habitat types and associated acreages found on Bayou Sauvage NWR 21
Table 3. Socioeconomic profile - U.S. Census, 2005 American Community Survey 29
Table 4. Summary of projects 70
Table 5. Bayou Sauvage NWR step-down management plans related to the goals and
objectives of the CCP 72
Table 6. Comparison of alternatives by management issues for Bayou Sauvage NWR 85
Table 7. Summary of environmental effects by alternatives, Bayou Sauvage NWR 114

I. Background

INTRODUCTION

This Draft Comprehensive Conservation Plan and Environmental Assessment (Draft CCP/EA) for Bayou Sauvage National Wildlife Refuge (NWR) was prepared to guide management actions and direction for the refuge. Fish and wildlife conservation will receive first priority in refuge management. Wildlife-dependent recreation will be allowed and encouraged as long as it is compatible with, and does not detract from, the mission of the refuge or the purposes for which it was established.

A planning team developed a range of alternatives that best meet the goals and objectives of the refuge and could be implemented within the 15-year planning period. This Draft CCP/EA describes the Fish and Wildlife Service's proposed plan, as well as other alternatives considered and their effects on the environment. The Draft CCP/EA will be made available to state and federal government agencies, conservation partners, and the general public for review and comment. Comments from each entity will be considered in the development of the Final CCP.

PURPOSE AND NEED FOR THE PLAN

The purpose of the Draft CCP/EA is to develop a proposed action that best achieves the refuge purpose; attains the vision and goals developed for the refuge; contributes to the National Wildlife Refuge System (Refuge System) mission; addresses key problems, issues and relevant mandates; and is consistent with sound principles of fish and wildlife management.

Specifically, the plan is needed to:

- Provide a clear statement of refuge management direction;
- Provide refuge neighbors, visitors, and government officials with an understanding of Service management actions on and around the refuge;
- Ensure that Service management actions, including land protection and recreation/education programs, are consistent with the mandates of the Refuge System; and
- Provide a basis for the development of budget requests for operations, maintenance, and capital improvement needs.

FISH AND WILDLIFE SERVICE

The Fish and Wildlife Service (Service) traces its roots to 1871, with the establishment of the Commission of Fisheries which was involved with research and the culturing of fish. This once independent commission was renamed the Bureau of Fisheries and placed under the Department of Commerce and Labor in 1903.

The Service also traces its roots to 1886 with the establishment of a Division of Economic Ornithology and Mammalogy in the Department of Agriculture. In 1896, with a shift from research pertaining to the relationship of birds and animals to agriculture to the delineation of the range of plants and animals, the name was changed to the Division of the Biological Survey.

On June 30, 1940, the Department of Commerce, Bureau of Fisheries, was combined with the Department of Agriculture, Bureau of Biological Survey, and transferred to the Department of the Interior as the Fish and Wildlife Service. The name was changed to the Bureau of Sport Fisheries and Wildlife in 1956 and finally to the Fish and Wildlife Service in 1974.

The Service, working with others, is responsible for conserving, protecting, and enhancing fish and wildlife along with their habitats for the continuing benefit of the American people through federal programs relating to migratory birds, endangered species, interjurisdictional fish and marine mammals, and inland sport fisheries (142 DM 1.1).

As part of its mission, the Service manages more than 540 national wildlife refuges, covering over 95 million acres. These areas comprise the National Wildlife Refuge System, the world's largest collection of lands set aside specifically for fish and wildlife. The majority of these lands, 77 million acres, is in Alaska. The remaining acres are spread across the other 49 states and several United States territories. In addition to refuges, the Service manages thousands of small wetlands, national fish hatcheries, 64 fishery resource offices, and 78 ecological services field stations. The Service enforces federal wildlife laws, administers the Endangered Species Act, manages migratory bird populations, restores nationally significant fisheries, conserves and restores wildlife habitat, and helps foreign governments with their conservation efforts. It also oversees the Federal Aid program, which distributes hundreds of millions of dollars collected from excise taxes from the sale of fishing and hunting equipment to state fish and wildlife agencies.

NATIONAL WILDLIFE REFUGE SYSTEM

The mission of the National Wildlife Refuge System, as defined by the National Wildlife Refuge System Improvement Act of 1997 is:

> "...to administer a national network of lands and waters for the conservation, management, and where appropriate, restoration of the fish, wildlife and plant resources and their habitats within the United States for the benefit of present and future generations of Americans."

The National Wildlife Refuge System Improvement Act of 1997 (Improvement Act) established, for the first time, a clear legislative mission of wildlife conservation for the Refuge System. Actions were initiated in 1997 to comply with the direction of this new legislation, including an effort to complete comprehensive conservation plans for all refuges. These plans, which are completed with full public involvement, help guide the future management of refuges by establishing natural resources and recreation/education programs. Consistent with the Improvement Act, approved plans will serve as guidelines for refuge management for the next 15 years. The Improvement Act states that each refuge shall be managed to:

- Fulfill the mission of the Refuge System;
- Fulfill the individual purposes of each refuge;
- Consider the needs of wildlife first;
- Fulfill requirements of comprehensive conservation plans that are prepared for each unit of the Refuge System;
- Maintain the biological integrity, diversity, and environmental health of the Refuge System; and

- Recognize that wildlife-dependent recreation activities including hunting, fishing, wildlife observation, wildlife photography, and environmental education and interpretation are legitimate and priority public uses; and allow refuge managers authority to determine compatible public uses.

The following are just a few examples of the national network of conservation lands. Pelican Island National Wildlife Refuge, the first refuge, was established in 1903 for the protection of colonial nesting birds, such as the snowy egret and the brown pelican in the State of Florida. As a result of over-hunting, competition with cattle, and natural disasters, western refuges were established for species such as the American bison (1906), elk (1912), prong-horned antelope (1931), and desert bighorn sheep (1936). The drought conditions of the 1930s Dust Bowl severely depleted breeding populations of ducks and geese. Refuges established during the Great Depression focused on waterfowl production areas (i.e., protection of prairie wetlands in America's heartland). The emphasis on waterfowl continues today but it now includes protection of wintering habitat in response to a dramatic loss of bottomland hardwoods. By 1973, the Service had begun to focus on establishing refuges for endangered species.

Approximately 38 million people visited national wildlife refuges in 2002, most to observe wildlife in its natural habitats. As the number of visitors grows, there are significant economic benefits to local communities. In 2001, 82 million people 16 years of age and older fished, hunted, or observed wildlife, generating $108 billion in revenue. In 1995 a study was initiated on 15 refuges in an attempt to glean information pertaining to refuge visitation. The refuges in the study were Chincoteague (Virginia); National Elk (Wyoming); Crab Orchard (Illinois); Eufaula (Alabama); Charles M. Russell (Montana); Umatilla (Oregon); Quivira (Kansas); Mattamuskeet (North Carolina); Upper Souris (North Dakota); San Francisco Bay (California); Laguna Atacosa (Texas); Horicon (Wisconsin); Las Vegas (Nevada); Tule Lake (California); and Tensas River (Louisiana). The study, which concluded in 2002, revealed that visitation had grown 36 percent in that seven-year-period. At the same time, the number of jobs generated in surrounding communities as a result of refuge visitation grew from 87 to 120. More than $2.2 million were pumped into local economies. Other findings also validate the theory that communities near refuges benefit economically from the presence of the refuge. Expenditures on food, lodging, and transportation grew from $5.2 million to $6.8 million per refuge; a 31 percent increase during the study period. For each dollar spent on the Refuge System, surrounding communities benefited with a gain of $4.43 in recreation expenditures and $1.42 in job-related income (Caudill and Laughland, unpubl. data).

Volunteers continue to be a major contributor to the success of the Refuge System. In 2002, volunteers contributed more than 1.5 million man hours on refuges nationwide, a service valued at more than $22 million.

The wildlife and habitat vision for national wildlife refuges stresses that wildlife comes first; that ecosystems, biodiversity, and wilderness are vital concepts in refuge management; that refuges must be healthy and growth must be strategic; and that the Refuge System serves as a model for habitat management with broad participation from others.

The Improvement Act stipulates that comprehensive conservation plans be prepared in consultation with adjoining federal, state, and private landowners and that the Service develop and implement a process to ensure an opportunity for active public involvement in the preparation and revision (every 15 years) of the plans.

All lands of the Refuge System will be managed in accordance with an approved comprehensive conservation plan that will guide management decisions and set forth strategies for achieving refuge unit purposes. The plan will be consistent with sound resource management principles, practices, and legal mandates, including Service compatibility standards and other Service policies, guidelines, and planning documents (602 FW 1.1).

LEGAL AND POLICY CONTEXT

Legal Mandates, Administrative and Policy Guidelines, and Other Special Considerations

Administration of national wildlife refuges is guided by the mission and goals of the Refuge System, congressional legislation, presidential executive orders, and international treaties. Policies for management options of refuges are further refined by administrative guidelines established by the Secretary of the Interior and by policy guidelines established by the Director of the Fish and Wildlife Service. Select legal summaries of treaties and laws relevant to administration of the Refuge System and management of the Bayou Sauvage NWR are provided in Appendix C.

Treaties, laws, administrative guidelines, and policy guidelines assist the refuge manager in making decisions pertaining to soil, water, air, flora, fauna, and other natural resources; historical and cultural resources; and research and recreation on refuge lands. They also provide a framework for cooperation between Bayou Sauvage NWR and other partners, such as the Louisiana Department of Wildlife and Fisheries (LDWF), National Park Service (NPS), Audubon Society, Friends of Louisiana Wildlife Refuges, corporations, and private landowners, etc.

Lands within the Refuge System are closed to public use unless specifically and legally opened. No refuge use may be allowed unless it is determined to be appropriate and compatible. The refuge manager determines if a use is appropriate based on sound professional judgment; uses that are illegal, inconsistent with existing policy, or unsafe may not be found appropriate. When a use is determined to be appropriate, it must then be determined to be compatible before it is allowed on a refuge. A compatible use is one that, in the sound professional judgment of the refuge manager, will not materially interfere with or detract from the fulfillment of the mission of the Refuge System or the purposes of the refuge. All programs and uses must be evaluated based on mandates set forth in the Improvement Act. Those mandates are to:

- Contribute to ecosystem goals, as well as refuge purposes and goals;
- Conserve, manage, and restore fish, wildlife, and plant resources and their habitats;
- Monitor the trends of fish, wildlife, and plants;
- Manage and ensure appropriate visitor uses as those uses benefit the conservation of fish and wildlife resources and contribute to the enjoyment of the public; and
- Ensure that visitor activities are compatible with refuge purposes.

The Improvement Act further identifies six priority wildlife-dependent recreational uses. These uses are: hunting, fishing, wildlife observation, wildlife photography, and environmental education and interpretation. As priority public uses of the Refuge System, they receive priority consideration over other public uses in planning and management.

Biological Integrity, Diversity, and Environmental Health Policy

The Improvement Act directs the Service to ensure that the biological integrity, diversity, and environmental health of the Refuge System are maintained for the benefit of present and future generations of Americans. This policy is an additional directive for refuge managers to follow while achieving refuge purpose(s) and the Refuge System mission. It provides for consideration and protection of the broad spectrum of fish, wildlife, and habitat resources found on refuges and associated ecosystems. When evaluating the appropriate management direction for refuges, refuge managers will use sound professional judgment to determine their refuges' contribution to biological integrity, diversity, and environmental health at multiple landscape scales. Sound professional judgment incorporates field experience, knowledge of refuge resources, refuge role within an ecosystem, applicable laws, and best available science, including consultation with others both inside and outside the Service.

NATIONAL AND INTERNATIONAL CONSERVATION PLANS AND INITIATIVES

Multiple partnerships have been developed among government and private entities to address the environmental problems affecting regions. There is a large amount of conservation and protection information that defines the role of the refuge at the local, national, international, and ecosystem levels. Conservation initiatives include broad-scale planning and cooperation between affected parties to address declining trends of natural, physical, social, and economic environments. The conservation guidance described below, along with issues, problems, and trends, was reviewed and integrated where appropriate into this Draft CCP/EA.

This Draft CCP/EA supports, among others, the Partners-in-Flight Plan, the North American Waterfowl Management Plan, the Western Hemisphere Shorebird Reserve Network, and the National Wetlands Priority Conservation Plan.

North American Bird Conservation Initiative. Started in 1999, the North American Bird Conservation Initiative is a coalition of government agencies, private organizations, academic institutions, and private industry leaders in the United States, Canada, and Mexico, working to ensure the long-term health of North America's native bird populations by fostering an integrated approach to bird conservation to benefit all birds in all habitats. The four international and national bird initiatives include the North American Waterfowl Management Plan, Partners-in-Flight, Waterbird Conservation for the Americas, and the U.S. Shorebird Conservation Plan.

North American Waterfowl Management Plan. The North American Waterfowl Management Plan is an international action plan to conserve migratory birds throughout the continent. The plan's goal is to return waterfowl populations to their 1970s levels by conserving wetland and upland habitat. Canada and the United States signed the plan in 1986 in reaction to critically low numbers of waterfowl. Mexico joined in 1994, making it a truly continental effort. The plan is a partnership of federal, provincial/state and municipal governments, non-governmental organizations, private companies, and many individuals, all working towards achieving better wetland habitat for the benefit of migratory birds, other wetland-associated species and people. Plan projects are international in scope, but implemented at regional levels. These projects contribute to the protection of habitat and wildlife species across the North American landscape.

Partners-in-Flight Bird Conservation Plan. Managed as part of the Partners-in-Flight Plan, the Lower Mississippi River Ecosystem (LMRE) physiographic area represents a scientifically based land bird conservation planning effort that ensures long-term maintenance of healthy populations of native land birds, primarily non-game land birds. Non-game land birds have been vastly under-represented in conservation efforts, and many are exhibiting significant declines. This plan is voluntary and non-regulatory, and focuses on relatively common species in areas where conservation actions can be most effective, rather than the frequent local emphasis on rare and peripheral populations.

U.S. Shorebird Conservation Plan. The U.S. Shorebird Conservation Plan is a partnership effort throughout the United States to ensure that stable and self-sustaining populations of shorebird species are restored and protected. The plan was developed by a wide range of agencies, organizations, and shorebird experts for separate regions of the country, and identifies conservation goals, critical habitat conservation needs, key research needs, and proposed education and outreach programs to increase awareness of shorebirds and the threats they face.

Northern American Waterbird Conservation Plan. This plan provides a framework for the conservation and management of 210 species of waterbirds in 29 nations. Threats to waterbird populations include destruction of inland and coastal wetlands, introduced predators and invasive species, pollutants, mortality from fisheries and industries, disturbance, and conflicts arising from abundant species. Particularly important habitats of the southeast region include pelagic areas, marshes, forested wetlands, and barrier and sea island complexes. Fifteen species of waterbirds are federally listed, including breeding populations of wood storks, Mississippi sandhill cranes, whooping cranes, interior least terns, and Gulf Coast populations of brown pelicans. A key objective of this plan is the standardization of data collection efforts to better recommend effective conservation measures.

RELATIONSHIP TO STATE WILDLIFE AGENCY

A provision of the Improvement Act and subsequent agency policy is that the Service shall ensure timely and effective cooperation and collaboration with other state fish and game agencies and tribal governments during the course of acquiring and managing refuges. State wildlife management areas and national wildlife refuges provide the foundation for the protection of species, and contribute to the overall health and sustainment of fish and wildlife species in the State of Louisiana. Bayou Sauvage NWR is located in a region which includes several other state and federal conservation areas (Figure 1).

RELATIONSHIP TO THE LOUISIANA DEPARTMENT OF WILDLIFE AND FISHERIES

The Louisiana Department of Wildlife and Fisheries (LDWF) (http://www.wlf.louisiana.gov) is vested with responsibility for the conservation and management of wildlife in the state, including aquatic life, and is authorized to execute the laws enacted for the control and supervision of programs relating to the management, protection, conservation, and replenishment of wildlife, fish, and aquatic life, and the regulation of the shipping of wildlife fish, furs, and skins. LDWF's mission is to manage, conserve, and promote wise utilization of Louisiana's renewable fish and wildlife resources and their supporting habitats through replenishment, protection, enhancement, research, development, and education for the social and economic benefit of current and future generations; to provide opportunities for knowledge of and use and enjoyment of these resources; and to promote a safe and healthy environment for the users of the resources. LDWF is divided into seven divisions for management of the state's resources: Enforcement, Fur and Refuge, Public Information, Inland Fisheries, Marine Fisheries, Management and Finance, and Wildlife.

The state's participation and contribution throughout this planning process will provide for ongoing opportunities and open dialogue to improve the ecological sustainment of fish and wildlife in the State of Louisiana. An essential part of comprehensive conservation planning is integrating common mission objectives where appropriate.

Figure 1. Location of Bayou Sauvage NWR in relation to regional conservation area

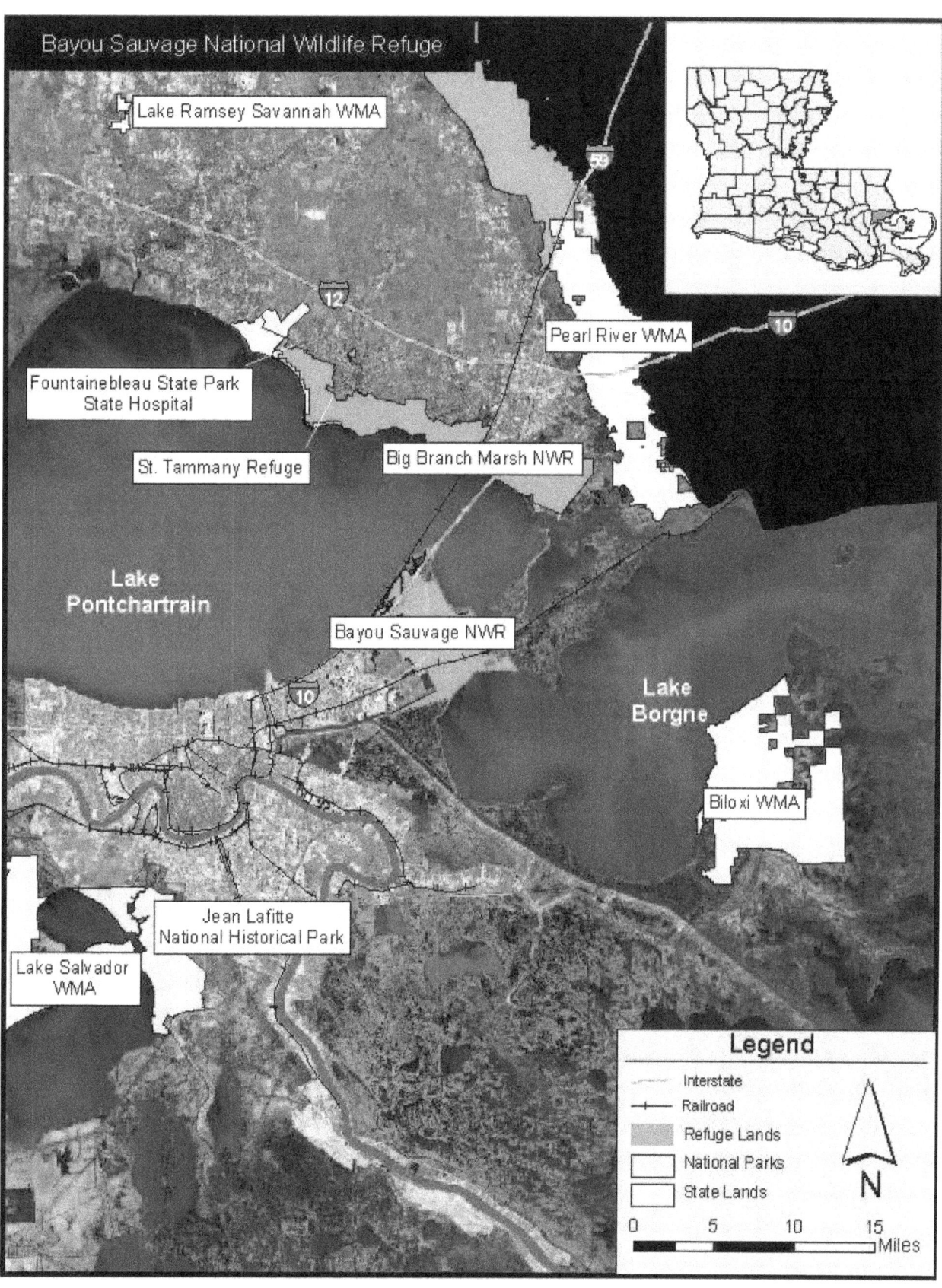

II. Refuge Overview

INTRODUCTION

Bayou Sauvage NWR is located in eastern Orleans Parish, Louisiana, and is entirely situated within the corporate limits of the city of New Orleans (Figure 2). It is the largest national wildlife refuge located in an urban area of the United States and is one of the last remaining marsh areas adjacent to the south shores of Lakes Pontchartrain and Borgne. The refuge consists of 22,265 acres of wetlands and is bordered on three sides by water: Lake Pontchartrain to the north, Chef Menteur Pass to the east, and Lake Borgne to the south. The western side of the refuge is bordered by the Maxent Canal and fast lands that consist of bottomland hardwood habitat and exotic species, such as Chinese tallow and china berry. Un-leveed portions of the refuge consist of estuarine tidal marshes and shallow water. The Hurricane Protection Levee System, along with roadbeds, created freshwater impoundments which altered the plant communities as well as the fish communities within these impoundments. Small forested areas exist on the low, natural ridges formed along natural drainages and along manmade canals.

Work on the this Draft CCP/EA was initiated in January 2007 and is scheduled for completion in late 2009. The Draft CCP/EA contains concepts to guide the development and implementation of land use and management programs as well as associated facilities for the next fifteen years. Consideration of the refuge's physical, biological, and cultural resources, along with the socioeconomic environment, refuge management and administration are taken into account and analyzed to produce an overview of the refuge along with the challenges it faces. The EA is being prepared in compliance with the National Environmental Protection Act (NEPA) guidelines. In addition to documenting the existing natural, environmental, and socio-economic setting, the EA evaluates the impact of the proposed and alternative actions, including the no action alternative, to facilitate selection of the management plan most suitable for implementation.

REFUGE HISTORY AND PURPOSE

Bayou Sauvage NWR is located within the corporate limits of the city of New Orleans, approximately 18 miles east of the central business district. Bayou Sauvage NWR is one of eight refuges managed as part of the Southeast Louisiana National Wildlife Refuge Complex. Prior to establishment of the refuge, area wetlands were threatened by urban expansion from the city of New Orleans. The refuge was authorized under House Resolution 5262, sponsored on July 28, 1986, by Louisiana Representatives John Breaux and Lindy Boggs. Authorization originated under a miscellaneous provision of the Emergency Wetland Resources Act of 1986 (Public Law 99-645), and on November 10, 1986, the bill establishing Bayou Sauvage NWR was signed into law by President Ronald Reagan.

The enacting legislation mandated that the Secretary of the Interior acquire 19,000 acres of land for the refuge within four years and complete a master plan for operation of the refuge within two years. In 2007, the refuge consisted of 22,265.12 acres in fee-title; 445 acres are managed through a Memorandum of Understanding with the city of New Orleans for management purposes; and there are 23,126 acres within the current acquisition boundary (Figure 2).

The purposes of the refuge were defined by the following authorities:

Figure 2. Current and acquisition boundaries of Bayou Sauvage NWR

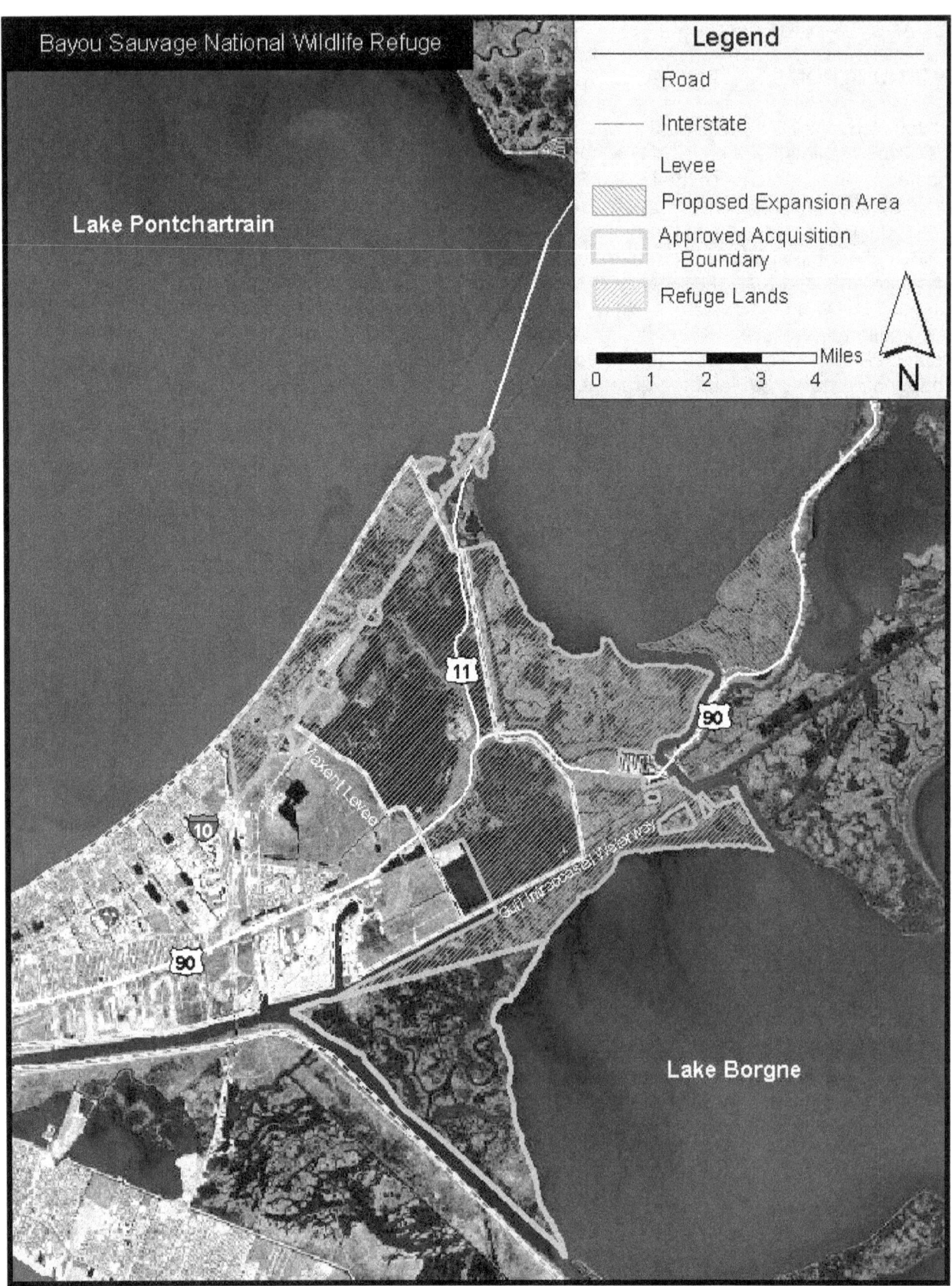

Emergency Wetlands Resources Act of 1986, 16 U.S.C. 3901 (b):
- For the conservation of the wetlands of the nation in order to maintain the public benefits they provide and to help fulfill international obligations contained in various migratory bird treaties and conventions.

North American Wetlands Conservation Act, 16 U.S.C. 4401 2(b):
- To protect, enhance, restore, and manage an appropriate distribution and diversity of wetland ecosystems and other habitats for migratory birds and other fish and wildlife in North America;
- To maintain current or improved distributions of migratory bird populations; and
- To sustain an abundance of waterfowl and other migratory birds consistent with the goals of the North American Waterfowl Management Plan and the international obligations contained in the migratory bird treaties and conventions and other agreements with Canada, Mexico, and other countries.

Legislation designated that the refuge should serve the following purposes:
- To enhance the populations of migratory, shore, and wading birds within the refuge.
- To encourage natural diversity of fish and wildlife species within the refuge.
- To protect the threatened and endangered species and otherwise to provide for the conservation and management of fish and wildlife within the refuge.
- To fulfill the international treaty obligations of the United States respecting fish and wildlife.
- To protect the archaeological resources of the refuge.
- To provide opportunities for fish and wildlife-dependent public uses and recreation in an urban setting.

SPECIAL DESIGNATIONS

The lands within Bayou Sauvage NWR were reviewed for their suitability in meeting the criteria for wilderness, as defined by the Wilderness Act of 1964 (Appendix H). No lands in the refuge were found to meet these criteria.

Although not within the refuge boundary, eastern Lake Pontchartrain and all of Lake Borgne were designated as critical habitat for the threatened Gulf Sturgeon in 2003. These waters provide juveniles, sub-adults, and adults feeding, resting, and passage habitat especially during winter months.

ECOSYSTEM CONTEXT

Bayou Sauvage NWR is located in the St. Bernard Delta of the Mississippi River, which is geographically located at the southern end of the Lower Mississippi River Ecosystem (LMRE). The LMRE includes the deltaic plain and associated marshes and swamps created by the meanderings of the Mississippi River and its distributaries. Prior to agricultural development, almost all of the Mississippi Delta was covered with flood plain forests. Today, only about 23 percent remains in forest, and the remaining forest is highly fragmented. The flood plain forests are primarily oak-gum-cypress cover type with co-dominant species of overcup, willow, Nuttall, water, swamp chestnut, and cherrybark oaks, as well as sweetgum, water tupelo, water hickory, willow, cottonwood, sycamore, sugarberry, red maple, box elder, bald cypress, and green ash. Cotton, soybeans, and rice are the most widespread crops but winter wheat, corn, sorghum, and sugar cane are also commonly cultivated. Although cleared of natural vegetation, flooded agricultural fields can provide important wildlife habitat.

Specifically, Bayou Sauvage NWR lies within the Gulf Coast Prairies and Marshes ecoregion of the LMRE. As the name implies, this ecoregion occupies the coastal zone of the Gulf of Mexico and is defined by coastal prairie and marsh communities. Louisiana's coastal marsh areas, in which Bayou Sauvage NWR is found, are comprised of salt, brackish, intermediate, and fresh marsh habitat types. Associated natural communities include cypress and cypress-tupelo swamps, live oak natural levee forests, and some bottomland hardwood forests.

According to the U.S. Geological Survey, Lake Pontchartrain and adjacent lakes in Louisiana form one of the larger estuaries in the Gulf Coast region. The estuary drains the Pontchartrain Basin, an area of over 12,000 km^2 situated on the eastern side of the Mississippi River delta plain. In Louisiana, nearly one-third of the state population lives within the 14 parishes of the basin.

REGIONAL CONSERVATION PLANS AND INITIATIVES

Bayou Sauvage NWR is a component of many regional and ecosystem conservation planning initiatives, which are described in the following paragraphs.

The National Estuary Program, established as part of the 1987 amendments to the Clean Water Act (CWA), seeks to protect and restore 28 designated estuaries of national significance that are deemed to be threatened by pollution, development, or overuse. The Barataria-Terrebone National Estuary Program focuses on two basin estuaries in southern Louisiana (Barataria to the south of New Orleans, and Terrebonne to the west), between the Mississippi and Atchafalaya Rivers. Federal agencies participating in the planning and assessment efforts include the Environmental Protection Agency (EPA), National Oceanic and Atmospheric Administration (NOAA), United States Geological Survey (USGS), Department of the Interior (DOI), and United States Department of Agriculture (USDA).

The Harmful Algal Bloom and Hypoxia Research and Control Act (Public Law 105-383 and Public Law 108-456) resulted in the establishment of a task force of federal and state agencies with responsibilities over activities in the Mississippi River basin, the Louisiana coastline, and the Gulf of Mexico. The task force includes eight federal and ten state agencies. This Mississippi River/Gulf of Mexico Watershed Nutrient Task Force has prepared an "*Action plan for Reducing, Mitigating, and Controlling Hypoxia in the Northern Gulf of Mexico*." The goal is to reduce the so-called "dead zone" in the coastal Gulf by half by 2015, and to reduce nitrogen loading to the Gulf by thirty percent.

As a result of The Pontchartrain Basin Restoration Act, a water management plan is being implemented which establishes environmental monitoring, implements restoration programs, and constructs restoration projects within the Lake Pontchartrain Basin. A partnership of the Lake Pontchartrain Basin Foundation, regional planning organizations, universities, and parish agencies is developing this management plan.

Two federal funding programs, the Wildlife Conservation and Restoration Program (WCRP) and the State Wildlife Grants Program (SWG), resulted in the State of Louisiana developing a Comprehensive Wildlife Conservation Strategy (CWCS). In December 2005, the LDWF, as part of its mission to manage, conserve, and promote wise utilization of Louisiana's fish and wildlife resources and their supporting habitats, released its *Comprehensive Wildlife Conservation Strategy (Wildlife Action Plan)*. The conservation actions and strategies in this plan were developed through public focus groups held across the state. Participants included invited conservation organizations, forestry and wildlife associations, federal and state agencies, industry, universities, and private citizens. The intent of the plan is to guide the conservation efforts of the LDWF over the next ten years.

The Coastal Wetlands Planning, Protection, and Restoration Act, CWPPRA, (Public Law 101-646) authorizes the development of comprehensive restoration and comprehensive conservation plans for our nation's coastlands. Forty percent of the coastal marshes of the continental United States covered by this law are in Louisiana. In February 2008, there were 164 CWPPRA restoration projects in Louisiana. Details for these restoration projects are available at the following website: http://www.lacoast.gov/projects/list.asp. The majority deal with hydrologic management, shoreline protection, and marsh creation.

Acting on the impetus of CWPPRA, the Governor's Office of Coastal Activities in Louisiana provides state leadership, direction, and coordination in the development and implementation of policies, plans, and programs which encourage multiple uses of the coastal zone and achieve a proper balance between development and conservation, restoration, creation, and nourishment of coastal resources. The following programs and activities have been established under this umbrella:

- Coastal Protection and Restoration Authority of Louisiana (CPRA)
- Coastal Wetland Forest Conservation and Use Science (CWFCU)
- Louisiana Coastal Wetlands Conservation and Restoration Task Force; and
- Wetlands Conservation and Restoration Authority.

The Coastal Protection and Restoration Authority of Louisiana (CPRA), has prepared a master plan, "*Integrated Ecosystem Restoration and Hurricane Protection: Louisiana's Comprehensive Master Plan for a Sustainable Coast,*" to incorporate hurricane protection and protection of coastal wetlands. The CPRA plan marshals Louisiana's Natural Resources and Transportation and Development departments (and other state agencies) to work closely with the Governor's Advisory Commission on Coastal Protection, Restoration, and Conservation and the Louisiana Recovery Authority (LRA) to integrate within a single state authority coastal restoration and hurricane protection.

The Coastal Wetland Forest Conservation and Use Science working group (CWFCU) provides information and guidelines for the long-term use, conservation, and protection of Louisiana's coastal wetland forest ecosystem. "*Coast 2050: Toward a Sustainable Coastal Louisiana*" is a plan prepared by the Louisiana Coastal Wetlands Conservation and Restoration Task Force and the Wetlands Conservation and Restoration Authority, a task force of federal, state, and local interests attempting to address Louisiana's massive coastal land loss problem.

The *Louisiana Native Plant Initiative* and the *Emergency Watershed Protection program* are two programs initiated by the USDA Natural Resources Conservation Service. The former program seeks to conserve vanishing native plants by identifying resource areas and developing partnerships with the Coastal Plain Conservancy, USGS National Wetlands Research Center, Barataria Terrebonne National Estuary Program, and state universities; while the later program removes debris from waterways and downed timber on forest lands.

The eight refuges that make up the Southeast Louisiana National Wildlife Refuge Complex are: Atchafalaya, Bogue Chitto, Bayou Sauvage, Breton, Bayou Teche, Delta, Big Branch Marsh, and Mandalay.

Comprehensive conservation plans are being prepared for each refuge to provide managers with a 15-year strategy and broad direction to conserve wildlife and their habitats, to achieve refuge purposes, and to contribute toward the mission of the Refuge System. In addition, the plans identify appropriate and compatible wildlife-dependent refuge uses available to the public, including hunting, fishing, wildlife observation, wildlife photography, and environmental education and interpretation.

ECOLOGICAL THREATS AND PROBLEMS

National wildlife refuges in the Lower Mississippi Valley serve as part of the last safety net to support biological diversity – the greatest challenge facing the Service. According to the LMRE Team, the greatest threats to biological diversity within the Lower Mississippi Valley include:

- loss of sustainable communities, including the loss of 20 million acres of bottomland hardwood forest;
- loss of connectivity between bottomland hardwood forest sites (e.g., forest fragmentation);
- effects of agricultural and timber harvesting practices;
- simplification of the remaining wildlife habitats within the ecosystem and gene pools;
- effects of constructing navigation and water diversion projects; and
- cumulative habitat effects of land and water resource development activities.

ALTERATIONS TO HYDROLOGY

There have been significant alterations in the region's hydrology due to flood control levees, urban development, river channel modifications, and degradation of aquatic systems from excessive erosion, sedimentation, and contaminants. A critical issue facing the refuge is land loss due to subsidence, erosion, major storm events, and salt-water intrusion. Compounding the situation, the area has experienced four major droughts over the past 15 to 20 years. During droughts, more saline water from Lake Pontchartrain has had to be introduced inside the impoundments to reduce subsidence. The highly organic soils lose elevation from compaction caused by loss of moisture during cycles of drought. In the past, these periods were fairly short and although some elevation was lost, subsequent rainfall purged the salts left in the soils.

The ability of the river/floodplain ecosystem to transport and assimilate nutrients and chemicals has also been impaired to the point that state and federal water quality standards are not met in many water bodies. This is compounded by industrial and urban runoff and leaks from oil and gas pipelines. These waste streams enter the refuge mainly through stormwater and non-point source runoff.

CLIMATE CHANGE

The culmination of recent findings on world climate has prompted the Service to include information on climate changes and sea level rise as critical issues facing national wildlife refuges, especially those located within coastal zones. According to the Environmental Defense Organization, on February 2, 2007, the international group of experts tasked with evaluating climate science—the Intergovernmental Panel on Climate Change—released their summary of the latest findings on global warming. Their report summarizes research conducted from about 2001 through the end of 2005 and concludes that "...numerous long-term changes in climate have been observed. These include changes in...the intensity of tropical cyclones." The report also finds that in the North Atlantic fiercer hurricanes are "correlated with increases of tropical sea surface temperatures." Additionally, John Huffman's report, *Estimates of Future Sea Level Rise*, developed four different scenarios to estimate sea level rise. These scenarios included a "conservative" scenario, which projects a sea level rise of 56.2 cm (22 in) by 2100; a "high" scenario, which projects a rise of 345 cm (11.5 ft) by 2100, and two mid-range scenarios projecting rises of 144 cm (4.8 ft) and 216cm (7 ft). Huffman predicts that the sea level rise at the end of this century is most likely to fall within the mid-range scenarios (~5-7 ft).

With the possibility of future habitat degradation due to world climate changes, the Service is investigating modeling national wildlife refuges using SLAMM (Sea Level Rise Affects Marshes Model) to predict how climate changes will affect different regions of the county, especially coastal regions. At this time the Service is still working to assess probable long-term effects for each refuge; monitoring the situation is advised until additional information is available.

URBANIZATION

Urban development (Bayou Sauvage NWR is located in east Orleans Parish, entirely within the corporate limits of New Orleans, a city with a present population of over 250,000 with a metro area population of approximately one million people) changes hydrology. Natural landscapes allow water to slowly and gradually filter into the ground. Rooftops, driveways, roads, and other surfaces associated with urban development are nonporous, causing water to accumulate above the surface and to run off in large volumes and at higher velocities, causing flooding and erosion. Because of the variety of pollutants associated with urban runoff–oil and grease from automobiles; nutrients and pesticides from lawns and gardens; sediment from construction sites; bacteria from pets and improper sewage disposal; household debris, etc.–urban development results in reduced water quality.

Urbanization is an ever-present threat to both refuge wildlife and habitat. The refuge is surrounded by industry and housing to the south and west. Three major highways (Interstate10, U.S. 90 and U.S. 11) traverse the refuge, leaving it vulnerable to environmental effects associated with urban trash dumping. The old Recovery 1 landfill located south of U.S. Highway 90, adjacent to the refuge, continues to be a potential threat for hazardous waste pollution. In addition, both an airport and drag racing track have been proposed as potential new developments adjacent to the refuge.

Another potential source of pollution exists in the form of pipelines within and adjacent to the refuge. These pipelines contain both petroleum products and natural gas. These include Collins Pipeline Company, Creole Pipeline Company, Barnwell Production Company, and Southern Natural Gas Company.

PROLIFERATION OF INVASIVE PLANTS AND ANIMALS

The introduction of exotic or nonnative plants on the refuge has threatened the natural aquatic vegetation important to aquatic systems, and has choked waterways to a degree that often prevents recreational use. Chinese tallow (*Sapium sebiferum*) is a tree that grows and spreads rapidly, is difficult to kill, and tends to take over large areas by out-competing native plants. It was introduced from Asia and is planted widely as an ornamental tree. Birds disperse the seeds, which have spread within the refuge where it is a significant threat to woody species. This species has been especially invasive around the natural ridge levee.

Non-native wildlife is an issue of which the refuge administration has struggled with for many years. Animals such as nutria compete with native wildlife for limited resources and many, like feral hogs, have caused extensive habitat damage and alterations. Presently, the refuge has a trapping program that allows nutria and hog populations to be controlled, thus reducing damage to habitat and food supplies.

PHYSICAL RESOURCES

CLIMATE

Climate in this region is subtropical with mild winters and hot, humid summers. Temperatures average 81.6 °F in summer and 54.0 °F in winter. Sporadic afternoon thunderstorms occur almost daily in summer with rainfall averages 61.03 inches per year. The maximum 24-hour rainfall for the area is 10.0 to10.5 inches with a recurrence interval of 25 years. According to a recent Weather Channel special report, the New Orleans area is the most vulnerable in the country when it comes to hurricanes. With the gradual warming of Gulf of Mexico waters, hurricanes and tropical storms from the Gulf are likely to be more severe and more frequent. This leaves the New Orleans area, located just above sea level, extremely vulnerable.

CLIMATE CHANGE AND GLOBAL WARMING

The Intergovernmental Panel on Climate Change (IPCC) recently concluded that warming of the climate is undeniable and could cause changes in our stewardship of land. Examples of potential changes are altered fire regimes, rain and snowfall patterns, access to water resources, hydrology in rivers and wetlands, frequency of extreme weather events, and rising sea level at coastal refuges.

Global climate change poses risks to human health and to terrestrial and aquatic ecosystems. Important economic resources such as agriculture, forestry, fisheries, and water resources also may be affected. Warmer temperatures, more severe droughts and floods, and sea level rise could have a wide range of impacts. All these stresses can add to existing stresses on resources caused by other influences such as population growth, land-use changes, and pollution.

According to NOAA and NASA data, the Earth's average surface temperature has increased by about 1.2 to 1.4°F since 1900. The ten warmest years in the twentieth century have all occurred within the past 15 years, with the warmest two years being 1998 and 2005. Some climate models, based on emissions of greenhouse gases, primarily carbon dioxide, methane, and nitrous oxide, predict that average surface temperatures could increase from 2.5 to 10.4°F by the end of this century. Increases in atmospheric CO_2 are attributed largely to human activities, which have grown rapidly since 1945. The burning of fossil fuels adds 5.6 billion tons of carbon, and deforestation contributes another 0.4 to 2.5 billion tons of carbon, to the atmosphere each year.

Global warming, resulting in melting of glaciers and ice sheets, will cause sea levels to rise. Globally, sea level has risen 4 to 10 inches during the past century. NASA estimates that yearly, 50 billion tons of ice is melting from the Greenland ice sheet. NASA aerial surveys show that more than 11 cubic miles of ice is disappearing from the ice sheet annually. Considering that land less than 10 meters above sea level contains 2 percent of the world's land surface but 10 percent of its population, major impacts could be felt by large numbers of people living on the low lying coastlands, particularly the Gulf and East Coast states.

Changes in coastal wetlands due to sea-level rise were modeled for Bayou Sauvage NWR using the Sea Level Affecting Marshes Model (SLAMM). This model simulates the dominant processes involved in wetland conversions and shoreline modifications during long-term sea-level rise (Clough and Park 2006, www.warrenpinnacle.com/prof/SLAMM). Dramatic changes are projected for Bayou Sauvage NWR's marshes and other near-shore habitats under the 1-meter sea-level rise scenario. Swamp and freshwater marshes in the northwest and middle sections of the refuge would likely convert to open water, and dike failure is likely in some areas (Nieves 2008, Bayou Sauvage SLAMM Analysis).

In addition to the rising seas, the effects of climate change and global warming will be changes in weather/rainfall patterns, decreases in snow and ice cover, rising sea levels, and stressed ecosystems. For the southeastern United States and the Bayou Sauvage NWR region, this can mean extreme precipitation events; greater likelihood of warmer/dryer summers and wetter/reduced winter cold; and, alterations of ecosystems and habitats due to these changes in weather patterns–to name but a few possibilities. For example, a recent study of the effects of climate change on eastern United States bird species concluded that as many as 78 bird species could decrease by at least 25 percent; while as many as 33 species could increase in abundance by at least 25 percent due to climate and habitat changes.

GEOLOGY AND TOPOGRAPHY

The geological history of the refuge dates to the Pleistocene Epoch when coarse, gravelly terraces were fluvially deposited through upland river valleys now occupied by the Tchefuncte and Pearl Rivers, north and east of the refuge. The depositional age of the Pleistocene sediments underlying the refuge is from 35,000 to less than 25,000 years ago.

Between 4,500 and 700 years ago, the area was characterized by phases of Mississippi River sedimentation and delta lobe abandonment associated with the St. Bernard Delta cycle. The advancing delta lobes deposited prodelta silts and clays and delta font sands, silts, and clays. The distributary channels, associated with delta formation and responsible for shoreline progradation, left a network of relict natural levee deposits on the refuge; the most noticeable of these is the Bayou Sauvage natural levee ridge. The crests of these natural levees form topographic ridges and provide a firm and stable substrate.

As the Mississippi River sub-deltas developed, marshes became established along the base of the natural levees and in the inter-levee basins. The buildup of organic material from the marsh and swamp vegetation and the slow, constant subsidence has produced a sequence of peat deposits and organic rich clays in these areas. After the abandonment of the Bayou Sauvage delta lobe around 200 years ago, natural subsidence characterized by marsh deterioration and shoreline erosion accelerated in the absence of Mississippi River sedimentation.

The construction of massive navigation and flood control works has essentially stopped the natural processes of the river. Historical flooding into the alluvial plain provided fish spawning sites, nutrient and sediment exchange, and a wealth of aquatic and wetland habitats. The river is now stabilized, fixed in place, and unable to move and function as the dynamic system that both created and destroyed habitats such as riffles, oxbows, sand bars, willow banks, and side channels. Consequently, the river and its tributaries and distributaries are now denied access to the flood plain, so crucial physical and biological interactions between the rivers and flood plains no longer exist.

Natural patterns of erosion and sedimentation have been greatly altered. Erosion rates are increased on both upland and alluvial soils. Sedimentation is increased in swamps, brakes, oxbow lakes, and other depressional areas. Sediment loading in streams and rivers is increased, disrupting natural patterns of aggravation and degradation.

The altered hydrology and sedimentation have disrupted natural geomorphic processes. Land and lake formation associated with river meandering and sedimentation is no longer occurring, restricting the formation of new oxbow lakes, meander lakes, and sloughs. Sediment transport from the Mississippi River and its distributaries to coastal marshes and bays has been greatly reduced, and the interface between fresh and salt water grossly modified. These hydrologic changes have reduced the formation of new deltas and associated coastal marshes and significantly increased the erosion and subsidence of existing marshes.

SOILS

The majority of the refuge soils are in the Clovelly-Lafitte-Gentilly soil association which is characterized as level, very poorly drained soils that have a thick to thin mucky surface layer underlain by clayey sediments. These soils exist at elevations ranging from 0 to approximately 1 foot above sea level and are naturally flooded most of the year. Only the Bayou Sauvage natural levee ridge, which reaches a maximum height of less than three feet, contains a Sharkey-Commerce soil association which is slightly better drained and rated fair to good as potential habitat for woodland wildlife. All of the soils on the refuge are poorly suited to construction of roads, buildings, and dry trails, but are ideal for wetland plants and wildlife.

HYDROLOGY AND WATER QUALITY AND QUANTITY

The natural hydrology of the refuge has been altered considerably by human activities including construction of roads, railroads, levees, spoil deposits, and canals. Natural drainage provided by the Bayou Sauvage freshwater channel network, surface runoff, and estuarine tidal channels was adversely impacted by construction of hurricane flood protection levees in the mid-1950s. Flap-gated culverts were installed in the East Flood Protection Levee to facilitate drainage from the leveed areas but were not capable of providing adequate drainage, thus runoff and precipitation are often impounded inside the leveed areas. Presently, the only means available of lowering water levels in the refuge are via drainage into the Maxent Canal and discharge at two of the pump stations on the Gulf Intracoastal Waterway, or manually opening the flap gates in the protection levee when water levels are very low in Lake Pontchartrain.

Rainfall is the main source of water for the fresh marshes. During dry periods some areas of the refuge may dry up totally. Adding brackish water from Lake Pontchartrain can provide some relief, but introducing too much brackish water damages freshwater grasses and other plants. Tides on the refuge have an average diurnal range of 1.0 foot with a variation from 0.45 feet in Lake Pontchartrain, north of Chef Menteur Pass, to 1.1 feet in Lake Borgne, near the Pass. Salinities in tidal areas range from 3.95 to 3.89 parts per thousand (ppt) in Lake Pontchartrain to 5.38 ppt near the juncture of Chef Menteur Pass and the Gulf Intracoastal Waterway.

Headwater flooding from the Mississippi River has been eliminated. Backwater flooding has been reduced in extent and duration in all major backwater areas, and distributary flooding has been eliminated or restricted to designated outlets. Headwater and backwater flood events from alluvial valley tributaries have also been reduced in extent, frequency, and duration. Conversely, the frequency and duration of flooding has increased in all non-leveed areas. The floodplain available for flood water storage has been reduced by 90 percent and the flood storage capacity has been reduced from 60 to 12 days of mean daily discharge.

Under normal conditions, water inside the refuge is basically fresh. During Hurricane Katrina, some of the hurricane protection levees failed and introduced saline waters for a prolonged period. The Maxent Levee was overtopped by a 12- to13-foot storm surge and failed. Three of four refuge pumps were lost and the screw gate water control structures were compromised. The entire refuge, including relict ridges, was inundated for four weeks. It was a time of extremes; after the waters were pumped off or receded, drought conditions lasting more than a year worsened conditions. Salinity readings taken in water inside the levees ranged from 17 ppt up to the high 20s. Most of the freshwater vegetation was killed – 80 to 90 percent of the hardwoods are now dead. Present salinity in the water column is about 5 ppt, and salt levels are probably higher in the root zone.

Urban development also adversely affects hydrology and water quality in Bayou Sauvage NWR.

The Environmental Protection Agency has identified the Mississippi Delta as an area of significant concern for surface and groundwater quality. The region's abundant rainfall, finely textured alluvial soils, and intensive cultivation have contributed to serious non-point source pollution problems. An estimated 12-45 tons of soil per acre are lost from agricultural lands in the LMAV each year leading to increased water turbidity, siltation, pollution from pesticide and herbicide run-off, toxicity to fish and other aquatic organisms, oxygen depletion, and eutrophication. High pathogen loads have led to the closure of many of the shellfish grounds at the coast.

There is little long-term water quality data available for the refuge, although the USGS has done several water quality investigations on Lake Pontchartrain, one of the largest lakes in Louisiana and immediately contiguous to the refuge. Storm water runoff (particularly urban storm water runoff in the vicinity of New Orleans) is the largest contributor to the pollution of Lake Pontchartrain, followed by wastewater discharge and industrial and agricultural runoff. Sediment samples collected in Lake Pontchartrain show increased contaminant levels (metals, pesticides, and PCB's) in the vicinity of New Orleans. Similar results would be expected for the waters and sediments of Bayou Sauvage NWR. In 2002, the State of Louisiana classified the Bayou Sauvage from the New Orleans hurricane levee to Chef Menteur Pass, a length of about three miles, as fully supporting two uses: the protection and propagation of fish, shellfish, and wildlife; and recreation.

AIR QUALITY

The Clean Air Act (CAA) of 1970 (as amended in 1990 and 1997), required the U.S. Environmental Protection Agency (EPA) to implement air quality standards to protect public health and welfare. National Ambient Air Quality Standards (NAAQS) were set for six pollutants commonly found throughout the United States: lead, ozone, nitrogen oxides (NO_x), carbon monoxide (CO), sulfur dioxide (SO_2), and particulate matter less than 10 and 2.5 microns in diameter (PM_{10} and $PM_{2.5}$).

The Louisiana Department of Environmental Quality operates National Ambient Monitoring Stations (NAMS) and State and Local Ambient Monitoring Stations (SLAMS) to measure ambient concentrations of these pollutants. Areas that meet NAAQS are designated "attainment areas," while areas not meeting the standards are termed "non-attainment" areas. While no pollutant monitoring data are available for Bayou Sauvage NWR, per se, air quality is monitored on a regular basis in the city of New Orleans and vicinity. The monitoring results indicate that all of the New Orleans area qualifies as an attainment area for all monitored pollutants, and that air quality has improved since 1990 (Table 1). Currently, only the Baton Rouge area is in non-attainment of EPA's 8-hour ozone NAAQS.

Table 1. Air quality statistics around Bayou Sauvage NWR

Air Quality Statistics by City, 2005												
Metropolitan Statistical Area	2000 Population	CO 8-hr (ppm)	Pb Qmax (µg/m³)	NO₂ AM (ppm)	O₃ 1-hr (ppm)	O₃ 8-hr (ppm)	PM₁₀ Wtd AM (µg/m³)	PM₁₀ 24-hr (µg/m³)	PM₂.₅ Wtd AM (µg/m³)	PM₂.₅ 24-hr (µg/m³)	SO₂ AM (ppm)	SO₂ 24-hr (ppm)
New Orleans, LA MSA	1337726	2	0.82	0.009	0.103	0.083	21.1	41	12.0	32	0.003	0.032
National Ambient Air Quality Standards --		9	1.50	0.053	0.125	0.085	50	150	15	65	0.030	0.140

Air Quality Statistics by Parish/County, 2005												
Parish/County	2000 Population	CO 8-hr (ppm)	Pb Qmax (µg/m³)	NO₂ AM (ppm)	O₃ 1-hr (ppm)	O₃ 8-hr (ppm)	PM₁₀ Wtd AM (µg/m³)	PM₁₀ 24-hr (µg/m³)	PM₂.₅ Wtd AM (µg/m³)	PM₂.₅ 24-hr (µg/m³)	SO₂ AM (ppm)	SO₂ 24-hr (ppm)
Jefferson Parish (Kenner, Marrero)	455466	IN	0.13	0.009	0.100	0.083	ND	ND	11.8	32	IN	IN
Orleans Parish (City Park Tulane)	484674	2	0.09	IN	0.089	0.068	21.1	41	12.0	30	ND	ND
Plaquemines Parish	26757	ND	ND	ND	ND	ND	ND	ND	IN	IN	ND	ND
St. Bernard Parish (Arabi, Meraux)	67229	ND	0.82	ND	0.096	0.079	ND	ND	10.7	IN	0.003	0.032
St. Charles Parish (Hanhville)	48072	ND	0.04	ND	0.092	0.076	IN	IN	IN	IN	ND	ND
St. John the Baptist Parish (Garyville)	43044	ND	ND	ND	0.094	0.077	ND	ND	ND	ND	ND	ND
St. Tammany Parish	191268	ND	0.04	ND	ND	ND	ND	ND	ND	ND	ND	ND
St. James Parish (Convent)	21216	ND	ND	ND	0.103	0.078	ND	ND	IN	IN	ND	ND
National Ambient Air Quality Standards --		9	1.50	0.053	0.125	0.085	50	150	15	65	0.030	0.140

Following Hurricane Katrina, the National Resources Defense Council collected ambient air samples in Orleans and St. Bernard Parishes in October and November 2005. Samples were analyzed for both mold spores and heavy metals. The levels of mold spores found in the flooded areas of New Orleans were very high and posed a health threat to people with allergies, asthma, and other respiratory disease. The most common types of mold detected were Cladosporium and Aspergillus/Penicillium species. High concentrations of metals (e.g., lead, arsenic, and chromium) in ambient air samples were also found. Thick clouds of dust from drying sediment deposited by the flooding were observed during the sampling. In Orleans Parish, lead concentrations in ambient air samples exceeded the EPA national standard of 1.5 µg/m³. Arsenic and chromium concentrations in ambient air samples collected in Orleans and St. Bernard Parishes were significantly higher than EPA health-based screening levels. The concentrations of all three metals were higher than previous monitoring data collected prior to Hurricane Katrina. It is unknown where and for how long these moldy, dusty conditions persisted (or will persist) and to what extent residents are (or will be) exposed to the mold and dust contamination during cleanup activities.

BIOLOGICAL RESOURCES

HABITAT

The refuge staff manages eight management units that consist of emergent marsh, both tidally influenced and impounded, plus natural levee ridges, spoil banks and shallow open water bodies, which constitute a wide range of habitats within the refuge boundaries (Table 2). These habitats allow for good biological productivity and high species diversity of both terrestrial and aquatic organisms. The freshwater lagoons, bayous, and ponds provide an excellent habitat for fish and large numbers of shore and wading birds, ducks, and other waterfowl.

Most of the Bayou Sauvage NWR is located inside massive hurricane protection levees, built to hold back storm surges and prevent flooding in the low-lying city of New Orleans. The levees interrupt natural water flow patterns and challenge refuge managers to maintain productive wetland habitats in this altered environment. A network of pumps and flap gates provides a means of regulating water levels seasonally to encourage the summer growth of emergent grasses that, in turn, provide waterfowl food supplies in winter.

The refuge contains a variety of different habitats, including freshwater marshes, brackish marshes, bottomland hardwood forests, lagoons, canals, borrow pits, chenieres (former beach fronts) and natural bayous (Figure 3). The lower lying portions of the levee backslopes support bottomland hardwood and swamp communities. The low lying, frequently flooded basins are dominated by emergent vegetation, which are exposed to a salinity gradient, ranging from fresh in the upper ends of the basin or near the base of natural levees to brackish near the Lakes. These salinity gradients are responsible for the creation of distinct plant communities arranged in roughly parallel zones between the swamp-hardwood communities and the open waters.

Table 2. Habitat types and associated acreages found on Bayou Sauvage NWR

Habitat Type	Acres
Fresh Marsh	4,838
Non - Fresh Marsh	7,574
Water	6,062
Forest	2,652
Swamp	307
Scrub/Shrub	2,048

The refuge's marsh zones are classified as fresh, intermediate, and brackish; with fresh and intermediate zones confined primarily to the leveed areas of the refuge. The tidal marshes are dominated by wiregrass. The leveed wetlands are more diverse with dominant vegetation species being wiregrass, fall panicum, switchgrass, sprangletop, and coastal waterhyssop. The freshwater bodies are characterized by coontail, water-celery, and southern niad. This variety of aquatic vegetation species provides a diverse habitat for aquatic organisms and food for migratory waterfowl. A wading bird rookery can be found in the scrub/shrub habitat of the refuge from May until July, while tens of thousands of waterfowl winter in its bountiful marshes. The marshes along Lakes Pontchartrain and Borgne serve as estuarine nurseries for various fish species, crabs, and shrimp. Freshwater lagoons, bayous, and ponds serve as production areas for largemouth bass, crappie, bluegill, and catfish.

Figure 3. General habitat types on Bayou Sauvage NWR

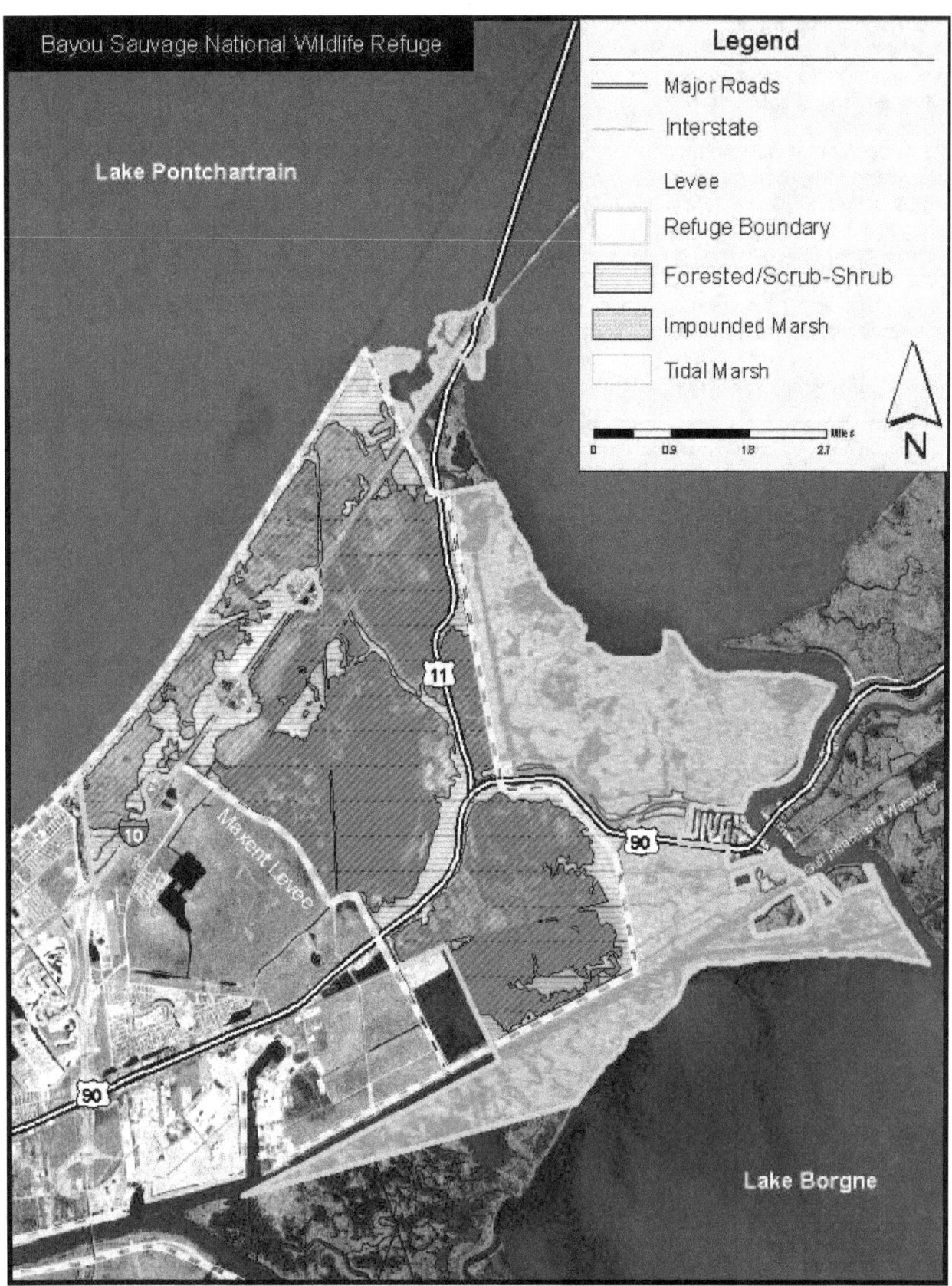

Vegetation communities within the refuge are representative of those communities found in an abandoned delta lobe within the Mississippi Deltaic Plain and can be grouped into three major categories: terrestrial, wetland, and aquatic. Regional landforms affect the distribution of the vegetation primarily through control of the periodic flooding and salinity.

Terrestrial vegetation, often characterized by live oak and mixed hardwood communities, is associated with higher natural levee ridges, which are well-drained and typically above the reach of saline waters. The continued subsidence of the ridges, in addition to the saltwater intrusion due to major storms and an extended drought over the past 15 to 20 years has continually compromised the integrity of the area to support hardwood communities. Prior to the summer of 2005, the natural levee ridge was a maritime bottomland hardwood forest dominated by live oak (*Quercus virginiana*) and sugar berry (*Celtis laevigata*).

Marshes are categorized as either impounded (leveed wetlands) or tidal waters. Prior to Hurricane Katrina the impounded marshes were primarily fresh with only a small area of intermediate marsh between Turtle Bayou and the East Hurricane Flood Protection Levee and brackish marsh in the tidal wetlands. The dominant vegetation is wiregrass, fall panicum (*Panicum dichotomiflorum*), switchgrass (*P. virgatum*), sprangletop (*Leptochloa fascicularis*), and coastal water hyssop/bagscale (*Sacciolepis striata*) occupying the low flats. The tidal wetland areas are dominated by wiregrass with marsh aster (*Aster subulatus*), saltmarsh lythrum (*Lythrum lineare*), Olney bulrush, and saltmarsh bulrush. Smooth cordgrass dominated edges of marsh ponds, and hogcane (*Spartina cynosuroides*) may dominate higher elevations along natural levees.

According to the Post Hurricane Katrina Refuge Damage Assessment, prior to Hurricane Katrina, the total area of freshwater and brackish marsh (including open water) was 21,717 acres, with the remaining 1,053 acres being upland margins along levees and berms. According to the Post Hurricane Katrina Refuge Damage Assessment, comparison of pre- and post-hurricane imagery showed conversion of 658 acres of freshwater and brackish marsh to open water, which amounted to an overall marsh loss of 11 percent. Most of the marsh loss occurred in freshwater marsh, particularly within Units 3 and 5. Total marsh area lost for these two units was 763 acres, or 21 percent of pre-storm marsh area in these units. This loss comprised 44 percent of all marsh lost within the refuge (Figure 4).

Prior to Hurricane Katrina, the refuge staff had been countering natural forces with vegetative plantings and creating "fences" for holding sediment with organic materials such as used Christmas trees, coir logs, and hay bales. When sediments build, they can quickly vegetate with submerged aquatics and subsequently various emergent marsh plant species. Unfortunately, all progress was destroyed during the 2005 storm season. No large scale dredging projects occur in the vicinity of the refuge to create a beneficial spoil source. Bayous and drainages within the refuge which have silted-in could provide small amounts of beneficial spoil for building up relict ridges.

WILDLIFE

Bayou Sauvage NWR was established in April 1990, to provide wintering habitat for migratory birds and waterfowl. It is the largest such urban refuge in the Refuge System and is home to 340 species of birds. Appendix I contains a list of wildlife species of concern and/or significance for management purposes.

Figure 4. Impacts of Hurricane Katrina on Bayou Sauvage NWR

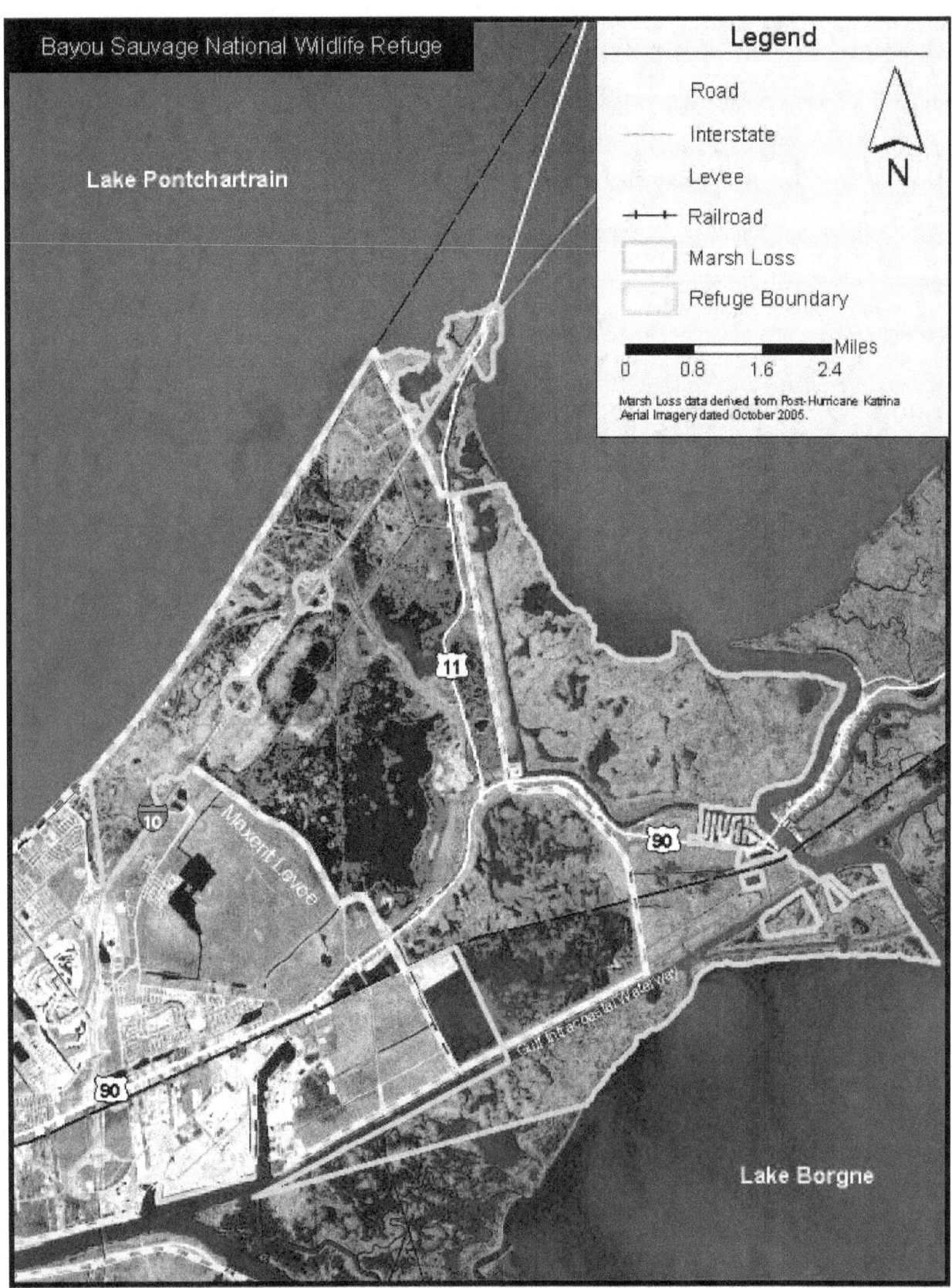

Migratory birds

Bayou Sauvage NWR is recognized as an important area for migratory waterfowl and other water birds that depend on shallow water with submerged and emergent herbaceous aquatic plants. The refuge lies within the Gulf Coast Joint Venture (GCJV), which was established as one of the original joint ventures under the NAWMP. The purpose of the NAWMP and GCJV was to formally establish a federal-state-private partnership for the conservation and perpetuation of waterfowl populations. Since its inception, the NAWMP and GCJV have expanded to embrace "all bird" conservation. The GCJV has divided the western Gulf Coast into six initiative areas for addressing habitat/population needs and objectives unique to those areas. Bayou Sauvage NWR lies within the Mississippi River Coastal Wetlands Initiative Area described by Wilson, Manlove, and Esslinger (2002) and includes waterfowl population and habitat objectives. The GCJV is currently developing priority bird lists and habitat/population objectives for other bird groups.

Prior to Hurricane Katrina, surveys documented an average of 25,000, with peaks of up to 40,000, migratory waterfowl using the refuge. Peak numbers were observed during periods of ample rainfall that facilitated natural food production in the impounded areas. In drier years, numbers dropped to around 10,000 to15,000 ducks. Moist-soil management began in the 1990s and waterfowl numbers increased during this period. Since 2000, the number of neotropical species has decreased consistently, not only on the refuge, but in the Lake Pontchartrain area in general. Christmas bird counts show losses of water birds since 2000. The decrease is probably a result of reduced moist soil plant production caused by droughts and hurricanes. Not only is emergent vegetation production less, but certain species of submerged aquatic vegetation (SAV) are also lost during periods of higher salinities associated with droughts.

The total number of waterfowl lost within the refuge as a result of Hurricane Katrina is based on total loss of marsh acreage, is 867, which is an 8.9 percent reduction in overall carrying capacity. Within freshwater marsh, 1,089 acres of lost marsh translated to a loss of 545 waterfowl, or a 15.9 percent reduction in freshwater marsh carrying capacity. Within brackish marsh, 658 acres of lost marsh translated to a loss of 322 waterfowl, or an 11 percent reduction in carrying capacity for brackish marsh. Based on these results, the heaviest loss of waterfowl in freshwater marsh was, as expected, in Units 3 and 5. Less expected was the high number of birds lost within brackish marsh Unit 1.

The most common species observed is gadwall with widgeon, shoveler, mallard, teal, and pintail occurring in smaller numbers. In December 2006, Unit 6 was full of ruddy ducks, a phenomenon not observed previously. Few geese are observed during surveys.

Because the refuge is within an urban area with restrictions on hunting and weapons, the entire refuge is a sanctuary. However, some consideration is being given to opening portions of the refuge outside the Hurricane Levee Protection System to youth waterfowl hunting.

Wood ducks, mottled ducks, and black-bellied whistling ducks nest in the area. Limited mottled duck nesting occurs on the levees. The range of black-bellied whistling ducks has increased eastward in recent years. A wood duck box program is successfully providing nesting for both wood ducks and black-bellied whistling ducks. Significant concern has been expressed, particularly in Texas, over apparent population decline of mottled ducks. While the decline is either not shared or is much less in Louisiana, the entire west Gulf Coast population is managed as one. In an effort to gain a better understanding of the population status and trends, there is renewed emphasis being placed on a multi-state pre-season banding program that was started in 1994, and in developing and conducting annual breeding/production surveys.

The location of shallow-water and moist-soil habitats adjacent to the Mississippi River and Lake Pontchartrain make Bayou Sauvage NWR attractive to shorebirds. Refuge wetlands provide important migratory shorebird habitat when dewatered or when natural drying occurs and coincides with spring and fall migration. Receding water exposes mudflats rich in invertebrate prey. In the past, large numbers of shorebirds have congregated in Unit 6; Units 3 and 5 have also been used but with less regularity than Unit 6 when water levels are optimum. The refuge is in the Gulf Coastal Prairie area of the lower Mississippi/western Gulf Coast region of the Shorebird Conservation Plan. No highly imperiled species use the refuge except possibly accidentally. Marbled godwit and Sanderling are species of high concern listed in the shorebird plan that potentially use the refuge area.

The emergent marsh habitat supports marsh birds, the highest priority species being king rail, clapper rail, yellow rail, sora, pied-billed grebe, horned grebe, least bittern, and American bittern. These birds need a mosaic of open, shallow water with emergent vegetation. Secretive marsh bird surveys before Hurricane Katrina revealed large numbers of nesting king and clapper rails and to a lesser degree gallinules and least bitterns. Numbers of marsh birds are down since Hurricane Katrina.

Wading birds that utilize the abundant forage resources in the shallow water habitats on the refuge are common. Over the past years, the wading bird rookery on the refuge had moved to trees on adjacent land when trees died from prolonged exposure to deep water in Unit 6; those trees on adjacent lands are now also dead from Hurricane Katrina's winds and floods. The refuge is presently used as a feeding/resting area with limited nesting. Priority species of regional concern expected to occur in the area include little blue heron, tri-colored heron, yellow-crowned night heron, and white Ibis.

A number of gulls and terns use the refuge for loafing and feeding. Priority species of regional concern possibly occurring on the refuge are Forster's tern and black tern.

Other water birds of management concern that feed in the area are the eastern brown pelican, which is observed year-round but does not breed on the refuge; the American coot and white pelican winter in the area.

The position of Bayou Sauvage NWR as an oasis in the midst of development makes it an important resting and feeding area to trans-Gulf migratory songbirds. The area is located in the Gulf Coastal Prairie area in Bird Conservation Region 37 (BCR 37). According to the BCR Plan, high-priority birds of concern common to the refuge are prothonotary warbler, sedge wren, Swainson's warbler, and painted bunting.

Most of the trees and freshwater vegetation were killed by the storm surge and saltwater intrusion associated with the 2005 storm season. Management to encourage the development of vertical structure (trees) would be beneficial.

Threatened and Endangered Species

The endangered eastern brown pelican (*Pelecanus occidentalis*) is a year-round resident of southeast Louisiana. The number of nesting brown pelicans has substantially increased despite loss of nesting habitat. Although they do not nest on the refuge, brown pelicans frequently use the area for feeding and loafing. An occasional West Indian manatee, an endangered species, is observed in the waters in the area during warm months, but departs during colder months. Eastern Lake Pontchartrain and all of Lake Borgne were designated as critical habitat for the threatened Gulf sturgeon in 2003. These waters provide juveniles, subadults, and adults feeding, resting, and passage habitat especially during winter months. The bald eagle (*Haliaeetus leucocephalus*) winters on the refuge and nests in the area.

Other Wildlife

Common mammals are white-tailed deer, squirrels, otter, raccoon, feral hog, nutria and mink. All terrestrial species suffered during and after Hurricane Katrina. The population of these species declined as a result of the storm. Some sign is observed of these species after the storm, but not in abundance like before Hurricane Katrina. Large numbers of alligators and turtles existed on the refuge; however, these species also experienced a population decline as a result of Hurricane Katrina.

Fisheries

A diversity of freshwater and saltwater species is found on the refuge. Common freshwater species are bass, catfish, mullet, crappie, minnows, and bream. Saltwater species are flounder, red fish, speckled sea trout, crabs, and shrimp. Fish assemblages in Lake Pontchartrain change seasonally depending on the balance between the amount of freshwater entering the lake from drainages and the amount of saltier Gulf waters that dominate during times of little rainfall.

Presently, most fishing in the refuge is by bank fishers. Anglers are seeking brackish water species deposited in the impoundments during the storm surge. Speckled sea trout fishing and crabbing have increased while large mouth bass and blue gill have declined. Before January 2007, salinities were 13 to15 ppt. January 2007 was the first time salinity readings dropped to below 10 ppt since the storm season of 2005.

CULTURAL RESOURCES

Indigenous Native Americans were present in the area dating back to 1800 B.C. The original inhabitants were nomadic hunters, who later gave way to sedentary mound building cultures. In 1699, Bienville, a French explorer, explored and named the areas surrounding Lake Pontchartrain. It is likely that Bienville and his party were the first Europeans to investigate this area. Mathurin and Perier Dreaux were among the first settlers to make their home in this area. In the 1720s they were given a land grant located on the Bayou Sauvage natural levees. The property was named Gentilly. This is associated with the westernmost portion of present day Bayou Sauvage.

Historical records reveal that the majority of the refuge area saw little settlement and development prior to the twentieth century. Even after that date, most settlement in the area occurred on lands just outside of the present refuge boundary. Possibly the earliest significant historic occupation in the area seems to have been the plantation established by Barthelemy Lafon in approximately 1809. Early maps of the area indicate that the *Habitation Lafon* was located along the south side of Bayou Sauvage, just east of Turtle Bayou.

There are numerous archaeological sites located on the refuge. The study of the Big and Little Oak Island sites began in 1935 and still continues. One of the most extensive studies was conducted by Professor Shenkel at University of New Orleans in the 1980s. During this study several pits were dug and many artifacts were discovered. These artifacts were thought to be a product of the Tchefuncte culture, a widespread people located primarily in the Pontchartrain basin. The Tchefuncte were the first people to widely use ceramics and were hunter-gatherers. The Tchefuncte culture is classified as virilocal or patrilocal in structure and their organizational structure is defined as small bands, which typically consisted of 25 to 50 individuals.

In 1993 a Phase I Archaeological Survey identified eight archaeological sites and one "Spot Find" on refuge property or potential property. Two sites recognized for their archaeological significance, Big Oak Island and Little Oak Island, have been placed on the National Register of Historic Places because of their ability to contribute to the understanding the history of the region. Three sites, Turtle Bayou, Bayou Sauvage, and Madere, are on natural levees of Bayou Sauvage or its distributaries. These three sites have not been extensively examined and all have the potential for containing significant cultural remains.

SOCIOECONOMIC ENVIRONMENT

Regional Demographics and Economy

According to the 2005 American Community Survey, the population of the eight-parish, New Orleans Metropolitan Statistical Area (MSA) was 1.3 million, and the population of the city of New Orleans (which is synonymous with Orleans Parish) was 437,186 persons. Between its maximum population of 627,525 in 1960 and 2005, the population of New Orleans slowly declined. Hurricane Katrina resulted in a dramatic drop in population in New Orleans. In July 2006, the U.S. Census Bureau estimated a population of 223,388 in the city, a decline of 54 percent, compared to an estimated of 437,186 in 2005, prior to Hurricane Katrina (Table 3).

However, the population of New Orleans is recovering from Hurricane Katrina. As of March 2007, there had been a rebound in population to 255,000 people – a 14 percent increase from the July 2006 estimate. The Census Bureau estimated the entire New Orleans MSA population at that time to be just over one million residents. Given the socio-economic and geographic links within the MSA parishes, these population changes will impact the local economy and the public use of Bayou Sauvage NWR. In recent years, the refuge has had approximately 150,000 visitors a year (generating about $15 million), drawn from the regional population and tourists who visit New Orleans. The 2005 census survey estimated that within the New Orleans MSA there were 218,000 elementary and high school students, all of whom could benefit from the refuge's environmental education programs.

The economy of New Orleans is characterized by a relatively large number of low and moderate wage jobs associated with tourism, retail trade, and related services. The 2005 American Community Survey found 24.5 percent of the people in Orleans Parish lived in poverty, seventh highest among large counties in the country. The median household income of $30,771 for Orleans Parish is far below the national average of $46,242.

New Orleans has always been primarily a commercial center, with manufacturing playing a secondary role in its economic life. The busy port, besides adding to the city's cosmopolitan atmosphere, is the foundation of the metropolitan economy, influencing many aspects of urban life. The economy of New Orleans has historically been regulated by its location on one of the most productive river systems in the world. Its key location on the Mississippi River and its close proximity to the Gulf of Mexico encourage an economy based largely on shipping and port-related industry. Exports include grain, petroleum, petrochemicals, and agricultural products. Today, the economy of New Orleans is driven by tourism, with the port economies down significantly. Tourism visits to New Orleans were down sharply in the aftermath of Hurricane Katrina, with many conventions cancelled and hotels closed or being used for aid workers. The numbers of scheduled airline flights into the city are still below the levels prior to Hurricane Katrina. Community leaders have been working hard to restore the tourism economy and important strides are being made with the reopening of most hotels and the refurbishment of the Louisiana Superdome and the Convention Center.

Table 3. Socioeconomic profile - U.S. Census, 2005 American Community Survey

Characteristic	City of New Orleans (Orleans Parish)	St Bernard Parish	New Orleans MSA	United States
Demographic				
Population (number)	437,186	64,576b	1,292,774	288,378,137
Total Land Area (sq. miles)	180.6	465.0	3153.4	3,537,438
Population Density (pop./sq. mile)	2420	139	410	82
Race/Ethnicity (% of Population)				
White	28.0	86.4	57.0	74.4
Black/African American	67.5	10.5	37.7	12.1
Hispanic/Latino (of any race)	3.1	5.5	5.0	14.5
Asian	2.4	1.5	2.4	4.3
Education (% of population over 25)				
High School degree	82.3	80.5	83.5	84.2
College degree	31.4	10.9	25.6	27.2
Economic				
Median Household Income	$ 30,771	$ 34,858	$ 39,879	$ 46,242
Per capita Income	$ 21,998	$ 18,441	$ 22,540	$ 25,035
Families below poverty level (%)	21.8%	--	14.5%	10.2%
Individuals below poverty level (%)	24.5%	21.0%	17.8%	13.3%

REFUGE ADMINISTRATION AND MANAGEMENT

LAND PROTECTION AND CONSERVATION

The conservation priorities identified for Bayou Sauvage NWR include emphasis on restoration of habitats for migratory birds, shore and wading birds, and efforts to enhance and maintain a diverse balance of wildlife species.

The refuge now totals 22,265 acres, with a current approved acquisition boundary of 23,126 acres. This initial acquisition was made possible through a partnership agreement between The Conservation Fund, city of New Orleans, and the Service. There are several parcels of land that lie within the existing refuge boundary that are not owned by the Service. Several of these parcels compromise refuge management due to conflicting management purposes and disturbance to wildlife. Acquisition of these parcels would eliminate access issues, improve management options and tighten some unclear and confusing boundary issues.

VISITOR SERVICES

The priority public uses of the refuge are fishing, wildlife observation, wildlife photography, and environmental education and interpretation. The issues facing the Visitor Services Program center on the re-establishment of services post Hurricane Katrina. Several primary public use areas of the refuge are currently closed due to storm damage. Using the Final CCP and the visitor services plan, the refuge will establish a plan for restoration of public services and access. The locations of current public use facilities at Bayou Sauvage NWR are illustrated in Figure 5.

Fishing and Hunting

The primary objectives of Bayou Sauvage NWR are to provide habitat for the protection of fish and other wildlife. Fishing is one of the main public uses of the refuge. Access to and recreational use of the refuge resources are permitted in designated areas and in accordance with state and federal regulations. Further, the use of these resources is subject to the following conditions: Bayou Sauvage NWR is open 30 minutes before legal sunrise until 30 minutes after legal sunset. Sport and recreational shell fishing are permitted from February 1 through October 31.

There are several public access points for fishing activities. There is a handicap accessible fishing pier on Highway 90 at the Wayside Park location along the Bayou Sauvage waterway. Prior to Hurricane Katrina, this site was rarely if ever used for fishing and this is not expected to change unless the bayou can be deepened to improve fish habitat. Bank fishing at non-designated "pull offs" along Highway 11 was popular with anglers prior to Hurricane Katrina; it is expected that this will not change as the recovery from the hurricane continues. The Highway 11 boat launch provides boating access to anglers with 25 hp or less engines. The Madere Marsh Unit off of Highway 90 is a popular site for anglers to catch bait. Opportunities for crawfishing also abound at the Joe Madere Marsh site. Before Hurricane Katrina, there was also fishing from along the Maxent Canal, at the Ridge Trail site, which is in an area just outside of the refuge. The Ridge Trail site has not re-opened to the public. However, the site will be opened by the time the CCP document is released. Salt marsh fishing occurred at the refuge on both sides of the Gulf Intracoastal Waterway prior to Hurricane Katrina and still remains popular. Crabbing has been historically popular at the Crabbing Bridge Road Site. The most commonly found fish on the refuge are bass, catfish, bream, redfish, speckled sea trout, and gar.

Bayou Sauvage NWR serves as one of the last remaining non-hunted sanctuaries in the area for wildlife and presently is not opened to hunting. However, the refuge is considering opening the marshes outside of the Hurricane Protection Levee System to limited youth waterfowl hunting.

Wildlife Observation and Photography

Prior to Hurricane Katrina, wildlife viewing opportunities abounded on Bayou Sauvage NWR. The refuge is part of the "America's Wetland Birding Trail." The Ridge Trail boardwalk was a popular destination for visitors and tourists to view the diverse flora and fauna of Bayou Sauvage NWR. The Ridge Trail offered a first-hand view of three habitat types: bottomland hardwood forest, swamp, and marsh. While walking the trail, one could likely see a variety of birds, both resident and/or neotropical, depending on the season, as well as the ever-present birds of prey, such as hawks and turkey vultures. A myriad of reptiles and amphibians were commonly seen, as well as a variety of mammals, such as raccoons, squirrels, and rabbits. The end of the board walk had an observation deck with a viewing scope overlooking an old cypress swamp. From this deck, visitors could see wading birds, ducks, and perhaps a bald eagle. The boardwalk and observation deck were destroyed during Hurricane Katrina, but are being rebuilt as part of the recovery process.

Wildlife photography and viewing opportunities are also available along the north and south Maxent Levees. Birders, in particular, took advantage of these locations. The Bayou Sauvage Bikeway, a hard-surfaced 4.5 mile bike trail, was damaged by Hurricane Katrina and may be reopened as a rougher, "dirt bike" type trail. The bike path offers excellent views of wildlife for photographers and visitors. While walking or riding along the path, visitors may see wading birds, alligators, marsh rabbits, or other resident wildlife.

The universally accessible Wayside Park Pier offers a close look at a portion of the actual historical Bayou Sauvage waterway. Nearby, before Hurricane Katrina, Joe Madere Marsh offered several marked canoe trails and excellent opportunities to view ducks, shorebirds, marshbirds, raptors, and alligators, as well as lush marsh grasses.

Environmental Education

Prior to Hurricane Katrina, the environmental education program consisted of an off-site (classroom visits) component and an on-site component. Currently offered classroom programs include the following:

"Endangered Species" is a program intended primarily for students in grades 4-6. This program provides a look at why species become endangered and the Fish and Wildlife Service's role in protecting them. It features endangered species items confiscated by the Service's wildlife inspectors, and rangers bring live endangered species to the classroom as well.

"Creature Features" is a program for students in grade levels K-3, which offers students a fun and educational lesson in how animals adapt to and survive in their environment. Live animals are featured as well as a "modeling" component where the adaptations of a wetland animal are demonstrated as a student is dressed up in articles based on that animal.

Both the "Endangered Species" and the "Creature Features" programs were popular before Hurricane Katrina and are in more demand since Hurricane Katrina, probably due to more "advertising" of the programs, and the fact that we cannot yet resume our on-site environmental education curriculum.

On-site Programs:
Prior to Hurricane Katrina, the refuge offered two major on-site programs to the public. "Habitat Is Where It's At," was for students in grades 4-6, and is a wetlands education curriculum which takes place at the Ridge Trail Site. This is a three-part program consisting of a nature walk, dip netting in the nearby Maxent canal, and a van tour of the refuge featuring wildlife viewing and education about management and challenges facing an urban refuge.

"Wetlands Investigator" is a program made possible by a National Fish and Wildlife Foundation grant. It was created to offer educational opportunities to underserved students in the metro New Orleans area, particularly those in close proximity to Bayou Sauvage NWR. Students in grades 2-3 came to the refuge and made an exploratory trek on the boardwalk, identifying flora and fauna, and then they went on a swamp tour at the former "Swamp Tour Site" and where they observed flora and fauna up close and got a first-hand view of the marshes of the refuge.

To get information to teachers about these opportunities, the education staff mails information to schools in the metro New Orleans area, distributes an informational sheet at special events, and issues press releases.

It is anticipated that on-site environmental education program offerings will be significantly re-tooled to reflect habitat changes after Hurricane Katrina and to highlight the recovery of the refuge's ecosystems. An effort will also be made to tie the refuge's natural processes and resources more closely to larger issues of coastal preservation in the state.

Interpretation

An ambitious slate of weekend interpretive programs was offered at Bayou Sauvage NWR prior to Hurricane Katrina, with peak programming occurring in approximately 2002. Refuge programs were scaled back due to reduced staffing and the development and expansion of programs at Big Branch Marsh NWR. Much of the staffing capability for these outings was provided by the Southeast Louisiana NWR Complex's full-time student intern/SCA program. Some of these programs included:

- Interpretive canoe tours were offered through the Joe Madere Marsh unit of the refuge, and occasionally from the Highway 11 boat launch site or from the Maxent Levee near Blind Lagoon, as dictated by water levels. These tours were free to the public, and reservations were taken in advance. Usually a maximum of 12 canoes per trip was used.

- Interpretive nature walks, including nighttime or "moonlight" walks, were also offered at the Ridge Trail boardwalk.

- Interpretive bike tours were offered on the Bayou Sauvage Bikeway. These trips were not as popular as anticipated. Participants had to transport their own bikes to the refuge, and some participants were looking more for a "ride" than an interpretive tour.

- Birding tours were offered at the Ridge Trail and other sites on the refuge, including the Maxent Levee. These were sometimes conducted by volunteers from local birding clubs, and were fairly popular during certain seasons.

- <u>Junior Refuge Manager Program</u> was offered at the Ridge Trail pavilion on selected Saturdays mainly during spring and fall. Nature study booklets were developed at two different levels (ages 6-9 and 10-12) and keyed to numbered stops set up at the pavilion and along the Ridge Trail boardwalk. A staff person greeted and oriented participants at the pavilion, and showed a 3-minute interpretive film about the Refuge System as an introduction. Participants then followed the sequence of stops in the booklet, observing and answering questions about the resources along the way. At the conclusion, the booklets were "graded" and participants received a Bayou Sauvage Junior Refuge Manager badge.

Non-personal interpretation opportunities were also offered. Some of these opportunities included:

- The Ridge Trail boardwalk featured approximately 20 black and white 9 x 12 trailside interpretive signs focusing on selected flora and fauna present along the route. There was also a 2 x 3 wayside on bottomland hardwoods, and a 2 x 3 wayside entitled "Bayous" near an overlook of the Bayou Sauvage waterway. That panel explained the origin of the term "bayou" and the geologic significance of the waterway. The majority of these signs was destroyed by Hurricane Katrina.

- The Wayside Park (Highway 90 Pier) kiosk still has a 3 x 3 interpretive panel in good shape entitled "Bayou Sauvage – Highway to the Past," which provides a sketch of the historical significance of the waterway as a transportation route into New Orleans.

- The Highway 11 Boat Launch kiosk featured a standard 3 x 3 panel on Waterfowl Migration and a 2 x 3 panel entitled "Be a Better Boater," with recommendations for environmentally friendly boating practices. The kiosk, brochure box, and panels were destroyed by Hurricane Katrina, and were frequent targets of vandalism prior to that.

- At the Crabbing Bridge, a kiosk with a 3 x 3 "you are here" type panel indicates the start of the Bayou Sauvage Bikeway. It is in good shape. Another 3 x 3 panel is entitled "Crabs and Crabbing," with blue crab biology, crabbing tips, and other information about this pastime. It was badly defaced by spray paint. The kiosk was damaged by Katrina and was removed.

- At Exit 251 (swamp tour exit) of I-10, at the opposite end of the bike path was a kiosk that had a "you are here" panel similar to the one at the Crabbing Bridge. It was likely stolen after Hurricane Katrina. On the south side of the exit, at the swamp tour, was a kiosk that originally had a Refuge System panel. That panel was later replaced by a refuge centennial panel, which featured a map of all Louisiana national wildlife refuges. The exit and the swamp tour are now closed and the kiosk panels have been removed.

Figure 5. Location of public use areas on Bayou Sauvage NWR

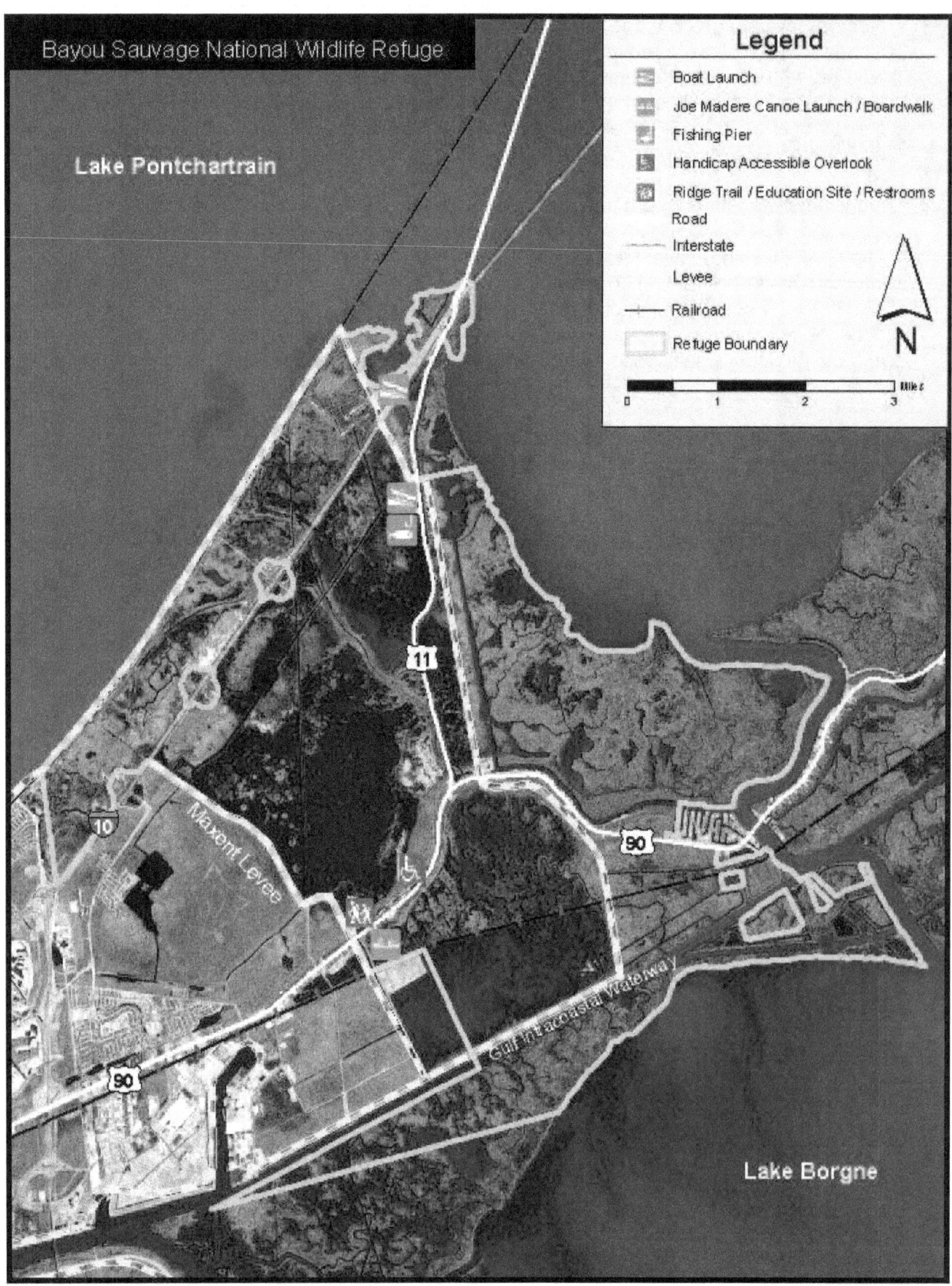

PERSONNEL, OPERATIONS, AND MAINTENANCE

Refuge administration refers to the operation and maintenance of refuge programs and facilities, including construction. Refuge personnel are not assigned solely to Bayou Sauvage NWR, but support the eight refuges in the Southeast Louisiana NWR Complex. Six positions share responsibility for Bayou Sauvage, Breton, and Delta NWRs. The Complex staff consists of 27 permanent full-time employees (Figure 6 See Chapter 5 under Funding and Personel). The refuge also benefits from the help of interns and volunteers.

The major management activities on the refuge include wetland restoration projects, law enforcement, wildlife monitoring, environmental education, and providing public uses when they are compatible with refuge purposes.

III. Plan Development

SUMMARY OF ISSUES, CONCERNS, AND OPPORTUNITIES

The planning team identified a number of issues, concerns, and opportunities related to fish and wildlife protection, habitat management and restoration, visitor and educational services, and refuge administration. Issues and concerns are based on the professional judgment of the team and on recommendations and discussions with personnel from other conservation agencies and refuges. Also, issues and concerns arising from a February 2007 review of the refuge's biological program and a March 2007 review of the refuge's visitor services program were considered. Comments from the public made at a public scoping meeting held in June 2007, and comments mailed to the refuge, were considered. Key issues included: restoration of the refuge due to damages from Hurricane Katrina, migratory bird and waterfowl nesting habitats, invasive species of plants and animals, refuge access, law enforcement, and re-establishing volunteer and environmental education programs. The planning team considered federal and state mandates, as well as applicable local ordinances, regulations, and plans.

All public and advisory team comments were considered; however, some issues important to the public fall outside the scope of the decisions made within this planning process. The team considered all issues that were raised throughout the planning process. This plan attempts to balance the competing opinions relating to important issues. The team identified the issues that, in its best professional judgment, are most significant to the refuge. A summary of the significant issues follows.

FISH AND WILDLIFE POPULATION MANAGEMENT

Threatened and Endangered Species

The protection of threatened and endangered plants and animals is an important responsibility delegated to the Service and its national wildlife refuges. A number of federal threatened and endangered species are thought to use, or have the potential to use, Bayou Sauvage NWR. These include the eastern brown pelican, West Indian manatee, and Gulf sturgeon. Although the refuge does not actively manage for these transient species, it does offer protection and habitat.

Invasive and Nuisance Species

An "invasive species" is defined as a species that is non-native (or alien) to the ecosystem under consideration, and whose interdiction causes or is likely to cause economic harm, environmental harm, or harm to human health (Executive Order 13112). These species are normally introduced by direct or inadvertent human actions.

Both plant and animal nuisance and invasive species currently occur on the refuge. Animal species, such as nutria and feral hogs, compete with native species for limited food supplies and can be destructive to habitats. Removal of hogs has been accomplished by trappers working under a special use permit issued by refuge management. Removal of nutria is through private trappers enrolled in the state's nutria removal program.

Nuisance and invasive plant species include the Chinese tallow tree, water hyacinth, cogon grass, and the dodder plant. One commenter mentioned the need to control water hyacinth to reduce the threat of choked waterways to a degree that permits recreational use. Another commenter mentioned the need to conserve natural aquatic vegetation important to aquatic systems and to reduce the destructiveness of tallow trees around the natural ridge levee. Because of the opportunistic and resilient nature of these species, they have thrived after Hurricane Katrina.

Resident Wildlife

While the Service's primary goal is the protection of federal trust species, the refuge's purposes include improving natural diversity of resident fish and wildlife species. Therefore, it is the responsibility of the refuge to manage resident wildlife within the refuge boundaries. This management needs to be performed in conjunction with, and not to the detriment of, migratory, shore, and wading birds within the refuge. An array of wildlife species indigenous to the LMRE inhabit Bayou Sauvage NWR. The most widely recognized species include white-tailed deer, squirrel, rabbit, otter, raccoon, and mink. Resident reptiles and amphibians include alligators, various snakes, frogs, skinks, and turtles.

A commenter at the public scoping meeting suggested establishing a relocation trapping program to restore the wildlife diversity of the refuge. Habitat restoration must take place before this comment can be given full consideration.

Migratory Birds

A primary purpose of the refuge is to provide wintering and nesting habitats for migratory and resident waterfowl, wading birds, and migrating song birds. The operation and management of the refuge provides for the basic needs of these species, including feeding, resting, and breeding. Management measures include planting vegetation and managing moist-soil in eight different water management units that cater to a variety of different species. Comments from the biological review team and the public expressed a desire to support and expand these efforts. A major issue facing the refuge is the reduction in migrating waterfowl utilizing the refuge because of recent drought conditions and previous hurricane damage to critical habitats. Several comments were made that the freshwater marsh should be re-established to improve waterfowl use and diversity on the refuge.

The biological review team also identified a need to properly survey and monitor resident and breeding waterfowl (i.e., mottled duck and marsh birds) populations to determine population numbers and to identify management needs. Nesting boxes for wood ducks and black-bellied whistling ducks exist and are used on the refuge and are a good source of valuable breeding information. These surveys would help evaluate impacts of previous management actions, as well as uncontrollable factors, such as weather and outside pollution sources.

HABITAT MANAGEMENT

The refuge is located in the physiographic region known as the LMRE. The LMRE includes the deltaic plain and associated marshes and swamps created by the meanderings of the Mississippi River and its distributaries. Prior to the 1920s, the lands that now make up the refuge were annually recharged by flooding of the Mississippi River, which created primarily brackish marsh habitats. Today, eight moist-soil water management units made up of fresh, intermediate, and brackish marsh are situated between Lakes Pontchartrain and Borgne. A small section of bottomland hardwood forest also exists along the natural ridge levee. The freshwater units' primary source of fresh water is precipitation, while the intermediate and brackish units receive tidal flows from the nearby lakes.

Moist-soil Water Management

Moist-soil management refers to management of land to provide moist-soil conditions during the growing season to promote the natural production of beneficial plants. Seeds produced by these plants often attract and concentrate waterfowl and other wetland wildlife species. Moist-soil impoundments provide plant and animal foods that are a critical part of the diet of wintering and migrating waterfowl and have become a significant part of management efforts on many refuges. Preferred moist-soil plants provide seeds and other plant parts (e.g., leaves, roots, and tubers) that generally have low deterioration rates after flooding, and provide substantial energy and essential nutrients less available to wintering waterfowl in common agricultural grains (i.e., corn, milo, and soybeans). Moist-soil impoundments also support diverse populations of invertebrates, an important protein source for waterfowl. The plants and invertebrates available in moist-soil impoundments provide food resources necessary for wintering and migrating waterfowl to complete critical aspects of the annual cycle, such as molt and reproduction. Due to the highly organic nature of the soils at Bayou Sauvage NWR, water management is a highly complex undertaking. It has been further complicated by the residual salts remaining from Hurricane Katrina.

The eight water management units are managed to control water depths and to cater to resident and migratory waterfowl. Habitat management of the refuge includes planting grasses and trees to provide food and nesting resources, using Christmas trees and breakwater dikes as shoreline erosion control, and some prescribed burning to control invasive plants and underbrush. As mentioned in the Physical and Biological Resource sections of this plan, Hurricane Katrina greatly impacted waterfowl, neotropical migratory birds, and resident wildlife habitats. One major issue is restoration of the freshwater marsh habitat after Hurricane Katrina. The refuge staff seeks to re-establish the diversity of the refuge to that observed prior to Hurricane Katrina by restoring the freshwater marsh units and reforesting the natural levee ridge. The refuge staff plans to enhance management of the freshwater units by exploring alternatives to reduce saltwater intrusion and soil salinities, and by the introduction of fresh waters other than precipitation to fresh marsh units.

Several comments were made by public stakeholders and members of the biological review team that reinforced the need to restore damaged habitats and to re-establish freshwater marsh to enhance fish and wildlife diversity.

Fire Management

Fire plays a role in shaping the wildlife habitats of Bayou Sauvage NWR. Fire management consists of both wildland fire suppression and prescribed burning activities. Prescribed burning is the application of fire by man to achieve land use objectives under specific conditions. In contrast, wildland fires that occur on the refuge are started by lightning strikes or from human activities under non-prescribed conditions. Wildfires occur every year on the refuge. During the period from 1990 to 2006, there were 101 wildfires that burned over 2,000 acres on the refuge. A majority of the wildfires were human-caused fires rather than natural lightning strikes.

There are many challenges to prescribed burning on Bayou Sauvage NWR. The biggest challenge is managing smoke in the presence of a major interstate (I-10) and highways (U.S. 11 and 90), which bisect the refuge, and the proximity of the refuge to residential areas and downtown New Orleans. In addition to the challenges of smoke management, water levels can also limit the window of opportunity for prescribed burning in certain units of the refuge.

Prescribed burning is used as a management tool in units inside the hurricane protection levees. Currently, no prescribed burning is used in the marshes outside the protection levees primarily because these brackish marshes are subsiding. There is little scientific data to support burning subsiding marshes. Within the protection levees, prescribed burning is used in selected units to encourage more desirable waterfowl food plant species, such as three-square, millet, and foxtail, over undesirable species, such as cattails. In units where native waterfowl foods are abundant, less prescribed burning is applied. Fire effects have been monitored over time at Bayou Sauvage NWR and have shown that the amount of native plant species, such as panicums, foxtails, and millets, has increased over time from the prescribed burning program. Although waterfowl response is usually good after a burn in the marsh, other factors such as overall health of the marsh or loss of plant materials for sedimentation can also play a role.

Another challenge to the fire management program of Bayou Sauvage NWR is the amount of debris deposited on the refuge following Hurricane Katrina in 2005. Marsh vegetation rolled up by wind and water formed lines of debris, known as "rack lines," within the refuge. These lines are mostly made up of the organic materials of the marsh. In order to maintain the original native vegetation, they will not be burned. However, there are numerous rack lines in the refuge made up of mostly man-made, wood-based products. These rack lines will be burned to improve access for the removal of debris. These rack lines occur mainly outside the protection levee system adjacent to the Intracoastal Water Way. Concerns have been expressed over the potential health risks to the public from inhaling smoke generated by burning hazardous materials.

RESOURCE PROTECTION

Cultural Resources

In addition to its biological assets, the refuge has cultural sites relating to human settlement that date back as far as 2,200 years. Several archaeological investigations have been performed over the years on refuge lands and have produced artifacts and evidence that range from the Tchefuncte culture habitation to the Civil War. These resources are not currently featured as public use areas due to the likelihood of theft and other adverse affects. It is unlikely that these areas will be open to the public. However, with the increased demand for public recreation and the economic value of artifacts, it may be necessary to increase law enforcement patrol frequency in these areas.

Pollution Prevention

Bayou Sauvage NWR is located adjacent to urban and industrial areas. Several sources of pollution may be present on the refuge caused by off-refuge sources. Pollutants such as heavy metals can have long-term effects when deposited into the soil column and bio-concentrated through the food chain. Pollutant effects on water quality also are exacerbated by drought, salt water intrusion, and flooding. Presence of any high contaminant levels should be identified and documented. Recovery One, an abandoned landfill owned by the city of New Orleans located in close proximity to refuge lands, is not presently being monitored. LDEQ should make determinations of any leaching that could cause contamination.

Refuge management has taken steps to reduce dumping by installing road gates, thereby managing after-hours access. A commenter suggested one way to combat noise pollution issues and the constant threat of continued urbanization is to acquire a strip of land to be managed as a buffer zone.

Six uses of refuge lands have been identified in the Improvement Act as priority public uses of refuges as long as they are compatible with refuge purposes. These uses, which include hunting, fishing, wildlife observation, wildlife photography, and environmental education and interpretation, must be determined appropriate and compatible for each specific refuge.

Fishing and Hunting

Fishing and hunting opportunities are of great public interest. Several stakeholders expressed the desire to include hunting as one of the public uses of the refuge. Presently, the refuge is not opened to hunting. However, the refuge is considering opening the marshes outside of the Hurricane Protection Levee System to limited youth water fowl hunting. With the loss of wetland habitat caused by urban development and coastal erosion, Bayou Sauvage NWR serves as one of the last remaining non-hunted sanctuaries in the area for wildlife.

Most of the waterways inside the Hurricane Protection Levee System have been impacted by increased salinity levels caused by saltwater intrusion from Hurricane Katrina. Areas that once had a diversity of freshwater aquatic species now only yield a few brackish species. Several recommended actions were suggested to improve fishing opportunities and access to fishing areas on the refuge. These included increasing signage to indicate refuge-approved fishing areas, restoring fishing piers and access roads, and performing maintenance dredging to improve fishing opportunities.

Wildlife Observation and Photography/Environmental Education and Interpretation

Prior to Hurricane Katrina, wildlife viewing and photography opportunities were plentiful on Bayou Sauvage NWR. Several trails, boardwalks, and piers provided diverse flora and fauna observation opportunities to visitors. Most of these structures and trails were severely damaged by Hurricane Katrina. The visitor services review team and public stakeholders have recommended repairing and restoring these viewing areas to their pre-Hurricane Katrina condition. Additional recommendations included installing kiosks to describe wildlife viewing opportunities, redesigning the tear sheets indicating the good birding/wildlife viewing areas, and developing an observation tower off of the Maxent Levee.

The environmental education programs offered by the refuge include both on-site and off-site classroom components. Because environmental education is a legislated purpose of the refuge, this plan should include a visionary look at how this purpose will be addressed. Recommendations from the visitor service team included task items to be completed now, intermediately, and long-term. These included the need to look at staffing options, re-establishing weekend programs, maintaining an accurate teacher contact database, and re-establishing the intern program as environmental education support.

The refuge has participated in various off-site outreach events over the years. Regular events have included the annual Earth Fest at the Audubon Zoo, the Sportsman's Show at the Louisiana Superdome, the Mayor's Earth Day in downtown New Orleans, and the Wildfowl Carvers Show in Westwego (suburban New Orleans). Other venues have included conventions and conferences held in New Orleans, special events at the Louisiana Nature Center, shopping malls, and teacher fairs held at Six Flags and other locations around town. Refuge staff and volunteers, including the Friends of Louisiana Wildlife Refuges, Inc., have staffed these events.

Media outreach occurs in the form of press releases, radio and television interviews, and phone contacts. Special events and interpretive programs have also been subjects of press releases and newspaper stories. Prior to Hurricane Katrina, a reporter assigned to the New Orleans East area was always eager to print stories in that edition of the *Times Picayune*. Refuge staff have appeared on TV morning shows to promote special events, and on radio talk shows to discuss post-Hurricane Katrina refuge status.

Congressional outreach has consisted of inviting local senators and representatives and their staffs to special events, and for special tours of the refuge. Congressional staffers have also been present for visits by Secretary Norton and Secretary Kempthorne.

The visitor services review team recommended holding special events to celebrate the reopening of refuge public use areas, developing a Bayou Sauvage NWR exhibit at the local zoo, and maintaining contacts at local newspapers, radio, and television stations.

REFUGE ADMINISTRATION

Law Enforcement

The demand for recreation access and the dumping and vandalism problems encountered by the refuge have prompted a recommendation for additional law enforcement presence on the refuge. Several public comments proposed possible resolutions to dumping and theft such as additional officer presence, installing cameras, and cutting back hedges around parking areas.

Staffing Needs

The staff that administers Bayou Sauvage NWR is also responsible for the management of Delta and Breton NWRs. As part of the eight-refuge Southeast Louisiana Refuge Complex, these same staff support activities and issues on all of the refuges. The staff presently assigned to Bayou Sauvage NWR consists of a refuge manager and a refuge operations specialist. The park rangers and maintenance staff share their work duties on several of the refuges. Future staff positions needed to operate Bayou Sauvage, Delta, and Breton NWRs are an assistant manager, an additional law enforcement officer, and a biologist.

Additional funding and facilities are needed to meet the refuge's goals and vision for the next 15 years. This plan details these needs by establishing goals, objectives, and strategies.

Wilderness Review

Refuge planning policy requires a wilderness review as part of the comprehensive conservation planning process. The results of the wilderness review are included in Appendix H.

IV. Management Direction

INTRODUCTION

The Service manages fish and wildlife habitats by considering the needs of all resources in decision-making. However, first and foremost, fish and wildlife conservation assumes priority in refuge management. A requirement of the Improvement Act is for the Service to maintain the ecological health, diversity, and integrity of refuges. Public uses are allowed if they are appropriate and compatible with wildlife and habitat conservation. The Service has identified six priority wildlife-dependent public uses. These uses are: hunting, fishing, wildlife observation, wildlife photography, and environmental education and interpretation.

The proposed comprehensive conservation plan for managing the refuge over the next 15 years is described below. This proposed management direction contains the goals, objectives, and strategies that will be used to achieve the refuge vision.

Three alternatives for managing the refuge were considered:

A - No Action (Current Management)

B - Restore and Improve Ecological Diversity and Augment Visitor Services (Proposed)

C - Custodial Management, while Maximizing Visitor Services

Each of these alternatives is described in Section B, Environmental Assessment. The Service chose Alternative B (Restore and Improve Ecological Diversity and Augment Visitor Services) as the proposed management direction.

Implementing the proposed alternative will result in the restoration and improvement of refuge resources needed for wildlife and habitat management, while providing opportunities for a variety of additional compatible wildlife-dependent recreation, education, and interpretive activities. This alternative would also allow the refuge to provide law enforcement protection that adequately meets the demands of an urban environment.

VISION

Bayou Sauvage NWR, which includes a diversity of flora and fauna, provides habitat for the protection of fish and wildlife and provides opportunities for fish- and wildlife-dependent public use and recreation adjacent to a major urban center. Staff and volunteers, with the active participation of partners, strive to maintain, identify, conserve, manage, and enhance refuge habitats to increase public awareness of environmental issues affecting the refuge. The management of wildlife and habitat on the refuge is an active, science-driven, comprehensive endeavor that includes research projects to meet information needs of the refuge, and aims to conserve the natural health and beauty of the land for future generations.

GOALS, OBJECTIVES, AND STRATEGIES

The goals, objectives, and strategies presented are the Service's response to the issues, concerns, and needs expressed by the planning team, the refuge staff and partners, and the public, and are presented in hierarchical format. Chapter V, Plan Implementation, identifies the projects associated with the various strategies.

These goals, objectives, and strategies reflect the Service's commitment to achieve the mandates of Improvement Act, the mission of the Refuge System, and the purposes and vision of Bayou Sauvage NWR. The Service intends to accomplish these goals, objectives, and strategies within the next 15 years.

FISH AND WILDLIFE POPULATION MANAGEMENT

Goal 1. Identify, conserve, manage, and restore populations of native fish and wildlife species with emphasis on migratory birds and threatened and endangered species.

Discussion: Bayou Sauvage NWR is home to a large variety of resident fish and wildlife species, in addition to a wide diversity of habitats providing feeding, nesting, and resting for many species of resident and migratory birds, including many species of waterfowl, shorebirds, marsh birds, wading birds, and songbirds. Starting in 2000, the populations of these species began to decrease. This decrease was primarily attributed to damage to food sources and habitats due to drought and major storms. The key to the conservation and restoration of these species' populations is increased monitoring that can be used to direct adaptive management of critical habitats.

Recovery and protection of threatened and endangered plants and animals are important responsibilities delegated to the Service and its national wildlife refuges. Federal threatened and endangered species such as the Gulf sturgeon, eastern brown pelicans and West Indian manatee are thought to use, or could use, the refuge lands.

Objective 1.1: Over the 15-year life of the CCP, increase monitoring of waterfowl and other migratory birds in order to assess and adapt habitat management strategies/actions.

Discussion: Currently the refuge conducts one midwinter waterfowl survey and one other aerial waterfowl survey annually. Due to the decrease in migration numbers over the past several years and the destruction of habitat due to natural disasters, it is important to increase monitoring to determine the overall health of the ecosystem. This additional monitoring will help assess the need for habitat recovery, allowing refuge staff to actively adapt habitat management strategies to focus on critical needs.

Strategies:

- Participate in Secretive Marsh Bird surveys using standardized protocols in select management units.
- Conduct aerial waterfowl surveys every three weeks from November 1 to February 1.
- Participate in midwinter waterfowl survey.
- Participate in Christmas Bird Count: provide one (1) staff and boat to facilitate surveys in marsh and waterways.
- Conduct monthly rookery counts of wading birds during the March to June time period each year.

Objective 1.2: Over the 15-year life of the CCP, consult with the Service's Ecological Services Office on potential impacts of refuge programs/actions on threatened and endangered species.

Discussion: The Service is the principal federal agency charged with protecting and enhancing more than 800 species of migratory birds that spend all or part of their lives in the United States. In addition, the Service and the National Oceanic and Atmospheric Administration share responsibility for administration of the Endangered Species Act of 1973, which combines both United States and foreign species. "Trust species" for the Service are those covered by the many laws and mandates designating federal responsibility for their protection and conservation. In addition, plans such as bird conservation plans for waterfowl, shorebirds, songbirds, etc., contain lists of birds of concern which are targeted for management purposes. Management programs on Bayou Sauvage NWR target those migratory and resident birds that depend on marsh, trees, and other habitats occurring on the refuge. No federally listed threatened or endangered species reside on the refuge, although some species may use the area temporarily.

Strategy:

- Consult with the Service's Ecological Services Office through the Section 7 process to evaluate potential impacts of refuge programs and actions on threatened and endangered species.

Objective 1.3: Provide nest cavities for wood ducks and black-bellied whistling tree ducks to support 100 hatchlings per year.

Discussion: Natural nesting cavities have become scarce. Many refuges provide nesting habitat by placing nesting boxes in the appropriate habitats. The refuge would like to provide and maintain at least 25 boxes. These boxes will be checked periodically to determine how many were used and the amount of reproduction that occurred.

Strategy:

- Install and ensure that a minimum of twenty-five nest boxes are cleaned and available prior to January of each year.

Objective 1.4: Over the 15-year life of the CCP, participate in the State of Louisiana Nutria Control program. Actively promote the nutria control program and seek assistance from area trappers to reduce nutria populations on refuge lands consistent with the state's Nuisance Animal Control Plan.

Proactively seek assistance in implementing an aggressive eradication program for feral hogs consistent with the refuge's Nuisance Animal Control Plan.

Discussion: While the Service strives to provide habitat diversity for a range of native wildlife, there are non-native or nuisance species that are destructive to critical habitat and out-compete native wildlife for available food resources. Bayou Sauvage NWR has several documented non-native nuisance animal species. Animals like feral hogs compete with native wildlife for limited resources and others, like nutria, have caused extensive habitat damage and alterations. Control of these species' populations is imperative to maintaining habitats for federal trust species and other native wildlife.

Strategies:

- Conduct yearly evaluations of nutria and feral hog populations on refuge lands using established monitoring protocols.
- Partner with area trappers to reduce nutria and feral hog populations.

Objective 1.5: Over the 15-year life of the CCP, increase monitoring of endemic wildlife species in order to assess and adapt habitat management strategies/actions.

Discussion: The Improvement Act includes the need to manage for biological diversity and integrity in addition to federal trust species (e.g., migratory birds, and threatened and endangered species). Common wildlife observed on the refuge includes white-tailed deer, squirrel, otter, raccoon, and mink. All terrestrial species suffered during and after the 2005 hurricane season. Signs have been observed of these species, but not in the abundance before Hurricane Katrina. Large numbers of alligators and turtles once existed on the refuge. Both reptiles and amphibians have diminished in number. The refuge currently is collecting observational data of alligator presence and general size classes. Game fish harvests are being monitored. However, this monitoring needs to be expanded to allow the refuge staff to actively adapt habitat management strategies to focus on additional wildlife and critical habitat needs.

Strategies:

- Work with the Service's Fisheries Office to establish monitoring needs and protocols for yearly assessment of fish populations.
- Conduct yearly nighttime alligator surveys using established protocols and methods.
- Work with state herpetologist to identify and monitor reptile and amphibian populations.
- Conduct monthly creel surveys to identify species of game fish being harvested.

HABITAT MANAGEMENT

Goal 2. Restore and maintain fresh and brackish marsh systems and hardwood ridges to ensure healthy and viable ecological communities, with emphasis on migratory birds and threatened and endangered species. Develop a Habitat Management Plan.

Discussion: Historically, seasonal flooding from the Mississippi River recharged the refuge's aquatic systems and created a broad range of dynamic habitats that supported diverse fish and wildlife resources. The natural hydrology of this area was changed with the construction of man-made levees, installed to protect New Orleans from periodic river flooding and, later, hurricane protection levees to protect against major storm surges. The loss of this annual flooding regimen and disruption of tidal flows detrimentally impacted the wetland habitats and wetland-dependent species.

The position of Bayou Sauvage NWR as an oasis in the midst of urban development makes it an important resting and feeding area to trans-Gulf migratory songbirds, as well as waterfowl and shorebirds. Moist-soil management began in the 1990s and waterfowl numbers increased during this period. Consistently since 2000, numbers of waterfowl have decreased not only on the refuge, but in the Lake Pontchartrian basin area in general. Christmas bird counts also show lower numbers of other waterbirds since 2000. The decrease is probably a result of reduced moist-soil plant production caused by droughts and hurricanes. Not only is emergent vegetation production less, but certain species of submerged aquatic vegetation were also lost due to higher salinity levels in the water following the Hurricane Katrina storm surge.

Objective 2.1: Over the 15-year life of the CCP, acquire lands that provide resource and public use values from willing sellers by: fee title purchase, donation, mitigation purchase and transfer, or other viable means.

Discussion: The current acquisition boundary consists of approximately 30,126 acres. The refuge has approximately 22,265.12 acres in fee-title; 445 acres are managed through a Memorandum of Understanding with the city of New Orleans for management purposes; approximately 6,900 acres of privately owned land are included in the refuge's acquisition boundary; this could potentially be added to the refuge through donation, mitigation, or purchase from willing sellers. If funds and willing sellers become available, the refuge will attempt to acquire these lands in accordance with current Service policy.

Strategies:

- Complete minor expansion package (10 percent) for acquisition of lands.
- Through partners, explore potential for congressionally authorized major acquisition boundary expansion.

Objective 2.2: Develop and implement a habitat management plan by the year 2010.

Discussion: The need to develop and implement a habitat management plan was identified in the scoping stage of the CCP process. This management plan will identify resource needs and establish habitat restoration programs based on goals, objectives, and strategies identified in the CCP.

Strategy:

- Designate staff to develop and implement a habitat management plan. This plan should be completed by the year 2010.

Objective 2.3: Actively work to restore hardwood forest over the 15-year life of the plan.

Discussion: Prior to the summer of 2005, the natural levee ridge was a maritime bottomland hardwood forest dominated by live oak and sugar berry. The continued subsidence of this ridge, in addition to the saltwater intrusion due to major storms and an extended drought over the past 15 to 20 years, has continually compromised the integrity of the area to support hardwood communities. This has also allowed an invasive plant species, Chinese tallow, to opportunistically spread along this ridge, making it increasingly difficult for the propagation and restoration of natural vegetative species.

Strategies:

- Control Chinese tallow tree through mechanical and/or chemical means.
- Conduct mechanical and/or chemical site preparation and plant suitable native woody shrub and tree species.
- Re-establish cypress along shorelines of Bayou Sauvage and marsh edge.

Objective 2.4: Re-establish and restore fresh marsh habitat over the 15-year life of the CCP.

Discussion: Prior to Hurricane Katrina, the impounded marshes were primarily freshwater, with only a small area of intermediate salinity marsh between Turtle Bayou and the East Hurricane Flood Protection Levee and brackish marsh in the tidal wetlands. The damage incurred from the 2005 hurricane season included saltwater intrusion into the fresh impoundments, causing most of the fresh water vegetation and the trees to be killed. Restoration of these wetlands is especially difficult since wetlands depend on a dynamic interface of hydrologic regimes to maintain water, vegetation, and animal complexes and processes. An additional element that makes this restoration difficult, given the recent drought history, is that the only source of fresh water for these units is precipitation.

Strategies:

- Manage water levels to promote marsh growth and establishment while maintaining sufficient soil hydration to reduce/eliminate subsidence occurring through oxidation of organic materials.
- Restore Bayou Sauvage channel depth by removing infill material and providing an alternative outlet for excess water removal at the eastern end of the channel under Highway 11.
- Restore emergent marsh through beneficial use of dredged and/or other materials.
- Conduct vegetative plantings.
- Establish and monitor vegetation transects to assess impacts of management and restoration actions.
- Use organic materials such as Christmas trees and wood chips to create organic wave breaks and build marsh platforms.
- Investigate alternative methods of plant propagation and establishment such as floating cribs.
- Investigate alternative reliable sources of fresh water such as wetland assimilation of treated wastewater effluents.
- Investigate potential for use of select management units for water storage capability as supply for other management units.

Objective 2.5: Over the 15-year life of the CCP, submit project proposals for funding through the Coastal Wetlands Planning, Protection, and Restoration Act (CWPPRA) program.

Discussion: The CWPPRA (Public Law 101-646) authorizes the development of comprehensive restoration and comprehensive conservation plans for our nation's coastlands. Forty percent of the coastal marshes of the continental United States covered by this law lie in Louisiana. In February 2008, there were 164 CWPPRA restoration projects in Louisiana. The majority deal with hydrologic management, shoreline protection, and marsh creation. The most recent CWPPRA project on the refuge involved the installation of a rock breakwater dike along the Bayou Chevee and Lake Pontchartrain bank as shoreline protection and brackish tidal marsh restoration.

Strategy:

- Seek additional partnerships and opportunities for restoration through beneficial use of dredge disposal and alternative shoreline protection measures such as oyster reef blocks.

Objective 2.6: Over the 15-year life of the CCP, increase efforts to control invasive plant species.

Discussion: Bayou Sauvage NWR has several documented native and non-native invasive and exotic plant species. These invasive and exotic species were a problem prior to the 2005 hurricane season, but have proliferated and thrived in the absence of the native species killed by saltwater intrusion. These invasive species impact the refuge's ability to carry out desired wildlife and habitat management objectives and at times also reduce the range of visitor service activities. Many invasive plant species are difficult to control without applying chemical treatments. The moist-soil conditions conducive to providing quality habitat for migratory waterfowl management frequently encourages germination of those invasive species. If Bayou Sauvage NWR is to restore habitat ravaged by past natural disasters, a major part of this will consist of controlling invasive plant species, such as Chinese tallow trees, cogon grass, and water hyacinth.

Strategies:

- Proactively seek funding through the Service's invasive species control program for additional control efforts.
- Work with educational institutions, non-profit groups, and other organizations to promote recruitment and use of volunteers in control efforts.

Objective 2.7: Over the 15-year life of the CCP, manage and maintain prescribed and wildfire response programs to achieve healthy and viable wildlife and plant communities on the refuge.

Discussion: Fire management on the refuge consists of both wildfire suppression and controlled burning activities. Prescribed burning is the application of fire by man to achieve land use objectives under controlled conditions. In contrast, wildfires that occur on the refuge are started by lightning strikes or mainly from human activities under non-controlled conditions. Wildfires occur every year on the refuge. During the period from 1990 to 2006, there were 101 wildfires that burned over 2,000 acres on the refuge.

Strategies:

- Burn areas identified by biologists as available water level and other conditions allow.
- Promote and maintain desired vegetative communities through application of prescribed fire and reduce hazardous fuels and fuel levels as needed.
- Respond appropriately to all wildfires on refuge due to close proximity of neighbors, and state and federal critical infrastructure.

VISITOR SERVICES

Goal 3. Provide public use opportunities consistent with the Refuge System mission that capitalize on the unique urban proximity of Bayou Sauvage NWR.

Discussion: The Improvement Act states that compatible wildlife-dependent recreational uses are the priority public uses of the Refuge System (e.g., hunting, fishing, wildlife observation, wildlife photography, and environmental education and interpretation) and will receive enhanced consideration over the other general public uses. The Service will permit other uses only when they have been proven to be both appropriate and compatible (See 605 FW 1, General Guidance, and 603 FW 1, Appropriate Refuge Uses).

Bayou Sauvage NWR is the largest urban refuge in the Refuge System. A variety of indigenous wildlife inhabits the refuge. Some of the more notable wildlife species are those easily seen by the general public, such as alligators, large wading birds, and waterfowl. The refuge sport fisheries and crawfish populations provide sustainable recreational fishing opportunities. The introduction of limited waterfowl hunting is also being evaluated. Since the 2005 hurricane season, a large portion of the refuge's recreational areas have been temporarily closed to public access. As on-going recovery efforts are completed, the refuge will gradually be reopened.

Objective 3.1: Develop and implement a visitor services management plan by the year 2012.

Discussion: The need to develop and implement a visitor services management plan was identified in the visitor services review, held in the scoping stage of the CCP process. This management plan will identify resource needs and establish visitor service programs based on goals, objectives, and strategies identified in the CCP.

Strategy:

- Designate staff to develop and implement a visitor services management plan. This plan should be completed by the year 2012.

Objective 3.2: Over the 15-year life of the CCP, maintain and, where possible, expand interpretive opportunities on the refuge.

Discussion: Interpretive opportunities communicate important fish, wildlife, habitat, and other resource issues to visitors of all ages and abilities. The Refuge System tailors messages and delivery methods to specific audiences, presents them in appropriate locations, and encourages visitors to take positive actions supporting refuge goals and the Refuge System mission (See 605 FW 7, Interpretation). Prior to the 2005 hurricane season, the refuge offered a diverse slate of guided and unguided interpretive trails, bike paths, and kiosks. Many of the trails' interpretive panels, signs, and kiosks were damaged or destroyed by high winds and storm surge and need to be replaced. As on-going recovery efforts are completed, the interpretive areas will gradually be reopened with newly developed and installed interpretive panels, signs, and kiosks. There is also a need to establish a contact station or visitor center on the refuge to provide additional refuge education and interpretive opportunities.

Strategies:

- Establish a visitor center or contact station on the refuge, possibly at I-10, Exit 251, or the Ridge Trail site, which will provide interpretive displays and materials to aid visitor understanding of refuge resources and management issues.
- Implement personal interpretive opportunities and expand where possible through partnerships, including guided nature walks, canoe tours, birding tours, and similar programs.
- Develop and install new kiosks, waysides panels, and trail signs with appropriate interpretive messages at Ridge Trail site, Madere Marsh, Highway 11 launch, and Wayside Park.

Objective 3.3: Over the 15-year life of the CCP, develop a new slate of environmental education programs that emphasizes refuge restoration activities and the diversity of water management regimes in the aftermath of Hurricane Katrina, and that also addresses larger coastal conservation issues.

Discussion: As described in Chapter II, prior to Hurricane Katrina, the environmental education program consisted of an off-site (classroom visits) component and an on-site component. These programs focused on endangered species, wetland habitats, and wildlife. The visitor services review identified the need to incorporate environmental education elements that focus on post-Hurricane Katrina recovery, the diversity of ecosystems found on the refuge, and coastal wetlands conservation. The review also identified the need to re-establish weekend education programs when staffing is available.

Strategies:

- Select grade levels to target, and then establish curriculum-based programs that address appropriate state grade level expectations for those grades.
- Seek grant support and partnerships to fund bus transportation to the refuge for those schools in need.
- Communicate the diversity of fresh and brackish water ecosystems found under this water management regime.
- Maintain contacts with area school systems to promote programs and gain teacher input in program design.

Objective 3.4: Over the 15-year life of the CCP, expand wildlife observation and wildlife photography opportunities where possible to highlight both fresh and brackish water ecosystems through the addition of facilities.

Discussion: Wildlife observation and wildlife photography (reference 605 FW 4, Wildlife Observation, and 605 FW 5, Wildlife Photography) are appropriate wildlife-dependent recreational uses of refuge lands, when compatible. Prior to Hurricane Katrina, wildlife viewing opportunities abounded on Bayou Sauvage NWR. The refuge is part of America's Wetland Birding Trail. The Ridge Trail boardwalk was a popular destination for visitors and tourists to view Bayou Sauvage NWR's diverse flora and fauna. The Ridge Trail offered a first-hand view of three habitat types: bottomland hardwood forest, swamp, and marsh. Several restoration activities will need to be completed before the trails and walkways will be available to the public. However, as on-going recovery efforts are completed, the trails and walkways will gradually be reopened to re-establish these opportunities.

Strategies:

- Promote levee-top walking trails/routes via signage.
- Reopen bike path to "trail bikes" if access can be re-established at exit 251 and/or Crabbing Bridge.
- Consider other opportunities for public access at exit 251, including boat tour possibilities (concession- or Service-operated).
- Revise bird lists every 5 years to reflect habitat and population changes after Hurricane Katrina.
- Reopen Joe Madere Marsh Boardwalk and Canoe Launch.

Objective 3.5: Where possible, over the 15-year life of the CCP, provide and improve fishing opportunities on the refuge.

Discussion: The primary objectives of Bayou Sauvage NWR are to provide habitat for the protection of fish and other wildlife. Fishing is one of the main public uses of the refuge; where appropriate and compatible, the best fishing opportunities are made available to the public. Currently, access to and recreational use of the refuge's resources are permitted in designated areas and in accordance with state and federal regulations, subject to the following conditions: Bayou Sauvage NWR is open 30 minutes before legal sunrise until 30 minutes after legal sunset. Sport and recreational shell fishing are permitted from February 1 through October 31.

There are several public access points for fishing activities. There is a handicap accessible observation pier on Highway 90 at the Wayside Park location. The Highway 11 boat launch provides access to anglers whose boat engines are 25 hp or less. The Madere Marsh Unit off of Highway 90 is a popular site for fishermen to catch bait. Opportunities for crawfishing also abound at the Madere Marsh site.

Strategies:

- Explore ways to improve roadway access to the Crabbing Bridge area through acquisition or partnerships.
- Consider fisheries management actions that would improve fishing opportunities on the refuge, such as stocking.
- Consider dredging Bayou Sauvage NWR's waterway to improve fishing habitat.
- Consider opportunities for fishing access at former swamp tour site at exit 251.

Objective 3.6: Evaluate the feasibility of opening up the marshes outside the hurricane protection levee to limited hunting.

Discussion: Presently, the refuge is not opened to hunting and it has not occurred since refuge establishment. However, the refuge is considering opening the marshes outside of the Hurricane Protection Levee System to limited youth waterfowl hunting. With the loss of wetland habitat caused by urban development and coastal erosion, Bayou Sauvage NWR serves as one of the last remaining non-hunted sanctuaries in the area for wildlife.

Strategies:

- Evaluate acceptability of providing hunting opportunities.
- Petition city of New Orleans for permission to hunt within city limits.
- Open tidal marsh outside Hurricane Protection Levee System to youth waterfowl hunting.

Objective 3.7: Over the 15-year life of the CCP, maintain and expand an active volunteer program to enhance all aspects of refuge management including resident interns, volunteers with recreational vehicles, Friends of Louisiana Wildlife Refuges' members, and local volunteers.

Discussion: The refuge's volunteer program is part of the overall volunteer program of the Southeast Louisiana NWR Complex. A volunteer coordinator housed at the complex office oversees the program. Through student interns, volunteers with recreational vehicles, local businesses, and friends groups, the refuge has had support to help with debris clean-up, vegetation and tree plantings, wildlife monitoring, and maintenance activities. The Friends of Louisiana Wildlife Refuges have also sought and received grants to support environmental education and interpretation on the refuge.

Strategies:

- Refine and implement improved recruitment methods, including web pages and contacts with local volunteer organizations.
- Specifically recruit local volunteers to be trained to assist with environmental education programs on a "semester" basis (12 weeks).
- Develop position descriptions for specific volunteer tasks, with timelines, to use in recruitment.
- Encourage and assist Friends of Louisiana Wildlife Refuges with membership recruitment throughout the greater New Orleans metropolitan area.
- Identify projects for potential friends group involvement.

- As funds allow, reactivate the resident intern/SCA program to support environmental education programming as well as other refuge functions.

Objective 3.8: Where possible, over the 15-year life of the CCP, increase public outreach to emphasize resource management practices and promote public use opportunities.

Discussion: The refuge has participated in various off-site outreach events over the years. Regular events have included the annual Earth Fest at the Audubon Zoo, the Sportsman's Show at the Louisiana Superdome, Mayor's Earth Day in downtown New Orleans, and the Wildfowl Carvers Show in Westwego (suburban New Orleans). Other venues have included conventions and conferences held in New Orleans, special events at the Louisiana Nature Center, shopping malls, and teacher fairs held at Six Flags and other locations around the city. The staff and volunteers, including the Friends of Louisiana Wildlife Refuges, Inc., have staffed these events.

Media outreach has occurred in the form of press releases, radio and television interviews, and phone contacts. Recent subjects have involved post Hurricane Katrina cleanup, temporary refuge closures, alligator feeding issues, and prescribed burns planned for the refuge. Special events and interpretive programs have also been subjects of press releases and newspaper stories. Prior to Hurricane Katrina, a reporter assigned to the New Orleans east area was always eager to print stories in that edition of the *Times Picayune*.

Strategies:

- Develop a tabletop display for offsite events that details post Hurricane Katrina restoration and water management activities.
- Revise the Bayou Sauvage NWR tear sheet/map.
- Develop a general brochure for the refuge.
- Seek additional outreach venues at off-site locations and events such as festivals.

Objective 3.9: Over the 15-year life of the CCP, develop a program to welcome and orient visitors to the refuge through directional and entrance signs, design and upkeep of facilities, and the provision of information regarding programs and facilities.

Discussion: At this time, there are no staffed facilities located on the refuge to welcome and orient visitors. This has been identified as a need in the visitor services review. Additionally, because of the destructive nature of the 2005 hurricane season, it is essential to replace missing or damaged entrance, directional, and boundary signs. This will better orient visitors to the various public use opportunities offered on the refuge.

Strategies:

- Replace all missing or destroyed entrance signs at major access points.
- Install secondary signs identifying major public use sites and facilities.
- Maintain current visitor information on the refuge website regarding facilities and programs.
- Seek additional outlets for distribution of refuge tear sheets and/or general brochure.
- Maintain contractual services for upkeep (e.g., trash and mowing) of visitor use areas so they are always clean and welcoming.

- Establish a visitor center or contact station on the refuge, possibly at I-10, Exit 251, or the Ridge Trail site, where visitors can speak with knowledgeable staff or volunteers, obtain maps and other refuge publications, and gain current information about recreational and educational opportunities.

REFUGE ADMINISTRATION

Goal 4. Protect the natural and cultural resources of the refuge and ensure visitor safety and facility integrity to fulfill the mission of the National Wildlife Refuge System.

Discussion: Protecting the natural and cultural resources of Bayou Sauvage NWR and ensuring the safety of all refuge visitors are fundamental responsibilities of the Refuge System. Bayou Sauvage NWR is one of eight refuges administered under the Southeast Louisiana NWR Refuge Complex. Six staff members are exclusively dedicated to Bayou Sauvage, Delta, and Breton Refuges. Because of the urban location of Bayou Sauvage NWR, law enforcement is essential and necessary to protect refuge resources including wildlife, habitat, and cultural resources. The safety and protection of visitors to the refuge are priorities.

Objective 4.1: Enforce all federal and state laws applicable to the refuge. Protect all known archaeological sites on the refuge from illegal take or damage in compliance with the Archaeological Resources Protection Act, the Native American Graves Protection and Repatriation Act, and the National Historic Preservation Act.

Discussion: The Service values and protects its archaeological and historical resources as defined in the National Historic Preservation Act of 1966, the Native American Grave Protection and Repatriation Act of 1990, and the Archaeological Resources Protection Act of 1979. There are various archaeological sites located on the refuge. One of the most extensive studies was conducted by Professor Shenkel at University of New Orleans in the 1980s. In 1993, a Phase I Archaeological Survey identified eight archaeological sites and one "Spot Find" on refuge property or potential property. Two sites recognized for their archaeological significance have been placed on the National Register of Historic Places because of their ability to contribute to an understanding of the region's history. There are still sites that have not been extensively examined and have the potential to contain significant cultural remains.

Strategies:

- Continue law enforcement patrols on all known sites to inspect for disturbances and illegal digging and/or looting.
- Within three years of CCP approval, acquire a written list and photos of inventoried items from the University of New Orleans.
- Within four years of CCP approval, develop literature of past archaeological and historical investigations on the refuge, and produce a brochure of the area's history.
- Within eight years of CCP approval, develop a plan to protect identified archaeological sites in conjunction with Native American tribes, State Historic Preservation Office, National Park Service Archaeologist, and Service Archaeologist.

Objective 4.2: Over the 15-year life of the CCP, maintain refuge boundary and identify unmarked areas.

Discussion: Because of frequent storm damage and vandalism, maintaining the current refuge boundary through sign replacement is a continuous need. This need is also perpetuated by funding constraints and active land acquisition within the refuge's acquisition boundary. The refuge would like to initiate an annual monitoring program to evaluate the need for boundary and directional signs on the refuge.

Strategies:

- Maintain existing refuge boundary signs.
- Evaluate all refuge signs on an annual basis and make required repairs, changes, updates, or upgrades.
- Evaluate, add, and replace signs at a rate of 10 percent per year.

Objective 4.3: Over the 15-year life of the CCP, provide visitor safety, protect resources, and ensure public compliance with refuge regulations.

Discussion: With only one law enforcement officer, Bayou Sauvage NWR's urban environment makes it extremely challenging to ensure visitor safety and facility integrity. In addition to the protection of wildlife and cultural resources, the law enforcement personnel must also deal with illegal drugs, vandalism, thefts, illegal dumping, and the safety of visitors. Additional law enforcement presence is essential to meeting this increasing demand.

Strategies:

- Conduct an internal and external review of the law enforcement program within four years.
- Develop and implement a law enforcement plan within seven years.
- After five years, review and improve law enforcement plan. Develop and work cooperatively with local, state and other federal law enforcement agencies to supplement resource protection.
- In an effort to establish a visual presence on the refuge, designate one full-time law enforcement officer to spend 100 percent of time on Bayou Sauvage NWR.
- Provide educational and outreach programs in local communities as part of preventive law enforcement effort to encourage voluntary compliance.

Objective 4.4: Over the 15-year life of the CCP, maintain existing equipment used as a part of refuge management.

Discussion: More than $3,000,000 worth of capitalized equipment exists for the complex of eight refuges. This equipment is used in all aspects of refuge administration, including habitat, wildlife, public use, protection projects, and management. Equipment is shared among the refuges of the complex instead of being assigned solely to one refuge. Project efficiency depends largely on age, condition, and maintenance of the equipment.

Strategies:

- Maintain more than $3,000,000 worth of capitalized equipment used in all aspects of refuge management, such as habitat, wildlife, public use, and protection.
- Within six years of CCP approval, develop an equipment maintenance plan for heavy equipment and watercraft.
- Maintain and replace equipment as needed.

V. Plan Implementation

INTRODUCTION

Refuge lands are managed as defined under the Improvement Act. Congress has distinguished a clear legislative mission of wildlife conservation for all national wildlife refuges. National wildlife refuges, unlike other public lands, are specifically dedicated to the conservation of the nation's fish and wildlife resources and wildlife-dependent recreational uses. Priority projects emphasize the protection and enhancement of fish and wildlife species first and foremost, but considerable emphasis is placed on balancing the needs and demands for wildlife-dependent recreation and environmental education.

To accomplish the purpose, vision, goals, and objectives contained in this CCP for Bayou Sauvage NWR, this section identifies projects, funding and personnel needs, volunteers, partnership opportunities, step-down management plans, and a monitoring and adaptive management plan review and revision on 23,000 acres of bottomland hardwoods and fresh and brackish marshes.

This CCP focuses on the importance of funding the operations and maintenance needs of the refuge to ensure the staff can achieve the goals and objectives identified and are crucial to fulfill the purpose for which the refuge was established. The refuge's role in protecting and providing habitat for migratory waterfowl, birds, and endangered species is critical. Proposed priority public use programs will establish and expand opportunities for wildlife-dependent recreation, but not without specialized staff and resources for operations and maintenance.

PROPOSED PROJECTS

Listed below are the proposed project summaries and their associated costs for fish and wildlife population management, habitat management, resource protection, visitor services, and refuge administration over the next 15 years. Price estimates are based over the same time period. This proposed project list reflects the priority needs identified by the public, planning team, and refuge staff based upon available information. These projects were generated for the purpose of achieving the refuge's objectives and strategies. The primary linkages of these projects to those planning elements are identified in each summary.

FISH AND WILDLIFE POPULATION MANAGEMENT

The refuge attracts 15 species of waterfowl, of which mottled ducks, black-bellied whistling tree ducks, and wood ducks nest on the refuge. Over 50,000 waterfowl and 340 bird species use the refuge during the year for resting and feeding. Shorebirds, wading birds, neotropical migratory songbirds, raptors, mammals, reptiles and amphibians, and numerous fisheries exist on the refuge. Endangered species occurring on or near the refuge are the eastern brown pelican, Gulf sturgeon, and manatee. The refuge marsh wetlands provide diverse habitats for large bird rookeries, nurseries, and spawning and feeding grounds for many aquatic species.

Project 1 – Monitor waterfowl use on refuge during migration.

The refuge is closed to all hunting. It is the only public area within the Lake Pontchartrain Basin that provides refuge for waterfowl to stage, rest, and feed without hunting pressure. The refuge will play a significant role monitoring waterfowl migration numbers by performing aerial waterfowl counts. Refuge staff will:

- Conduct annual waterfowl aerial surveys consisting of four to six aerial surveys contingent on weather conditions. Initial survey will be performed before hunting season begins and last survey will be conducted after hunting season ends.
- Coordinate with LDWF on migration numbers on refuge.

Project 2 – Provide nest cavities for wood ducks and black-bellied whistling tree ducks to support 100 hatchlings per year. Refuge staff will:

- Install and ensure that a minimum of twenty-five nest boxes are cleaned and available prior to January of each year.

Project 3 – Monitor species of concern, targeted species, and species of federal responsibility.

National wildlife refuges are mandated to manage for threatened and endangered species if they occur on the refuge. However, refuges are also responsible for management of all native species if the action does not negatively impact threatened or endangered species. Refuge management is geared toward managing the ecosystem as a whole.

- A faunal species list will be compiled from surveys conducted by Fish and Wildlife Service biologists and other researchers. This list will be made available to the public through the refuge website. Within the list, refuge staff will prioritize species based on regional and state lists of species of concern, at risk/target species identified by Partners in Flight, and other plans.
- Develop a wildlife inventory plan based on species selected as priority species.
- Mottled duck nesting will be surveyed and monitored.
- Neotropical bird observations and counts will be conducted.
- Partner with colleges and university researchers to conduct studies or research as requested.

HABITAT MANAGEMENT

The refuge habitat offers bottomland hardwoods, fresh and brackish water marshes, lagoons, and natural bayous. Rain is the sole source of freshwater for the areas inside the man-made hurricane protection levee. A series of pumps allow moist-soil management to occur and stimulate plant production. However, because rain is the sole source of freshwater, drought periods significantly impact plant production. The primary objectives of the refuge are to provide habitat for the protection of fish and wildlife and to provide opportunities for fish and wildlife-dependent public use and recreation.

Project 1 – Clear and mulch 184 acres of damaged bottomland hardwoods impacted by Hurricane Katrina within the Ridge Trail area. Refuge staff will:

- Identify, mark, and leave trees with potential nesting cavities 150 feet away from all structures, boardwalks, and parking areas

- Ensure all fallen and leaning trees less than 20 inches in diameter are mulched to ground level within the boardwalk area. Any tree regardless of size that is unsafe must be felled. Any limbs, root balls, tree tops, branches, or hanging limbs must be mulched to ground level as well.
- Ensure all stumps will be mulched to less than one foot throughout the entire area.
- Ensure all fallen trees, limbs, branches, or tree tops outside the boardwalk area must be mulched if less than ten inches in diameter.
- Ensure all mulch will be less than three inches in size.

This work in conjunction with reforestation and invasive species control efforts will return a bottomland hardwoods habitat to the refuge. It will require a contractor with the necessary equipment to complete the work. Estimated cost is $140,000.

Project 2 – Treat all Chinese tallow trees on refuge. This invasive species has overtaken portions of the refuge since Hurricane Katrina. Refuge staff will:

- Identify areas on the refuge known to have Chinese tallow trees present and create a map with locations.
- Complete work by Hack and Frill Injection or Cut Stump Treatment by Service-approved herbicides on all Chinese tallow trees greater than ¼-inch in diameter, and spot broadcast Foliar spray on remaining Chinese tallow tree seedlings greater than one-foot tall.
- Treat all areas starting with the Ridge Trail area due to the reforestation efforts planned.
- Foliar spraying may only occur during May and June.
- Monitor and observe success of treatment for the desired goal of results lasting for twenty-four months after treatment.

This work will allow native species to return and grow without the competition of the fast-growing Chinese tallow tree. A contractor will perform the work with a cost of $200,000.

Project 3 – Reforestation of the Ridge Trail area to native bottomland hardwood species. This area is the only area within the refuge to offer bottomland hardwood habitat. It is unique on the refuge and provides habitat diversity compared to the surrounding marsh areas. Refuge staff will:

- Ensure the area has been prepared by clearing and mulching area and treating invasive species prior to planting.
- All trees planted will be native to the area.
- The 20 acres within the boardwalk area will be planted using potted trees on a 15X15-foot grid. The remaining 164 acres will be planted using seedlings and on a 10X10-foot grid.

The cost of this project would be an estimated $100,000 and will require use of a contractor to perform the work. It will speed the return of bottomland hardwoods to the area.

Project 4 – Dredge Sauvage Bayou channel and use mined sediment on refuge as beneficial material to create new marsh.

- Dredge Sauvage Bayou channel for seven miles to increase flow, storage, navigation, and aquatic species use of the bayou.
- Use generated spoil from suction dredge and place as beneficial fill in available open ponds or bays, creating new marsh and reducing erosion.
- Stack sediment at elevation of 4' +MLG.

- Monitor areas for vegetation growth and inventory species.
- Identify wildlife use during, after completion, and in the future.
- Once new lands are formed, plant desired marsh grass if necessary.

The cost of the project would be $3,000,000. Planting can be accomplished using volunteers.

Project 5 – Dredge section of the Borrow Pit Canal from the Highway 11 boat launch to the Southern Natural Gas Pipeline canal to improve access.

- Perform dredging operation for a distance of 4.5 miles, starting at the Highway 11 boat launch.
- Use generated spoil from suction dredge and place as beneficial fill in available open ponds, creating acres of new marsh and reducing erosion.
- Stack sediment at elevation of 4' +MLG.
- Monitor areas for vegetation growth and inventory species.
- Identify wildlife use during, after completion, and in the future.
- Once new lands are formed, plant desired marsh grass if necessary.

The estimated cost to complete the work is $2,500,000.

Project 6 – Shoreline stabilization in the Bayou Chevee Marsh. This project is designed to protect currently exposed wetlands areas from erosive wave energy from Lake Pontchartrain, and to enhance the establishment of submerged aquatic vegetation in the ponds behind the rock dikes.

- Proposed CWPPRA project. Construct an approximately one-mile-long rock dike extending north along the shoreline from an existing dike.
- Monitor and inventory submerged aquatic vegetation.

Erosion from Lake Pontchartrain has become a serious problem. These outer boundaries of the refuge have eroded and water depths have increased making any regeneration of vegetation impossible. These areas are a priority to address or the refuge will continue to shrink in size.

The cost to the refuge for the hard structure will be none if it can be performed as a CWPPRA project. The estimated cost of the project is $3,000,000.

Project 7– Restore Maxent Levee to authorized height level from Highway 90 to I-10. This levee serves as protection for adjacent residential areas north of the refuge from flooding during storm events or periods of high water.

- Plan as a TVA project to restore entire Maxent Levee to the three feet height level as originally designed.
- Raise portions that have naturally eroded, subsided, or that have been damaged by wildlife

This levee is a very significant factor in flood protection for the refuge and neighbors that must be maintained to its designed level.

The estimated cost to restore the levee is $4,000,000.

Project 8 – Restore South Maxent Levee from Recovery One Landfill to the hurricane protection levee.

- Raise portions that have naturally eroded, subsided, or that have been damaged by wildlife.

The estimated cost to restore the levee is $2,500,000.

Project 9 – Perform marsh restoration in Unit 6. It has become too deep to allow vegetation to generate and contributes to erosion problems as erosive wave energy increases due to the open water.

- Plan as a U.S. Army Corps of Engineers (Corps) project and partnership.
- As the Corps performs levee work to increase the height of the levees surrounding the freshwater marshes of the refuge, they will generate spoil material. This material can be placed directly in the open water areas of Unit 6 to create marsh.
- Plan the placement of materials with the Corps.
- Monitor and inventory submerged aquatic vegetation.

The cost to the refuge will be nothing as the Corps will benefit with a site to place the spoil.

Project 10 – Conduct marsh restoration projects in Blind Lagoon. Vegetation plantings are needed to replace damaged and eroded areas of the marsh.

- Use project as a volunteer opportunity to partner with other agencies (private or public) to complete the work.
- Plant 150 acres of emergent vegetation 18" apart, such as California bulrush (*Scirpus californicus*).
- Monitor and inventory submerged aquatic vegetation.

The cost of the planting will be $3,600,000.

Project 11 – Conduct marsh restoration projects in Turtle Bayou. Vegetation plantings are needed to replace damaged and eroded areas of the marsh.

- Use project as a volunteer opportunity to partner with other agencies (private or public) to complete the work.
- Plant 75 acres of emergent vegetation 18" apart.
- Monitor and inventory submerged aquatic vegetation.

The cost of the planting will be $1,800,000.

Project 12 – Construct wave fetch protection in open water area near Little Oak Island. This open body of water has significant erosion due to wave fetch.

- Use project as a volunteer opportunity to partner with other agencies (private or public) to complete the work.
- Collect Christmas trees or other organic materials and deposit in a planned area or cribbing within the area.
- Create ten acres of containment of organic materials.
- Monitor and inventory submerged aquatic vegetation.

The cost of the project will be $750,000.

Project 13 – Conduct live oak planting on Little Oak Island. Reforest area impacted by Hurricane Katrina and heavy saltwater intrusion into the freshwater marsh.

- Use project as a volunteer opportunity to partner with other agencies (private or public) to complete the work.
- Plant five acres of Live Oaks ten feet apart.
- Monitor and inventory plantings.

The cost of the planting will be $30,000.

Project 14 – Replace pump engines and work over four pumps used to manage water levels inside the levees.

- Replace engines and work over pumps on refuge.

The cost of the pump engine replacement and pump work over will be $1,300,000.

Project 15 – Manage and maintain prescribed and wild fire response programs to achieve healthy and viable wildlife and plants on the refuge.

- Burn areas identified on prescribed burn map as available water level and other conditions allow.
- Gain desirable vegetation from prescribed burning.
- Respond and monitor all wildfires on refuge due to close proximity of neighbors, and state and federal critical infrastructure.

Through the use of fire, burned areas will have a greater diversity of vegetation and reduced vegetative density. Five fire fighters and equipment will be required to complete work at a cost of $30,000 annually.

Project 16 – Develop monitoring programs for marsh loss, restoration, shoreline fortification, water depth along outer boundary of refuge, submerged aquatic plants, and the impact of public use activities on the refuge to ensure healthy viable plant and animal communities and protect the integrity of refuge habitats.

- Develop historic GIS maps of soils, habitats, and boundaries.
- Establish salinity monitoring points and monitor monthly by taking readings, developing a spreadsheet database, and evaluating changes. Coordinate with marsh survivability plots and vegetation composition changes.
- Map vegetation types with the use of GPS and GIS to inventory special and unique areas of the refuge requiring special management or protection.
- Implement a marsh subsidence monitoring plan to monitor the effects of refuge habitat manipulations and the encouragement of wildlife plants, such as *Spartina alternaflora*. This species will show impacts of higher salinity to freshwater marsh resources and impacts to resources for wildlife on refuge.

Operational funds should be dedicated for trained personnel performing basic wildlife inventories and monitoring. One biologist and one technician are needed to perform inventorying, monitoring, and managing restoration and management programs. Monitoring protocols and procedures will be established with results that are recognizable and achievable. Sampling schemes will use photo points and transects to monitor changes from management actions. These monitoring programs will employ the use of field computers, data collectors, and numerous types of boats and GIS technology for documentation. An initial cost estimate of $100,000 and an annual estimate of $75,000 will be required.

RESOURCE PROTECTION AND REFUGE ADMINISTRATION

Project 1 – Provide adequate law enforcement protection for refuge resources, federal trust species, personnel, and the visiting public.

The refuge hosts approximately 150,000 visitors annually for fishing and wildlife-dependent recreation. Visitation is down but expected to increase as recovery from Hurricane Katrina occurs. General services have returned to the area, such as restaurants, lodging, gas stations, and various other businesses. However, the population surrounding the refuge is still low due to the high cost of living and rebuilding expenses. The refuge will conduct a law enforcement program review and revise the law enforcement plan. A full-time law enforcement position is needed to cooperate with state wildlife officers, local sheriff's office, and city officers to:

- Protect visitors from vandalism, burglary, assault, and otherwise provide a safe experience while on the refuge.
- Enforce refuge regulations.
- Rescue visitors who are lost and need aid.
- Protect refuge infrastructure, equipment, and cultural and natural resources.
- Conduct patrols in refuge-owned canals, bays, or ponds for illegal poaching or commercial harvest activities.

A refuge officer assigned specifically to Bayou Sauvage NWR is needed to achieve goals and perform law enforcement duties on the refuge. Cost would be $100,000 per year.

Project 2 – Maintain marked refuge boundary and other identifying and regulating signs.

- Conduct refuge boundary surveys on all lands and any new lands when acquired and post accordingly.
- All existing refuge boundaries will be inspected and reposted at a rate of 20 percent annually.
- Signs will be placed at all refuge entrance points along trails, waterways, and roads.
- Signs regulating the portions of the refuge as "closed" must be visible at all entrances to the portions closed.
- Replace all faded or damaged signs as observed even if they occur outside of the annual 20 percent boundary sign program.

Maintaining boundary and signs will cost $50,000 per year.

Project 3 – Perform wilderness review.

- Determine if any acquired lands deserve inclusion in the Wilderness System through a wilderness review.

Project 4 – Meet current and future needs to maintain infrastructure for public use and resource management on the refuge.

Bayou Sauvage NWR is managed from the Southeast Louisiana NWR Complex; equipment and maintenance responsibilities are shared.

- Staff shares equipment to maintain facilities with other refuges within the complex.

Project 5 – Conduct archaeological survey.

- Develop an archaeological survey in coordination with the regional archaeologist and the professional community.
- Map all known archaeological sites.
- Protect site from vandals.
- Staff will inventory and map all archaeological sites and utilize an Unanticipated Discovery Site Mitigation Plan when new sites are accidentally located.

Project 6 – Administer oil and gas program with efforts guided to protect surface habitat and wildlife on the refuge.

Bayou Sauvage NWR has minimal oil and gas activities. However, one significant pipeline known as the "Collins Pipeline," a major 16-inch high pressure pipeline, runs through the refuge and must be watched closely. Any release from this pipeline would result in a major spill event on the refuge and surrounding areas. All activities relating to oil and gas on the refuge must be requested through a special use permit.

- Ensure all companies operating on refuge are permitted, identified, and in compliance with refuge regulations.
- All activities are submitted for review and a determination is made by refuge manager if a special use permit is required for activities requested or performed.
- Issue special use permits and assess mitigation for impacts to the surface of the refuge if they cannot be reduced.
- Response to all spill events and releases are conducted prior to work performed by clean-up company to ensure methods are approved on refuge.
- Conduct routine inspections of field and facility to ensure that proper operating procedures are in place and no releases are occurring.
- Provide guidance for wildlife-oriented protection methods during spill events and releases.
- Ensure employees are trained in Service oil and gas policy.

VISITOR SERVICES

The refuge is located within the city limits of New Orleans and is the largest urban national wildlife refuge in the United States. The refuge is easily accessible from major highways, and its many waterways provide for additional access by boat. Upon its establishment, public use, and in particular the opportunity for educational programming, was identified as a major management goal. Prior to Hurricane Katrina, a well-developed environmental education program for visiting schools was in place and weekend interpretive outings for the general public were offered.

The east side of Orleans Parish was severely damaged due to flooding resulting from Hurricane Katrina. The high cost of recovery and rebuilding has made recovery slow. Many schools have reopened and programs are presently being conducted by park rangers in the schools. The primary refuge educational site at the Ridge Trail is repaired and will shortly reopen, and along with that will be a resumption of on-site environmental education emphasizing the changes and re-growth occurring in the storm's aftermath.

Project 1 – Complete a Visitor Services Plan

Each refuge in the Refuge System is required to develop a Visitor Services Plan. This "stepped-down" plan will set goals, determine measurable objectives, identify strategies, and establish evaluation criteria for all visitor services. Careful planning provides the visiting public with opportunities to enjoy and appreciate fish, wildlife, plants, and other resources.

Project 2 – Assure that Bayou Sauvage NWR is welcoming, safe, and accessible to visitors. Provide visitors with clear information on where they can go, what they can do, and how to safely and ethically engage in recreational and educational activities. Facilities will be safe, high-quality, clean, well-maintained, and accessible.

- Replace and/or maintain all refuge entrance and directional signs so they present a neat and well-cared for appearance to visitors.
- In the absence of a visitor contact station on the refuge, provide headquarters contact information and brochure availability at all major public use sites on the refuge.
- Maintain kiosks with up-to-date refuge information and interpretive materials and panels, emergency contact information, and "permitted activities" signs.
- Maintain parking areas, boat launches, boardwalks and trails, and other public facilities to a high degree of quality and appearance. Adequate facility maintenance will require either additional maintenance staff or use of contractual services.

Costs associated with adequately maintaining visitor sites and facilities per year are $100,000.

Project 3 – Improve and enhance fishing opportunities while minimizing conflicts between consumptive and non-consumptive users.

Quality fishing opportunities abound on Bayou Sauvage NWR as many visitors repeatedly fish and crab on the refuge. Hunting is presently closed on the refuge. However, there is a possibility of opening the refuge to limited youth waterfowl hunting in the marshes outside of the hurricane protection levee system. The refuge contains both impounded freshwater habitats and brackish marshes outside the hurricane protection levee system. A refuge-maintained launch on Highway 11 provides access to interior marshes, and several private launches may be used to reach exterior marsh areas. The refuge staff will:

- Annually inspect public use facilities used for fishing for compliance with safety concerns and repair and maintenance needs.
- Repair fishing docks at Highway 11.
- Repair boat launch at Highway 11
- Coordinate with Louisiana DOT to improve access to Crabbing Bridge Road.
- Carry out dredging project in Bayou Sauvage channel, and consider stocking to improve fishery at that location.

Project 4 – Provide opportunities for wildlife observation and wildlife photography.

Wildlife observation and wildlife photography opportunities on the refuge are available because of the excellent and diverse habitats for viewing waterfowl, shorebirds, wading birds, and a variety of other fauna and flora.

- Offer occasional birding tours led by refuge staff or volunteers.
- Provide photo blinds in locations that take advantage of seasonal concentrations of birds or other wildlife.
- Reestablish canoe tour routes through Madere Marsh to provide unique wildlife viewing opportunities.
- Consider re-establishment of wildlife-viewing boat tours, either by concession or by refuge staff.

Project 5 – Establish visitor contact facility on the refuge.

There is no visitor contact point or office on Bayou Sauvage NWR where visitors can contact refuge staff. The Complex headquarters in Lacombe, approximately 30 miles away, is the nearest point of contact. However, the refuge is situated along a busy Interstate highway that connects New Orleans to points east and north. It is also close enough to downtown tourist areas to easily attract those that fly into the city for visits. An established exit on I-10 affords a prominent potential location for a visitor center or contact station that could tell not only the refuge story but also the larger story of coastal land loss in Louisiana. Other potential sites exist also. Establishment of this facility will also aid management and law enforcement efforts on the refuge through regular staff presence.

- Assess suitability of I-10 site, Ridge Trail site on U.S. Highway 90, and/or other potential sites for refuge contact station/visitor center
- Develop staffing plan for visitor contact facility; seek additional full-time employees and/or develop volunteer staffing capacity through Friends of Louisiana Wildlife Refuges and independent volunteers so as to meet staffing needs for 7-day/week operation.
- Develop interpretive plan/themes for facility displays and for associated trails, boardwalks, kiosks.

The cost estimate to construct a visitor center is $4,000,000.

Project 6 – Increase public outreach, staff- or volunteer-led interpretive programming, non-personal interpretation, and environmental education programming to emphasize resource management practices.

Marsh restoration and other refuge habitat management programs can be a source of information for educating the public about refuge resources and management. Education on refuge management will be focused on first-hand observations where possible. Interpretation of refuge resources will promote understanding, appreciation, and stewardship of refuge resources.

- Develop formal, curriculum-based environmental education programs for students in Orleans and surrounding parishes that, through first-hand experiences, promote understanding, appreciation, and stewardship of refuge resources and support for refuge management practices.
- To complement on-site programming, provide relevant classroom educational programming with the same goals of promoting understanding and stewardship of refuge resources.

- Maintain liaison contacts with area school systems and curriculum coordinators to continuously upgrade refuge education programs in the classroom and on the refuge to match curriculum needs.
- Implement as staffing permits a regular program of staff or volunteer-led walks, canoe tours, birding tours, and other programs that interpret refuge resources and management to the general public. Cultivate contacts in local birding and environmental organizations to develop cadre of knowledgeable volunteers.
- Complete and install new interpretive signs and panels on kiosks and trails throughout the refuge.
- Develop general brochure of refuge and distribute.
- Supply refuge brochures, bird lists, general brochures, and quarterly events calendars to parish convention centers, state welcome centers, and other tourist hubs.
- Provide schedules of planned programs to local newspapers.
- Recruit full-time volunteer interns to supplement refuge staff in delivering school curriculum-based environmental education programs, refuge interpretive programs, and to assist refuge personnel in refuge management, while providing developmental experiences that allow students to explore future career opportunities with the Service.
- Recruit volunteers and volunteer groups, such as recreational vehicle campers, to supplement and assist refuge staff, and to provide education, visitor services, maintenance, and clerical duties.
- Maintain and develop agreements with the Friends of Louisiana Wildlife Refuges, Inc., to cooperate on projects and provide refuge support.
- Issue press releases on important events on the refuge, including public events and changes to public use programs (e.g., hunting and fishing).
- Update and maintain an interactive refuge web site with links to regulations brochures, bird lists, trail maps and guides, refuge maps, tear sheets, contacts for refuge assistance, signup for programs, etc.
- Develop and deliver refuge education programs for adults through civic groups and to neighborhood groups surrounding the refuge.
- Develop a monitoring plan with schools to evaluate educational program results and effectiveness relative to Grade Learning Expectations.
- Visit school career fairs to promote Student Career Employment and Student Temporary Employment Programs and Youth Conservation Corps Programs to increase Fish and Wildlife Service career awareness within the nearby community.

FUNDING AND PERSONNEL

The current Complex staffing chart includes staff identified for Bayou Sauvage NWR (Figure 6). The proposed staffing chart (Figure 7) will utilize identified staff to accomplish the proposed projects (Table 4).

Figure 6. Current staffing chart for Bayou Sauvage NWR and Southeast Louisiana NWR Complex

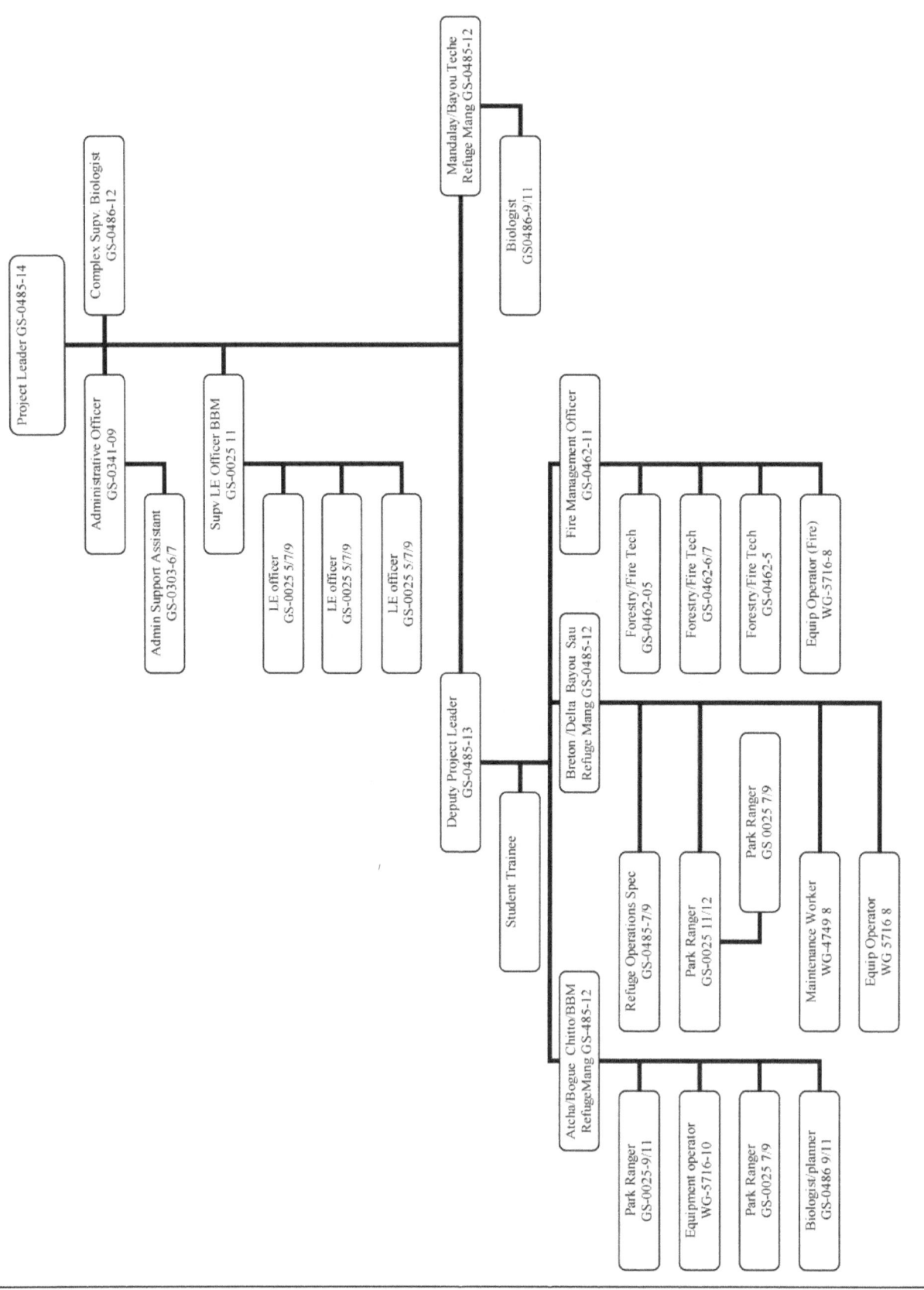

Figure 7. Proposed staffing chart for Bayou Sauvage NWR

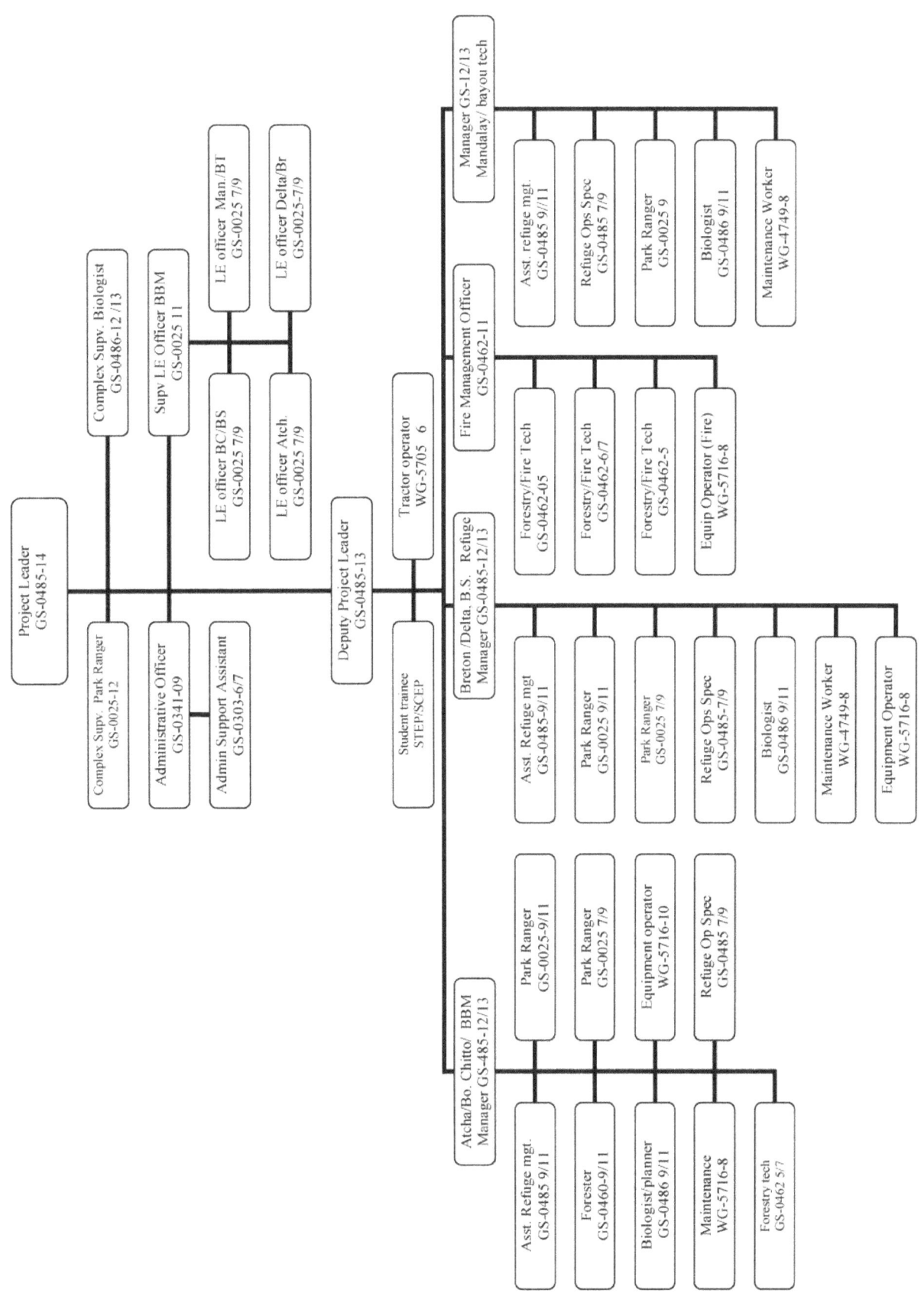

Table 4. Summary of projects

PROJECT NUMBER	PROJECT TITLE	FIRST YEAR COST	RECURRING ANNUAL COST
Populations 1	Aerial surveys of waterfowl on refuge	$20,000	$20,000
Populations 2	Provide nesting cavities for wood ducks	$15,000	$5,000
Populations 3	Monitor and manage other trust resource populations	$25,000	$0
Habitat 1	Clear and mulch Ridge Trail area	$140,000	$5,000
Habitat 2	Treat Chinese tallow trees with herbicide	$200,000	$10,000
Habitat 3	Reforestation of the Ridge Trail area	$100,000	$5,000
Habitat 4	Dredge Bayou Sauvage Bayou along the Ridge Trail area	$3,000,000	$0
Habitat 5	Dredge the Highway 11 pipeline canal	$2,500,000	$0
Habitat 6	Shoreline protection of Bayou Chevee, CWPRA proposal	$3,000,000	$0
Habitat 7	Restore Maxent Levee to designed height	$4,000,000	$0
Habitat 8	Restore south portion of Maxent Levee to designed height	$2,500,000	$0
Habitat 9	Marsh restoration of water management unit #6 as partnership with Corps	$10,000,000	$0
Habitat 10	Marsh restoration in Little Oak Island Lagoon	$1,200,000	$0
Habitat 11	Marsh restoration in Blind Lagoon	$3,600,000	$0
Habitat 12	Marsh restoration in Turtle Bayou	$1,800,000	$0
Habitat 13	Erosion/wave fetch protection in Little Oaks Island Lagoon	$750,000	$0
Habitat 14	Live Oak tree plantings in Little Oaks Island Lagoon	$30,000	$0

PROJECT NUMBER	PROJECT TITLE	FIRST YEAR COST	RECURRING ANNUAL COST
Habitat 15	Replace pump engines and work over pumps	$1,300,000	$30,000
Habitat 16	Manage prescribed burning plan	$30,000	$3,000
Habitat 17	Develop monitoring programs for each habitat of refuge	$100,000	$100,000
Protection 1	Provide adequate law enforcement for refuge resources, species, and visitors	$100,000	$100,000
Protection 2	Maintain marked boundary and signs	$50,000	$30,000
Protection 3	Wilderness determination	$10,000	$10,000
Protection 4	Maintain current and expanded infrastructure for public use and management capabilities	$100,000	$100,000
Protection 5	Archaeological survey	$100,000	$10,000
Protection 6	Administer oil and gas program	$5,000	$5,000
Visitor Services 1	Complete Visitor Services Plan	$10,000	$0
Visitor Services 2	Welcome and orient visitors	$100,000	$20,000
Visitor Services 3	Improve fishing opportunities	$15,000	$15,000
Visitor Services 4	Provide opportunities for wildlife observation and wildlife photography	$15,000	$15,000
Visitor Services 5	Construct Visitor Center	$4,000,000	$100,000
Visitor Services 6	Increase outreach and environmental education and interpretation	$80,000	$80,000

PARTNERSHIP/VOLUNTEER OPPORTUNITIES

A key element of this CCP is to establish partnerships with local volunteers, landowners, private organizations, and state and federal natural resource agencies. Partnerships are critically important to achieve refuge goals, leverage funds, minimize costs, reduce redundancy, and bridge relationships. In the immediate vicinity of the refuge, opportunities exist to establish and maintain partnerships with LDWF in law enforcement, local businesses, Orleans Parish, city of New Orleans, Nature Conservancy, Audubon Nature Institute, and the National Audubon Society.

The refuge staff can work with neighboring private landowners through the Partners Program or through agreements for managing neighboring land to complement the refuge management program.

STEP-DOWN MANAGEMENT PLANS

A CCP is a strategic plan that guides the future direction of the refuge. A step-down management plan provides more specific guidance on activities, such as habitat and visitor services management. Step-down plans (Table 5) are developed in accordance with the National Environmental Policy Act, which requires the identification and evaluation of alternatives and public review and involvement prior to their implementation.

Table 5. Bayou Sauvage NWR step-down management plans related to the goals and objectives of the CCP

Step-down Plans	Completion Date	Revision Date
Fisheries Management	1991	2011
Visitor Services	none	2012
Station Safety	2008	2023
Hunting Management	none	2023
Fire Management	2008	2013
Habitat Management	2010	2025
Wildlife Inventory	1996	2016
Marsh and Water Management	1998	2013
Sign Plan	none	2010
Nuisance Animal Control	1993	2014
Law Enforcement	1998	2012

MONITORING AND ADAPTIVE MANAGEMENT

Adaptive management is a flexible approach to long-term management of biotic resources that is directed over time by the results of ongoing monitoring activities and other information. More specifically, adaptive management is a process by which projects are implemented within a framework of scientifically driven experiments to test the predictions and assumptions outlined within a plan.

To apply adaptive management, specific surveying, inventorying, and monitoring protocols will be adopted for the refuge. The habitat management strategies will be systematically evaluated to determine management effects on wildlife populations. This information will be used to refine approaches and determine how effectively the objectives are being accomplished. Evaluations will include ecosystem team and other appropriate partner participation. If monitoring and evaluating indicate undesirable effects for target and non-target species and/or communities, then alterations to the management projects will be made. Subsequently, the CCP will be revised. Specific monitoring and evaluating activities will be described in the step-down management plans.

PLAN REVIEW AND REVISION

The CCP will be reviewed annually in development of the refuge's annual work plans and budget. It will also be reviewed to determine the need for revision. A revision will occur if and when conditions change or significant information becomes available, such as a change in ecological conditions or a major refuge expansion. The CCP will be augmented by detailed step-down management plans to address the completion of specific strategies in support of the refuge's goals and objectives. Revisions to the CCP and the step-down management plans will be subject to public review and NEPA compliance.

SECTION B. ENVIRONMENTAL ASSESSMENT

I. Background

INTRODUCTION

The Fish and Wildlife Service (Service) prepared this Environmental Assessment (EA) for Bayou Sauvage National Wildlife Refuge (NWR) in compliance with the National Environmental Policy Act (NEPA) and the National Wildlife Refuge System Improvement Act of 1997 (Improvement Act). The National Wildlife Refuge System Improvement Act requires the development of comprehensive conservation plans (CCPs) for all refuges. Following a public review and comment period on the Draft CCP/EA, a final decision will be made by the Service that will guide Bayou Sauvage NWR's management actions and decisions over the next 15 years, provide understanding about the refuge and management activities, and incorporate information and suggestions from the public and refuge partners.

The Draft CCP/EA proposes a management direction, which is described in detail through a set of goals, objectives, and strategies. The Draft CCP/EA addresses current management issues, provides long-term management direction and guidance for the refuge, and satisfies the legislative mandates of the Improvement Act. While the Draft CCP provides general management direction, subsequent step-down plans will provide more detailed management direction and actions.

The EA determines and evaluates a range of reasonable management alternatives. The intent is to support informed decision-making regarding future management of the refuge. Each alternative presented in this EA was generated with the potential to be fully developed into a Final CCP. The predicted biological, physical, social, and economical impacts of implementing each alternative are analyzed in this EA. This analysis assists the Service in determining if the alternatives represent no significant impacts, thus requiring the preparation of a Finding of No Significant Impact (FONSI), or if the alternatives represent significant impacts, thus requiring more detailed analysis through an Environmental Impact Statement and a Record of Decision. Following public review and comment, the Service will select an alternative to be fully developed for this refuge.

The CCP is needed to address current management issues, to provide long-term management direction for the refuge, and to satisfy the legislative mandates of the Improvement Act, which requires the preparation of a CCP for all national wildlife refuges.

PURPOSE AND NEED FOR ACTION

The function of the EA is to meet the purpose(s) of the refuge and the goals identified in the CCP (for which we evaluate each alternative). The purpose is to ensure that Bayou Sauvage NWR serves as an inviolate sanctuary for migratory, shore, and wading birds; conserves a variety of habitats to support native diversity of fish and wildlife species; protects rare, threatened and endangered species; protects and preserves archaeological and historical resources of the refuge; controls and eliminates exotic, invasive, and nuisance species; provides opportunities for wildlife-dependent public uses, recreation, and education in an urban setting that are appropriate and compatible; and provides for appropriate and compatible scientific research. The need of the EA is to adopt a 15-year management plan that provides guidance for future management and meets the mandates of the Improvement Act.

DECISION FRAMEWORK

Based on the assessment described in this document, the Service will select an alternative to implement the CCP for Bayou Sauvage NWR. If appropriate, the Final CCP will include a FONSI, which is a statement explaining why the selected alternative will not have a significant adverse effect on the environment. This determination will be based on an evaluation of the Service and Refuge System mission, the purpose(s) for which the refuge was established, and other legal mandates. Assuming no significant impact is found, implementation of the CCP will begin and will be monitored annually and revised as necessary.

PLANNING STUDY AREA

The Bayou Sauvage NWR is located within the corporate limits of the city of New Orleans, approximately 18 miles east of the central business district. Bayou Sauvage NWR is one of eight refuges managed as part of the Southeast Louisiana NWR Complex. Prior to establishment of the refuge, area wetlands were threatened by urban expansion from the city of New Orleans. The refuge was authorized under House Resolution 5262, sponsored on July 28, 1986, by Louisiana representatives John Breaux and Lindy Boggs.

The enacting legislation mandated that the Secretary of the Interior acquire 19,000 acres of land for the refuge within four years and complete a Master Plan for operation of the refuge within two years. By 2007, the refuge consisted of 22,265.12 acres in fee-title; 445 acres in a Memorandum of Understanding with the city of New Orleans for management purposes; and 23,126 acres within the current acquisition boundary.

This EA will identify management on refuge lands, as well as those lands proposed for acquisition by the Service.

AUTHORITY, LEGAL COMPLIANCE, AND COMPATIBILITY

The Service developed this Draft CCP/EA in compliance with the Improvement Act and Part 602 of the Service Manual (National Wildlife Refuge System Planning). The actions described herein also meet the requirements of NEPA. The staff achieved compliance with NEPA through the involvement of the public and the incorporation of the EA in the Draft CCP, with a description of the alternatives considered and an analysis of the environmental consequences of the alternatives (Chapters III and IV, Section B). When fully implemented, the CCP will strive to achieve the vision and purposes of Bayou Sauvage NWR.

The CCP's overriding consideration is to carry out the purposes for which the refuge was established. The laws that established the refuge and provided the funds for acquisition state the purposes. Fish and wildlife management is the first priority in refuge management, and the Service allows and encourages public use (wildlife-dependent recreation) as long as it is compatible with, or does not detract from, the refuge's mission and purposes.

COMPATIBILITY

The National Wildlife Refuge System Administration Act of 1966, as amended by the Improvement Act, states that national wildlife refuges must be protected from incompatible or harmful human activities to ensure that Americans can enjoy Refuge System lands and waters. Before activities or uses are allowed on a national wildlife refuge, the uses must be found to be compatible. A compatible use "...will not materially interfere with or detract from the fulfillment of the mission of the

Refuge System or the purposes of the refuge." In addition, "wildlife-dependent recreational uses may be authorized on a refuge when they are compatible and not inconsistent with public safety."

An interim compatibility determination is a document that assesses the compatibility of an activity during the period of time the Service first acquires a parcel of land to the time a formal, long-term management plan for that parcel is prepared and adopted. The Service has completed an interim compatibility determination for the six priority general public uses of the system, as listed in the Improvement Act. These uses are hunting, fishing, wildlife observation, wildlife photography, and environmental education and interpretation.

PUBLIC INVOLVEMENT AND THE PLANNING PROCESS

In accordance with Service guidelines and NEPA recommendations, public involvement has been a crucial factor throughout the development of the Draft CCP/EA for Bayou Sauvage NWR. This Draft CCP/EA has been written with input and assistance from interested citizens, conservation organizations, and employees of local and state agencies. The participation of these stakeholders and their ideas has been of great value in setting the management direction for Bayou Sauvage NWR. The Service, as a whole, and the refuge staff, in particular, are very grateful to each one who has contributed time, expertise, and ideas to the planning process. The staff remains impressed by the passion and commitment of so many individuals for the lands and waters administered by the refuge.

The development of the Bayou Sauvage NWR Draft CCP/EA was executed in accordance with refuge planning policy [602 FW 3.4C(1)] and NEPA. Initial planning began in January 2007, with the establishment of the core planning team and the preparation of the Team Charter and Work Plan. Through the planning process, and with input from local, state, and federal agencies, the public, and conservation associations, the planning team identified issues and concerns that were relevant to the current and future conservation and management of the refuge.

In February 2007, a biological review was completed that assessed the status of biological resources and programs currently in place on the refuge. This review also aided in identifying additional information needs and establishing preliminary management goals and objectives. The team that prepared the review was comprised of biologists, managers, conservation society members, and employees of local, state, and federal agencies. This review also served as an intergovernmental scoping meeting to obtain other government agency partners' participation in the CCP process. Issues discussed included habitat restoration and management, water quality, migratory birds, threatened and endangered species, other wildlife, fisheries, fire management, adjacent urbanization, and refuge staffing and equipment needs.

In March 2007, a visitor services review was conducted to evaluate the status of the existing public use programs, facilities, and opportunities. This review provided guidance for short, intermediate, and long-term recommendations for improving the quality of public use and educational services. These recommendations included: developing a current visitor services plan, restoring public use facilities, re-establishing environmental education and volunteer programs, and increasing law enforcement presence on the refuge to reduce dumping and vandalism.

Public involvement and input into the development of the Draft CCP/EA was initiated by the submission of a notice of intent (NOI). The NOI summarizing the intent of the refuge to begin the CCP process was published in the *Federal Register* on May 16, 2007 (72 FR 27585). A public scoping meeting was held June 18, 2007, to allow stakeholders the opportunity for their concerns to be considered in the refuge's future management.

The team directed the process of obtaining public input through a June 18, 2007 public scoping meeting at the Resurrection of Our Lord Church conference room in New Orleans East, Louisiana. The meeting was announced in the Times Picayune newspaper, New Orleans edition. Flyers were also distributed in the area surrounding the meeting location. This meeting gave interested stakeholders the ability to ask questions and register their concerns. The 13 attendees submitted 16 different questions or public comments. Three additional comment letters were sent to the refuge during this process.

A complete summary of the issues and concerns is provided in Section C, Appendix D, Public Involvement - Summary of Public Scoping Comments.

II. Affected Environment

For a description of the affected environment, see Section A, Chapter II, Refuge Overview.

III. Description of Alternatives

FORMULATION OF ALTERNATIVES

Alternatives are different approaches or combinations of management objectives and strategies designed to achieve the refuge's purpose, vision, and the goals identified in the CCP; the priorities and goals of the Lower Mississippi Valley Ecosystem Team; the goals of the Refuge System; and the mission of the Service. Alternatives are formulated to address the significant issues, concerns, and problems identified by the Service and the public during public scoping.

Three alternatives were identified and evaluated representing different approaches to provide permanent protection, restoration, and management of the refuge's fish, wildlife, plants, habitats, and other resources, as well as compatible wildlife-dependent recreation. Refuge staff assessed the biological conditions and analyzed the external relationships affecting the refuge. This information contributed to the development of refuge goals and, in turn, helped to formulate the alternatives. As a result, each alternative presents different sets of objectives for reaching refuge goals. Each alternative was evaluated based on how much progress it would make and how it would address the identified issues related to fish and wildlife populations, habitat management, resource protection and conservation, visitor services, and refuge administration. A summary of the three alternatives is provided in Table 6.

DESCRIPTION OF ALTERNATIVES

Serving as a basis for each alternative, a number of goals and sets of objectives were developed to help achieve the refuge's purpose and the mission of the Refuge System. Objectives are desired conditions or outcomes that are grouped into sets and, for this planning effort, consolidated into three alternatives. These alternatives represent different management approaches for managing the refuge over a 15-year time frame while still meeting the refuge purposes and goals. The three alternatives are summarized below. A comparison of each alternative follows the general description.

ALTERNATIVE A: CURRENT MANAGEMENT (NO ACTION)

This alternative is required by NEPA and is the "no-action" or "status quo" alternative in which no major management changes would be initiated by the Service. This alternative also provides a baseline to compare the current habitat, wildlife, and public use management to the two action alternatives (B and C).

Management emphasis would continue to be directed towards accomplishing the refuge's primary purposes. The staff would continue to restore and maintain emergent marsh, both tidally influenced and impounded; natural levee ridges; bottomland hardwood forest; and spoil banks and shallow open water bodies, all of which constitute a wide range of habitats within the refuge boundaries.

Current refuge management would continue to provide wintering and nesting habitats for migratory and resident waterfowl, wading birds and migrating song birds. The operation and management of the refuge would provide for the basic needs of these species, including feeding, resting, and breeding. Management measures include planting vegetation used for food, nesting and cover, and moist-soil management in eight different water management units that cater to a variety of different species; these measures would continue to be a priority. At least two aerial waterfowl surveys would continue to be conducted.

Only opportunistic, observational monitoring of reptiles and amphibians would be conducted, with emphasis on alligator presence and general size classes. Conservation of federally listed threatened and endangered species would continue to be achieved by consulting with established partnerships and the Service's Ecological Services Office on potential impacts of refuge programs and actions. The refuge staff would continue to control or slow the spread of exotic and/or invasive animal species by continued participation in the Louisiana Nutria Control Program and opportunistic application of the Nuisance Animal Control Plan for feral hogs. Additionally, the opportunistic control of invasive plant species, such as Chinese tallow and cogon grass, would continue as funding allows.

Fishing, wildlife observation, wildlife photography and environmental education and interpretation would continue to be the main focuses of the refuge's public use programs. These programs would be re-implemented with the same scope and continued at their pre-Hurricane Katrina level, as resources are available.

Land would be acquired from willing sellers within the current acquisition boundary and in accordance with current Service policy. Law enforcement on the refuge would continue at the current level. This includes being designated to uphold current regulations and for protection of wildlife, visitors, and cultural and historical resources. Refuge staff would continue to consist of a manager, a refuge operations specialist, two park rangers, and one maintenance position. These staff positions would continue to specifically support Delta, Breton, and Bayou Sauvage NWRs, along with supplementary support from the remainder of the Southeast Louisiana NWR Complex staff when needed.

ALTERNATIVE B: RESTORE AND IMPROVE ECOLOGICAL DIVERSITY AND AUGMENT VISITOR SERVICES (PROPOSED ALTERNATIVE)

The proposed action (Alternative B) was selected by the Service as the alternative that best signifies the vision, goals, and purposes of the refuge. Under Alternative B, the emphasis would be on restoring and improving refuge resources needed for wildlife and habitat management, while providing additional public use opportunities. This alternative would also allow the refuge to provide law enforcement protection that adequately meets the demands of an urban environment.

This alternative would focus on augmenting wildlife and habitat management to identify, conserve, and restore populations of native fish and wildlife species, with an emphasis on migratory birds and threatened and endangered species. This would partially be accomplished by increased monitoring of waterfowl, other migratory birds, and endemic species in order to assess and adapt management strategies and actions. The restoration of the fresh and brackish marsh systems and hardwood forest would be a vital part of this proposed action and would be crucial to ensuring healthy and viable ecological communities post Hurricane Katrina. This restoration would require increased wetland vegetation and tree plantings, the use of beneficial dredge, breakwater structures, and organic materials to promote re-establishment of emergent marsh and reduce wave energy erosion along Lakes Pontchartrain and Borgne. Improving and monitoring water quality and active moist-soil management would assist in re-establishing freshwater marsh habitat.

The refuge would more aggressively control and, where possible, eliminate invasive plant species by seeking funding through the Service's invasive species control program. The control of the Chinese tallow trees and cogon grass along the hardwood ridge would be a focal point. The control of nuisance wildlife would increase to include yearly population evaluations and more aggressive trapping programs for feral hogs and nutria.

Alternative B enhances the refuge's visitor services opportunities by: improving and providing additional fishing opportunities; considering providing limited hunting opportunities on the refuge; providing environmental education that emphasizes refuge restoration activities, coastal conservation issues and the diversity of water management regimes in the aftermath of Hurricane Katrina; establishing a visitor center or contact station on the refuge; developing and implementing a visitor services management plan, and enhancing personal interpretive opportunities. Volunteer programs and friends groups also would be expanded to enhance all aspects of refuge management and to increase resource availability.

Land acquisitions within the approved acquisition boundary would be based on importance of the habitat for target management species and public use value. The refuge headquarters would not only house administrative offices, but offer interpretation of refuge wildlife, habitats, and demonstrate habitat improvements for individual landowners. The headquarters facilities would be developed as an urban public use area with trails; buildings presently not being used and landscaping would be refurbished for visitor and community outreach.

In addition to the enforcement of all federal and state laws applicable to the refuge to protect archaeological and historical sites, the refuge would identify and develop a plan to protect all known sites. The allocation of one law enforcement officer to the refuge would not only provide security for these resources, but would also ensure visitor safety and public compliance with refuge regulations.

ALTERNATIVE C: CUSTODIAL MANAGEMENT, WHILE MAXIMIZING VISITOR SERVICES

Under Alternative C, the active management of the refuge resources would be employed to optimize public use opportunities. Staff and resources would be dedicated to increasing the public use activities of fishing, hunting, wildlife observation, wildlife photography, outreach, environmental education and interpretation. All purposes of the refuge and mandated monitoring of federal trust species and archaeological resources would be continued, but other wildlife management would be dependent on public interests.

This alternative would utilize a custodial habitat management strategy. Moist-soil units would not be actively managed and would be allowed to revert back to brackish tidal marsh. These units would also be maintained near full-pool level to facilitate public use opportunities, such as fishing and canoeing. Hardwood forest habitat in high public use areas would be restored and all other areas would recover naturally with no management intervention.

Increased wildlife observation, wildlife photography, and interpretation opportunities would result from the construction of an on-site visitor's center, canoe and birding tours, kiosks, and trail signs. Additionally, waterfowl and wildlife monitoring would be conducted periodically to identify high use areas for the visiting public to observe. Environmental education would be expanded by addressing a wide range of local and global environmental concerns and would be offered to a broader range of student groups and schools. New information brochures and tear sheets would be published to increase public outreach and to promote public use and recreational opportunities.

Land acquisitions within the approved acquisition boundary would be based on the importance of the habitat for public use. Administration plans would stress the need for increased maintenance of existing infrastructure and construction of new facilities that would benefit public use activities. The refuge would operate with the current level of staff. Law enforcement of refuge regulations and protection of wildlife and visitors would continue at current levels.

FEATURES COMMON TO ALL ALTERNATIVES

Although the alternatives differ in many ways, there are similarities among them as well, and some management programs and Service mandates would occur regardless of the alternative selected for implementation. To reduce the length and redundancy of individual alternative descriptions, these common features are summarized below.

- Resource Protection - Current enforcement of all federal and state laws applicable to the refuge to protect all known archaeological and historical sites would continue, including any efforts to increase resource protection through education and inventories. Certain mandated responsibilities such as protection of federal trust species, wetlands, prevention and control of invasive species, and payment of revenue sharing in lieu of taxes would be accomplished under all alternatives.

- Monitoring - Existing monitoring of waterfowl, other migratory birds and endemic species would continue. Monitoring activities may increase or decrease to meet other objectives under the various alternatives.

- Shoreline Restoration - All alternatives include seeking partnerships and opportunities for shoreline restoration through submission of proposals for funding through the Coastal Wetlands Planning, Protection and Restoration Act (CWPPRA).

- Management Plans - All alternatives include the development and implementation of visitor services and habitat management plans.

- Maintain Refuge Boundary - The existing refuge boundary and directional signs would be maintained as part of all alternatives.

- Law Enforcement - Law enforcement would provide visitor safety, protect resources, and ensure public compliance with refuge regulations under all alternatives. Enforcement presence varies under the various alternatives to meet specific objectives.

- Maintain Capitalized Equipment - All alternatives contain maintenance of refuge equipment, which is required to meet safety standards.

- Partnerships - Currently established partnerships with agencies, organizations, and individuals would continue to support refuge management programs.

- Prescribed Burns - Existing fire management, including prescribed burns, would continue. Fire management activities may increase or decrease to meet other objectives under the various alternatives.

COMPARISON OF THE ALTERNATIVES BY ISSUE

Table 6. Comparison of alternatives by management issues for Bayou Sauvage NWR

Issues	Alternative A (Current Management – No Action Alternative)	Alternative B Restore and improve ecological diversity and augment existing visitor services (Proposed Alternative)	Alternative C Little to no active water management while improving visitor services
Migratory Birds	Conduct midwinter waterfowl survey and one other aerial waterfowl survey.	Increase monitoring of waterfowl and other migratory birds in order to assess and adapt habitat management strategies/actions by the following: Conduct aerial waterfowl surveys every three weeks from Nov. 1 to Feb. 1. Participate in midwinter waterfowl survey. Participate in Christmas Bird Count by providing one staff and boat to facilitate surveys in marsh and waterways. Conduct monthly rookery counts of wading birds during time period March to June. Participate in Secretive Marsh Bird surveys using standardized protocols in select management units.	Conduct bi-weekly ground assessments of migratory bird use, identifying areas of bird concentration. Purpose of surveys is to identify high use areas for posting on refuge web-site, flyers, or other avenues in order to direct visiting public to observation areas.

Issues	Alternative A (Current Management – No Action Alternative)	Alternative B Restore and improve ecological diversity and augment existing visitor services (Proposed Alternative)	Alternative C Little to no active water management while improving visitor services
Threatened and Endangered Species	Consult with Ecological Services Office on potential impacts of refuge programs/actions on threatened and endangered species.	Same as Alternative A.	Same as Alternative A.
Migratory Birds Nesting	Provide nest cavities for Wood Ducks and Black-bellied Whistling Tree Ducks to support 100 hatchlings per year.	Provide nest cavities for Wood Ducks and Black-bellied Whistling Tree Ducks to support 100 hatchlings per year. Install and ensure a minimum of twenty-five nest boxes are cleaned and available prior to January of each year.	Provide nest cavities for Wood Ducks and Black-bellied Whistling Tree Ducks to hatchlings in wildlife observation areas.

Issues	Alternative A (Current Management – No Action Alternative)	Alternative B Restore and improve ecological diversity and augment existing visitor services (Proposed Alternative)	Alternative C Little to no active water management while improving visitor services
Invasive Species	Participate in State of Louisiana Nutria Control program. Continue opportunistic application of the refuges' Nuisance Animal Control Plan for feral hogs.	Participate in State of Louisiana Nutria Control program. Conduct yearly evaluations of nutria populations on refuge lands using established monitoring protocols. Actively promote nutria control program and seek assistance from area trappers to reduce nutria populations on refuge lands consistent with the refuge's Nuisance Animal Control Plan. Proactively seek assistance in implementing an aggressive eradication program for feral hogs consistent with the stations Nuisance Animal Control Plan.	Participate in State of Louisiana Nutria Control program. Continue opportunistic application of the refuge's Nuisance Animal Control Plan for feral hogs.

Issues	Alternative A (Current Management – No Action Alternative)	Alternative B Restore and improve ecological diversity and augment existing visitor services (Proposed Alternative)	Alternative C Little to no active water management while improving visitor services
Other Wildlife	Continue opportunistic, observational data of alligator presence and general size classes. Continue opportunistic, observational data of game fish being harvested.	Increase monitoring of endemic species in order to assess and adapt habitat management strategies/actions. Conduct yearly nighttime alligator surveys using established protocols and methods. Work with state herpetologist to identify and monitor reptile and amphibian populations. Conduct monthly creel surveys to identify species of game fish being harvested. Work with Fisheries Office to establish monitoring needs and protocols for yearly assessment of fish populations.	Conduct monthly ground assessments of alligators and monthly creel surveys, identifying areas of alligator concentrations and species of game fish being taken. Purpose of surveys is to identify areas for posting on refuge web-site, flyers, or other avenues in order to direct visiting public to observation areas and fishing opportunities.

Issues	Alternative A (Current Management – No Action Alternative)	Alternative B Restore and improve ecological diversity and augment existing visitor services (Proposed Alternative)	Alternative C Little to no active water management while improving visitor services
Land Acquisition	Acquire lands from willing sellers through fee title purchase.	Acquire lands that provide resource and public use values from willing sellers through fee title purchase, donation, mitigation purchase and transfer, or other viable means. Complete minor expansion package (10%) for acquisition of lands. Through partners explore potential for congressionally authorized major acquisition boundary expansion.	Acquire lands that provide increased public use values from willing sellers through fee title purchase, donation, mitigation purchase and transfer, or other viable means.
Habitat Management Plan	Develop and implement a habitat management plan by 2010.	Same as Alternative A.	Same as Alternative A.
Habitat Restoration	Allow hardwood forest to naturally recover with no intervention.	Actively work to restore hardwood forest. Control Chinese tallow tree through mechanical and/or chemical means.	Restore hardwood forest in high public use areas and allow remainder to recover naturally with no intervention.

Issues	Alternative A (Current Management – No Action Alternative)	Alternative B Restore and improve ecological diversity and augment existing visitor services (Proposed Alternative)	Alternative C Little to no active water management while improving visitor services
		Conduct mechanical and/or chemical site preparation and plant suitable native woody shrub and tree species. Reestablish cypress along shorelines of Bayou Sauvage and marsh edge.	
Habitat Restoration	Allow marsh habitat to recover naturally with no intervention.	Reestablish and restore fresh marsh habitat. Manage water levels to promote marsh growth and establishment while maintaining sufficient soil hydration to reduce/eliminate subsidence occurring through oxidation of organic materials. Restore Bayou Sauvage channel depth by removing infill material and provide alternative outlet for excess water removal at eastern end of channel under Highway 11. Conduct vegetative plantings.	Allow marsh habitat to recover naturally with no intervention. Maintain water levels near full pool when possible in order to facilitate public use opportunities such as fishing and canoeing.

Issues	Alternative A (Current Management – No Action Alternative)	Alternative B Restore and improve ecological diversity and augment existing visitor services (Proposed Alternative)	Alternative C Little to no active water management while improving visitor services
		Restore emergent marsh through beneficial use of dredge material or other materials.	
		Establish and monitor vegetation transects to assess impacts of management and restoration actions.	
		Use organic materials such as Christmas trees and wood chips to create organic wave breaks and build marsh platforms.	
		Investigate alternative methods of plant propagation and establishment such as floating cribs.	
		Investigate alternative reliable sources of fresh water such as wetland assimilation of treated effluent.	
		Investigate potential for use of select management units for water storage capability as supply for other management units.	

Issues	Alternative A (Current Management – No Action Alternative)	Alternative B Restore and improve ecological diversity and augment existing visitor services (Proposed Alternative)	Alternative C Little to no active water management while improving visitor services
Habitat Restoration	Submit project proposals for funding through the CWPPRA program.	Submit project proposals for funding through the CWPPRA program. Seek additional partnerships and opportunities for restoration through beneficial use of dredge disposal and alternative shoreline protection measures such as oyster reef blocks.	Same as Alternative A.
Invasive Species	Opportunistically control Chinese tallow and cogon grass when monies and time allow.	Increase efforts to control invasive plant species. Proactively seek funding through the Services invasive species control program for additional control efforts. Work with educational institutions, non-profit groups, and other organizations to promote recruitment and use of volunteers in control efforts.	Opportunistically control Chinese tallow and cogon grass when monies and time allow with efforts being targeted at public use areas.

Issues	Alternative A (Current Management – No Action Alternative)	Alternative B Restore and improve ecological diversity and augment existing visitor services (Proposed Alternative)	Alternative C Little to no active water management while improving visitor services
Fire Management	Manage and maintain prescribed and wild fire response programs to achieve healthy and viable wildlife and plants on the refuge.	Manage and maintain prescribed and wild fire response programs to achieve healthy and viable wildlife and plants on the refuge. Burn areas identified by biologist as available water level and other conditions allow. Promote and maintain desired vegetative communities through application of prescribed fire and reduce hazardous fuels and fuel levels as needed. Respond appropriately to all wildfires on refuge due to close proximity of neighbors, and state and federal critical infrastructure.	Manage and maintain prescribed and wild fire response programs to achieve enhanced visitor services opportunities.

Issues	Alternative A (Current Management – No Action Alternative)	Alternative B Restore and improve ecological diversity and augment existing visitor services (Proposed Alternative)	Alternative C Little to no active water management while improving visitor services
Visitor Services Plan	Develop and implement a Visitor Services Management Plan by 2012.	Same as Alternative A.	Same as Alternative A.
Interpretation	Maintain current limited slate of interpretive opportunities, primarily non-personal interpretation (e.g., panels, kiosks).	Maintain and where possible expand interpretive opportunities on the refuge. Establish a visitor center or contact station on the refuge, possibly at I-10, Exit 251, or the Ridge Trail site, that would provide interpretive displays and materials to aid visitor understanding of refuge resources and management issues. Implement personal interpretive opportunities and expand where possible through partnerships. Include guided nature walks, canoe tours, birding tours, and similar programs.	Maximize personal and non-personal interpretive opportunities, facilities, and programs on the refuge.

Issues	Alternative A (Current Management – No Action Alternative)	Alternative B Restore and improve ecological diversity and augment existing visitor services (Proposed Alternative)	Alternative C Little to no active water management while improving visitor services
		Develop and install new kiosks, waysides, and trail signs with appropriate interpretive panels/messages at Ridge Trail site, Madere Marsh, Highway 11 launch, and Wayside Park.	
Environmental Education	Re-implement a slate of environmental education programs with same scope and emphases as existing prior to Hurricane Katrina. (Programming is currently on hiatus due to storm damage.)	Develop a new slate of environmental education programs that emphasize refuge restoration activities and the diversity of water management regimes in the aftermath of Hurricane Katrina and also address larger coastal conservation issues. Select grade levels to target and then establish curriculum-based programs that address appropriate state Grade Level Expectations for those grades. Seek grant support and partnerships to fund bus transportation to refuge for schools in need.	Maximize offerings of environmental education programs that emphasize not only the brackish-water ecosystem in the aftermath of Hurricane Katrina, but that also address a wide range of local and global environmental concerns.

Issues	Alternative A (Current Management – No Action Alternative)	Alternative B Restore and improve ecological diversity and augment existing visitor services (Proposed Alternative)	Alternative C Little to no active water management while improving visitor services
		Communicate the diversity of fresh- and brackish-water ecosystems found under this water management regime.	
		Maintain contacts within area school systems to promote programs and gain teacher input in program design.	
Wildlife Observation and Photography	Reestablish and maintain current walking and canoeing access for wildlife observation and photography that existed prior to Hurricane Katrina.	Expand wildlife observation and photography opportunities where possible to highlight both fresh- and brackish-water ecosystems through the addition of facilities.	Maximize wildlife observation and photography opportunities through the addition of facilities, and also concession services if possible.
		Promote levee-top walking trails/routes via signage.	
		Reopen bike path to "trail bikes" if access can be re-established at Exit 251 and/or Crabbing Bridge.	
		Consider other opportunities for public access at Exit 251, including boat tour possibilities (concession or FWS-operated)	

Issues	Alternative A (Current Management – No Action Alternative)	Alternative B Restore and improve ecological diversity and augment existing visitor services (Proposed Alternative)	Alternative C Little to no active water management while improving visitor services
Fishing	Maintain existing fishing program and facilities.	Where possible, provide and improve fishing opportunities on the refuge. Explore ways to improve roadway access to the Crabbing Bridge area thru acquisition or partnerships. Consider fisheries management actions that would improve fishing opportunities on the refuge (i.e., stocking). Consider dredging of Bayou Sauvage waterway to improve fishing habitat. Consider opportunities for fishing access at former swamp tour site at Exit 251.	Maximize potential fishing opportunities through facilities development and fisheries management.

Environmental Assessment

97

Issues	Alternative A (Current Management – No Action Alternative)	Alternative B Restore and improve ecological diversity and augment existing visitor services (Proposed Alternative)	Alternative C Little to no active water management while improving visitor services
Hunting	The refuge is currently closed to hunting.	Evaluate the feasibility of opening up the marshes outside the Hurricane Protection Levee to limited hunting. Evaluate acceptability of providing hunting opportunities in Hunting Management Plan. Position city of New Orleans for permission to hunt within city limits. Open tidal marsh outside Hurricane Protection Levee System to youth water fowl hunting	Evaluate the feasibility of opening up the marshes outside the Hurricane Protection Levee to limited hunting.

Issues	Alternative A (Current Management – No Action Alternative)	Alternative B Restore and improve ecological diversity and augment existing visitor services (Proposed Alternative)	Alternative C Little to no active water management while improving visitor services
Volunteer Program and Friends Group	Maintain current volunteer program and Friends group status.	Maintain and expand an active volunteer program to enhance all aspects of refuge management including resident interns and volunteers with recreational vehicles, friends, and local volunteers. Refine and implement improved recruitment methods, including web pages and contacts with local volunteer organizations. Specifically recruit local volunteers to be trained to assist with environmental education programs on a "semester" basis (12 weeks). Develop position descriptions for specific volunteer tasks, with timelines, to use in recruitment. Encourage and assist Friends of Louisiana Wildlife Refuges, Inc., with membership recruitment throughout the greater New Orleans metro area. Identify projects for potential friends group involvement.	Maintain and expand an active volunteer program to support expanded recreation and visitor services, including resident interns, volunteers with recreational vehicles, friends, and local volunteers.

Issues	Alternative A (Current Management – No Action Alternative)	Alternative B Restore and improve ecological diversity and augment existing visitor services (Proposed Alternative)	Alternative C Little to no active water management while improving visitor services
		Reactivate the resident intern/SCA program, as funds allow, to support environmental education programming as well as other refuge functions.	
Outreach	Continue current outreach activities.	Increase public outreach to emphasize resource management practices and promote public use opportunities. Develop a tabletop display for offsite events that details restoration and water management activities after Hurricane Katrina. Revise the Bayou Sauvage NWR tear sheet/map. Develop a general brochure for the refuge. Seek out additional outreach venues at off-site locations and events such as festivals.	Increase public outreach to emphasize and promote public use and recreational opportunities.

Issues	Alternative A (Current Management – No Action Alternative)	Alternative B Restore and improve ecological diversity and augment existing visitor services (Proposed Alternative)	Alternative C Little to no active water management while improving visitor services
		Specifically target outreach to immediate refuge neighbors to encourage public use and develop possible partnership or volunteer opportunities. Promote public use opportunities to the metro New Orleans-area tourists through tourism centers and publications.	
Welcome and Orient Visitors	Maintain current status of program to welcome and orient visitors to the refuge through directional and entrance signs, design and upkeep of facilities, and the provision of information regarding programs and facilities.	Improve program to welcome and orient visitors to the refuge through directional and entrance signs, design, and upkeep of facilities, and the provision of information regarding programs and facilities. Replace all missing or destroyed entrance signs at major access points. Install secondary signs identifying major public use sites and facilities. Maintain current visitor information on refuge web site regarding facilities and programs.	Maximize efforts to welcome and orient visitors to the refuge through directional and entrance signs, design and upkeep of facilities, and the provision of information regarding programs and facilities.

Issues	Alternative A (Current Management – No Action Alternative)	Alternative B Restore and improve ecological diversity and augment existing visitor services (Proposed Alternative)	Alternative C Little to no active water management while improving visitor services
		Seek out additional outlets for distribution of refuge tear sheets and/or general brochure.	
		Maintain contractual services for upkeep (i.e., trash, mowing) of visitor use areas so they are always clean and welcoming.	
		Establish a visitor center or contact station on the refuge, possibly at I-10, Exit 251, or the Ridge Trail site, where visitors can speak with knowledgeable staff or volunteers, obtain maps and other refuge publications, and gain current information about recreational and educational opportunities.	

Issues	Alternative A (Current Management – No Action Alternative)	Alternative B Restore and improve ecological diversity and augment existing visitor services (Proposed Alternative)	Alternative C Little to no active water management while improving visitor services
Archaeological and Historical Site Protection	Enforce all federal and state laws applicable to the refuge. Protect all known archaeological sites on the refuge from illegal take or damage in compliance with the Archaeological Resources Protection Act, the Native American Graves Protection and Repatriation Act, and the National Historic Preservation Act.	Enforce all federal and state laws applicable to the refuge. Protect all known archaeological sites on the refuge from illegal take or damage in compliance with the Archaeological Resources Protection Act, the Native American Graves Protection and Repatriation Act, and the National Historic Preservation Act. Continue law enforcement patrols on all known sites to inspect for disturbances and illegal digging and or looting. Within 3 years of CCP approval, acquire a written list and photos of inventoried items from the University of New Orleans. Within 4 years of CCP approval, develop literature of past archaeological and historical investigations on the refuge, and produce a brochure of the area's history.	Same as Alternative A.

Issues	Alternative A (Current Management – No Action Alternative)	Alternative B Restore and improve ecological diversity and augment existing visitor services (Proposed Alternative)	Alternative C Little to no active water management while improving visitor services
		Within 8 years of CCP approval, develop a plan to protect identified archaeological sites in conjunction with Native American tribes, State Historic Preservation office, Park Service Archaeologist, and the Fish and Wildlife Service Archaeologist.	
Maintain Marked Refuge Boundary	Maintain marked refuge boundary and other directional signs.	Maintain refuge boundary and identify unmarked areas. Maintain existing refuge boundary signs. Evaluate all refuge signs on an annual basis and make required repairs, changes, updates, or upgrades. Evaluate, add, and replace signs at a rate of 10 percent per year.	Maintain refuge boundary and identify unmarked areas.

Issues	Alternative A (Current Management – No Action Alternative)	Alternative B Restore and improve ecological diversity and augment existing visitor services (Proposed Alternative)	Alternative C Little to no active water management while improving visitor services
Provide Visitor Safety, Protect Resources and Ensure Public Compliance with Refuge Regulations	Provide visitor safety, protect resources, and ensure public compliance with refuge regulations.	Provide visitor safety, protect resources, and ensure public compliance with refuge regulations. Conduct an internal and external review of law enforcement program within four years. Develop and implement law enforcement plan within seven years. After five years of law enforcement plan approval, review and improve plan as needed. Develop and work cooperatively with local, state and other federal law enforcement agencies to supplement resource protection. Designate one full-time law enforcement officer to spend 100% of his/her time dedicated to Bayou Sauvage NWR to establish visual presence on the refuge.	Same as Alternative A.

Issues	Alternative A (Current Management – No Action Alternative)	Alternative B Restore and improve ecological diversity and augment existing visitor services (Proposed Alternative)	Alternative C Little to no active water management while improving visitor services
		Provide educational and outreach programs in local communities as part of preventive law enforcement effort to encourage voluntary compliance.	
Maintain Capitalized Equipment for the Refuge Complex	Maintain existing equipment used as a part of refuge management.	Maintain existing equipment used as a part of refuge management. Maintain more than $3,000,000 worth of capitalized equipment used in all aspects of refuge management such as habitat, wildlife, public use, and protection. Within six years of CCP approval, develop an equipment maintenance plan for heavy equipment and water craft. Maintain and replace equipment as needed.	Same as Alternative A.

ALTERNATIVES CONSIDERED BUT ELIMINATED FROM FURTHER ANALYSIS

The alternatives' development process under NEPA and the Improvement Act is designed to allow consideration of the widest possible range of issues and potential management approaches. During the alternatives' development process, many different solutions were considered. The following alternative components were considered but not selected for detailed study in this Draft CCP/EA for the reason(s) described.

In addition to the three alternatives that were discussed and considered in this process, the following additional alternative was discussed:

Alternative D - Maximizing Resource Management with Minimum Public Use

In Alternative D, the focus would be placed on maximizing wildlife and habitat management. All funding and staffing support would be channeled towards this goal and all public use facilities and programs would cease to be maintained or encouraged. The inclusion of this alternative into the NEPA process was eliminated from further consideration because it was not compatible with one of the refuge's purposes, which dictates the need to provide wildlife-dependent public use opportunities. Additionally, this alternative would not be able to provide wildlife compatible recreational opportunities as required by the Improvement Act.

IV. Environmental Consequences

OVERVIEW

This section analyzes and discusses the potential environmental effects or consequences that could be reasonably expected by implementation of either of the three alternatives described in Chapter III of this EA. For each alternative, the expected outcomes are portrayed through the 15-year life of the CCP.

EFFECTS COMMON TO ALL ALTERNATIVES

A few potential effects would be the same for each alternative; these are summarized under seven categories: environmental justice, climate change, other management, land acquisition, cultural resources, refuge revenue-sharing, and other effects.

ENVIRONMENTAL JUSTICE

Executive Order 12898, "Federal Actions to Address Environmental Justice in Minority Populations and Low-Income Populations" was signed by President Clinton on February 11, 1994, to focus federal attention on the environmental and human health conditions of minority and low-income populations, with the goal of achieving environmental protection for all communities. The order directed federal agencies to develop environmental justice strategies to aid in identifying and addressing disproportionately high and adverse human health or environmental effects of their programs, policies, and activities on minority and low-income populations. The order is also intended to promote nondiscrimination in federal programs substantially affecting human health and the environment, and to provide minority and low-income communities with access to public information and opportunities for participation in matters relating to human health or the environment.

None of the management alternatives described in this EA would disproportionately place any adverse environmental, economic, social, or health impacts on minority and low-income populations. Implementation of any action alternative that includes public use and environmental education is anticipated to provide a benefit to the residents residing in the surrounding communities.

CLIMATE CHANGE

The Department of the Interior issued an order in January 2001 requiring federal agencies under its direction that have land management responsibilities to consider potential climate change impacts as part of long-range planning endeavors.

The increase of carbon within the earth's atmosphere has been linked to the gradual rise in surface temperatures commonly referred to as global warning. In relation to comprehensive planning for national wildlife refuges, carbon sequestration constitutes the primary climate-related impact to be considered in planning. The U.S. Department of Energy's *Carbon Sequestration Research and Development* (U.S. Department of Energy 1999) defines carbon sequestration as "...the capture and secure storage of carbon that would otherwise be emitted to or remain in the atmosphere."

The land is a tremendous force in carbon sequestration. Terrestrial biomes of all sorts—grasslands, forests, wetlands, tundra, perpetual ice, and desert—are effective both in preventing carbon emissions and in acting as a biological "scrubber" of atmospheric carbon monoxide. The conclusions of the

Department of Energy's report noted that ecosystem protection is important to carbon sequestration and may reduce or prevent the loss of carbon currently stored in the terrestrial biosphere.

Conserving natural habitat for wildlife is the heart of any long-range plan for national wildlife refuges. The actions proposed in this Draft CCP/EA would conserve or restore land and water, and would thus enhance carbon sequestration. This, in turn, contributes positively to efforts to mitigate human-induced global climate changes.

Changes in coastal wetlands due to sea-level rise were modeled for Bayou Sauvage NWR, using the Sea Level Affecting Marshes Model (SLAMM). This model simulates the dominant processes involved in wetland conversions and shoreline modifications during long-term sea-level rise (Clough and Park 2006, www.warrenpinnacle.com/prof/SLAMM). Dramatic changes are projected for Bayou Sauvage NWR's marshes and other near-shore habitats under the 1-m sea-level rise scenario. Freshwater marshes in the northwest and middle sections of the refuge would likely convert to open water, and dike failure is likely in some areas (Nieves 2008, Bayou Sauvage SLAMM Analysis).

OTHER MANAGEMENT

All management activities that could affect the refuge's natural resources, including subsurface mineral reservations, utility lines and easements, soils, water and air, and historical and archaeological resources, would be managed to comply with all laws and regulations. In particular, any existing and future oil and gas exploration, extraction, and transport operations on the refuge would be managed identically under each of the alternatives. Thus, the impacts would be the same.

LAND ACQUISITION

Funding for land acquisition from willing sellers within the approved acquisition boundary of Bayou Sauvage NWR would come from the Land and Water Conservation Fund, the Migratory Bird Conservation Fund, Corps of Engineers mitigation programs, fee title purchase, or donations from conservation and private organizations. Conservation easements and leases can be used to obtain the minimum interests necessary to satisfy refuge objectives if the refuge staff can adequately manage uses of the areas for the benefit of wildlife. The Service can negotiate management agreements with local, state, and federal agencies, and accept conservation easements. Some tracts within the refuge acquisition boundary may be owned by other public or private conservation organizations. The Service would work with interested organizations to identify additional areas needing protection and provide technical assistance if needed. The acquisition of private lands is entirely contingent on the landowners and their willingness to participate.

CULTURAL RESOURCES

All alternatives afford additional land protection and low levels of development, thereby producing little negative effect on the refuge's cultural and historic resources. Potentially negative effects could include logging, construction of new trails or facilities, and development of water impoundments. In most cases, these management actions would require review by the Service's Regional Archaeologist in consultation with the State of Louisiana Historic Preservation Office, as mandated by Section 106 of the National Historic Preservation Act. Therefore, the determination of whether a particular action within an alternative has the potential to affect cultural resources is an on-going process that would occur during the planning stages of every project.

Service acquisition of land with known or potential archaeological or historical sites provides two major types of protection for these resources: protection from damage by federal activity and protection from vandalism or theft. The National Historic Preservation Act requires that any actions by a federal agency which may affect archaeological or historical resources be reviewed by the State Historic Preservation Office, and that the identified effects must be avoided or mitigated. The Service's policy is to preserve these cultural, historic, and archaeological resources in the public trust, and avoid any adverse effects wherever possible.

Land acquisition by the Service within the current acquisition boundary would provide some degree of protection to significant cultural and historic resources. If acquisition of private lands does not occur and these lands remain under private ownership, the landowner would be responsible for protecting and preserving cultural resources. Development of off-refuge lands has the potential to destroy archaeological artifacts and other historical resources, thereby decreasing opportunities for cultural resource interpretation and research.

REFUGE REVENUE-SHARING

Annual refuge revenue-sharing payments to Orleans Parish would continue at similar rates under each alternative. If lands are acquired and added to the refuge, the payments would increase accordingly.

OTHER EFFECTS

Each of the alternatives would have similar effects or minimal-to-negligible effects on soils, water quality and quantity, noise, transportation, human health and safety, children, hazardous materials, waste management, aesthetics and visual resources, and utilities and public services.

SUMMARY OF EFFECTS BY ALTERNATIVE

The following section describes the environmental consequences of implementing each refuge management alternative. Table 7 summarizes and addresses the likely outcomes for the specific issues, and is organized by broad issue categories.

ALTERNATIVE A (CURRENT MANAGEMENT--NO ACTION)

The No Action Alternative would maintain the status quo and was developed using anticipated conditions in the area of Bayou Sauvage NWR over the next 15 years. It assumes that current conservation management and land protection programs and activities by the Service, federal, state, and local agencies, and private organizations would continue to follow past trends. This alternative is included for the purpose of comparison to baseline conditions and is not considered to be the most effective management strategy for achieving the vision and goals of the refuge.

In the No Action Alternative, wildlife population monitoring/surveys would be limited to current, primarily mandated species being monitored, without the benefit of additional focus on species of concern and species chosen as indicators of a healthy ecosystem. Restoration efforts would continue as small, experimental projects that could be easily destroyed by tropical storms and hurricanes, instead of larger projects with longer-lasting benefits. Public use programs would not change or increase with demand and would not be adapted based on the effects on refuge resources. Forestry and fire management programs would not be evaluated for efficiency and effectiveness.

Under Alternative A, negative impacts to soils, water, air, and other physical parameters would be mitigated to some extent, but not as much as in an adaptive management-based approach. The biological environment would remain protected, but certain systems could suffer if not systematically monitored using focused species as indicators. Management under Alternative A would not adversely impact socioeconomic values of the area, but the refuge would not achieve its potential for providing needed educational and wildlife-dependent recreational activities.

ALTERNATIVE B (PROPOSED ACTION – RESTORE AND IMPROVE ECOLOGICAL DIVERSITY AND AUGMENT VISITOR SERVICES)

Implementing Alternative B would be the most effective management action for meeting the purposes of Bayou Sauvage NWR. Monitoring and surveying would be conducted systematically after assessing which species should be targeted based on their population status and ability to indicate health of important habitat. Restoration efforts, wetland habitat management, the fire program, and forest management would reflect best management practices determined after examination of historical regimes, soil types and elevation, and the current hydrological system. Management actions would be monitored for effectiveness and adapted to changing conditions, knowledge, and technology. A Habitat Management Plan would be developed for future habitat projects and to evaluate previous actions.

Public use programs would be updated to educate visitors about the reasons for specific refuge management actions, and to provide quality experiences for refuge visitors. The refuge complex headquarters in Lacombe, Louisiana, would be developed to provide more visitors more information about Bayou Sauvage NWR. Options and opportunities would be explored to develop a visitor contact building on Bayou Sauvage NWR. In an increasingly developing region, Alternative B would strive to achieve a balanced program of wildlife-dependent recreational activities and protection of wildlife resources.

This alternative proposes to add 15 new positions to current staffing for the entire Complex (three of these new positions would have duties dedicated primarily to Bayou Sauvage NWR) in order to continue to protect refuge resources, provide visitor services, and attain facilities and equipment maintenance goals. No adverse effects to soils, water, air, and other physical parameters are expected under this alternative. The biological environment would improve as adaptive and best management practices are implemented. Socioeconomic values should also increase; the refuge would offer an oasis of undeveloped green space as a draw for the area's eco-tourist industry and for local residents searching for natural landscapes and environments.

ALTERNATIVE C (CUSTODIAL MANAGEMENT, WHILE MAXIMIZING VISITOR SERVICES)

Alternative C emphasizes managing the refuge for wildlife-dependent recreational uses. While this alternative fulfills some aspects of the Refuge Improvement Act of 1997, it falls short of fulfilling the entire Act, the mission of the Refuge System, the purposes of the refuge, and the goals of the Lower Mississippi River Valley Ecosystem and other conservation plans. Mandated species, such as threatened and endangered species, would continue to be monitored, but by focusing on species of interest only to the public, the status of other important species could be overlooked. Under Alternative C, because monitoring would not be based on indicator species or species of concern, any negative impacts to soil, water, air, and other physical parameters would be observed only when highly visible effects are manifested. Habitat restoration efforts would be accomplished to satisfy public use demands and would not occur in as efficient or timely manner as if planned using an ecosystem approach.

However, if the majority of staff time and funds support a state-of-the-art public use program, wildlife-dependent recreation, and environmental education and interpretation probably would be more successful than in the other alternatives. Refuge resources would be protected from overuse so that quality public use experiences would be maintained. The socioeconomic value of the refuge to the surrounding area would be the highest of the three alternatives.

Table 7. Summary of environmental effects by alternatives, Bayou Sauvage NWR

Bayou Sauvage NWR Issues	Alternative A (Current Management – No Action Alternative)	Alternative B (Proposed Alternative)	Alternative C
Wetland Habitat Restoration	Allow marsh habitat to recover naturally with no intervention.	Reestablish and restore fresh marsh habitat.	Allow marsh habitat to recover naturally with no intervention. Maintain water levels near full pool for public use opportunities.
	Slightly decreasing quality	Increasing quality	Slightly decreasing quality
Forest Habitat Restoration	Allow hardwood forest to naturally recover with no intervention.	Actively work to restore hardwood forest.	Restore hardwood forest in high public use areas and allow remainder to recover naturally.
	Decreasing quality	Increasing quality	Slightly increasing quality
Waterfowl	Conduct midwinter waterfowl survey and one other aerial waterfowl survey.	Increase monitoring of waterfowl and other migratory birds in order to assess and adapt habitat management strategies/actions.	Conduct bi-weekly ground assessments of migratory bird use, identifying areas of bird concentration for public use opportunities.
	Stable	Increasing quality	Stable
Neotropical Migratory and Breeding Birds	Conduct random, irregular monitoring as part of research studies.	Monitor during peak migration and breeding periods.	Conduct random, irregular monitoring as part of research studies.
	Stable	Increasing quality	Stable

Bayou Sauvage NWR Issues	Alternative A (Current Management – No Action Alternative)	Alternative B (Proposed Alternative)	Alternative C
Threatened and Endangered Species	Consult with Ecological Services Office on potential impacts of refuge programs/actions. **Stable**	Same as Alternative A. **Stable**	Same as Alternative A. **Stable**
Other Wildlife	Continue opportunistic, observational data of alligator presence and general size classes. Continue opportunistic, observational data of game fish being harvested. **Stable**	Increase monitoring of endemic species in order to assess and adapt habitat management strategies/actions. **Increasing quality**	Conduct monthly ground assessments of alligators and monthly creel surveys, in order to direct visiting public to observation areas and fishing opportunities. **Stable**
Fire Management	Maintain existing fire management program. **Stable**	Same as Alternative A. **Stable**	Maintain existing fire management program, unless it interferes with public use of highly visited areas. **Stable**
Exotic Plant Species	Opportunistically control Chinese tallow and cogon grass when monies and time allow. **Slightly Increasing quality**	Increase efforts to control invasive plant species. **Increasing quality**	Opportunistically control Chinese tallow and cogon grass when monies and time allow, with efforts being targeted at public use areas. **Slightly Increasing quality**

Bayou Sauvage NWR Issues	Alternative A (Current Management – No Action Alternative)	Alternative B (Proposed Alternative)	Alternative C
Invasive and Nuisance Species	Participate in State of Louisiana Nutria Control program. Continue trapping feral hogs with two contract trappers. Slightly Increasing quality	Participate in State of Louisiana Nutria Control program. Conduct yearly evaluations of nutria populations on refuge in order to assess and adapt management strategies and actions. Increase trapping staff to eliminate feral hogs. Monitor progress and increase eradication effort. Increasing quality	Participate in State of Louisiana Nutria Control program. Remove trappers and refuge staff support. Open refuge to public hog hunting. Slightly Increasing quality
Environmental Education, Outreach, and Interpretation	Re-implement a slate of environmental education programs with same scope and emphases as before Hurricane Katrina. Stable	Develop a new slate of environmental education programs that emphasize refuge restoration activities and the diversity of water management regimes in the aftermath of Hurricane Katrina and also address larger coastal conservation issues. Increasing quality	Maximize offerings of environmental education programs that emphasize the altered ecosystem of the refuge after Hurricane Katrina, but that also address a wide range of local and global environmental concerns. Increasing quality

Bayou Sauvage NWR Issues	Alternative A (Current Management – No Action Alternative)	Alternative B (Proposed Alternative)	Alternative C
Law Enforcement	Enforce all federal and state laws; post refuge boundaries.	Enforce all federal and state laws; dedicate law enforcement to spend 100 % of time on refuge and post 20 % of refuge boundary annually.	Same as Alternative A.
	Stable	Increasing quality	
Land Acquisition	Acquire lands from willing sellers through fee title purchase.	Acquire lands that provide resource and public use values from willing sellers by: fee title purchase, donation, mitigation purchase and transfer, or other viable means.	Acquire lands that provide increased public use values from willing sellers by: fee title purchase, donation, mitigation purchase and transfer, or other viable means.
	Slightly increasing quality	Increasing quality	Increasing quality

Bayou Sauvage NWR Issues	Alternative A (Current Management – No Action Alternative)	Alternative B (Proposed Alternative)	Alternative C
Welcome and Orient Visitors	Maintain current status of program to welcome and orient visitors to the refuge through use of directional and entrance signs, design and upkeep of facilities, and the provision of information regarding programs and facilities. **Stable**	Improve program to welcome and orient visitors to the refuge through use of directional and entrance signs, design and upkeep of facilities, and the provision of information regarding programs and facilities. **Slightly Increasing public use quality**	Maximize efforts to welcome and orient visitors to the refuge through use of directional and entrance signs, design and upkeep of facilities, and the provision of information regarding programs and facilities. **Increasing public use quality**
Outreach	Continue current outreach activities. **Stable**	Increase public outreach to emphasize resource management practices and promote compatible public use and recreational opportunities. **Slightly Increasing quality**	Increase public outreach to emphasize and promote compatible public use and recreational opportunities. **Slightly Increasing quality**
Public Uses	Continue to offer visitors fishing, wildlife observation, and wildlife photography opportunities. **Stable**	Expand to offer visitors additional fishing, wildlife observation, and wildlife photography opportunities. Petition city of New Orleans to allow youth waterfowl hunt outside levee system. **Slightly Increasing public use quality**	Maximize the number of visitors fishing, hunting, observing wildlife, and photographing wildlife. **Increasing public use quality; Decreasing biological quality**

UNAVOIDABLE IMPACTS AND MITIGATION MEASURES

Under Alternative A, the no action alternative, there are numerous unavoidable impacts, including inadequate monitoring and protection of aquatic and archaeological resources, inadequate monitoring of indicator species, and a public use program that lags behind increasing public use demands. Over time, if these issues are not addressed, they would continue to impact refuge resources.

Under Alternative C, the user-focused alternative, unavoidable impacts include inadequate protection of aquatic resources, inadequate monitoring of indicator and species of concern, ineffective habitat restoration, and unaddressed environmental issues. Over time, if these issues are not dealt with, refuge resources would deteriorate.

Alternative B, the proposed alternative, also has some unavoidable impacts. These are expected to be minor and/or of short duration. The refuge would use the measures described in the following sections to mitigate these impacts as much as possible.

WATER QUALITY IMPACTS FROM SOIL DISTURBANCE AND USE OF HERBICIDES

Soil disturbance and siltation due to water management activities; road maintenance; and construction of additional facilities would be expected to be minor and of short duration. To further reduce potential impacts, the refuge would use best management practices to minimize erosion and disturbance of soils.

Foot traffic on new and extended foot trails would be expected to have a negligible impact on soil erosion. To minimize the impacts from public use, the refuge would include informational signs directing trail users to remain on the trails to avoid causing potential erosion problems.

Long-term herbicide use for exotic plant control could result in a slight decrease in water quality in areas prone to exotic plant infestation. Through the proper application of herbicides, this would be expected to have a minor impact on the environment, with the benefit of reducing or eliminating exotic plant infestations. Use of insecticides for mosquito control would follow strict guidelines to reduce effects on non-target species.

WILDLIFE DISTURBANCE

Wildlife disturbance is an unavoidable consequence of any public use program, regardless of the activity. While some activities such as wildlife observation may be less disturbing than others, all public use activities proposed under the proposed alternative would be planned to avoid unacceptable levels of impact.

The known and anticipated levels of disturbance from the proposed alternative are not considered to be significant. Nevertheless, the refuge would manage public use activities to reduce impacts. Providing access for fishing opportunities would allow the use of a renewable natural resource without adversely impacting other resources. Potential hunting would also be managed with restrictions that ensure minimal impact on other resources. General wildlife observation could be designed to result in minimal disturbance to wildlife. If the refuge determined that impacts from the expected additional visitor uses would be above the levels that are anticipated, those uses would be discontinued, restricted, or rerouted to other less sensitive areas.

VEGETATION DISTURBANCE

Negative impacts could result from the creation, extension, and maintenance of trails that require clearing of vegetation. This would be expected to be a minor short-term impact.

Increased visitor use could increase the potential for introduction of new exotic species into areas when visitors fail to comply with boating regulations at boat ramps and other access points or with requests to stay on trails. The refuge would minimize this impact by enforcing regulations for access to the refuge's water bodies, and by installing informational signs directing users to stay on the trails.

USER GROUP CONFLICTS

As public use increases, unanticipated conflicts between different user groups could occur. If this should happen, the refuge would adjust its programs, as needed, to eliminate or minimize any public use issues. The refuge would use methods that have proven to be effective in reducing or eliminating public use conflicts. These include establishing separate use areas; different use periods; and limiting the numbers of users. These methods have been demonstrated to provide safe, quality, appropriate, and compatible wildlife-dependent recreational opportunities.

EFFECTS ON ADJACENT LANDOWNERS

Positive impacts to owners of adjacent private land that would be expected with implementation of the proposed alternative include higher property values, less intrusion of invasive exotic plants, and increased opportunities for viewing more diverse wildlife.

Adverse impacts on owners of adjacent private lands could include a higher frequency of trespass and noise associated with increased traffic. To minimize these potential impacts, the refuge would provide informational signs clearly marking refuge boundaries; maintain the refuge's existing parking facilities; use law enforcement; and provide increased educational efforts at the visitor center. Smoke from prescribed fires and wildfires could cause temporary discomfort and visibility; the fire program would employ methods to mitigate problems caused by smoke whenever possible and to forewarn neighbors of serious or deteriorating conditions.

Potential development of the refuge's buildings, trails, and other improvements could lead to minor short-term negative impacts on plants, soils, and some wildlife species. All construction activities would comply with the requirements of Section 404 of the Clean Water Act; the National Historic Preservation Act; Executive Order 11988, Floodplain Management; and other applicable regulatory requirements.

CUMULATIVE IMPACTS

A cumulative impact is defined as an impact on the natural or human environment that results from the incremental impact of the [proposed] action when added to other past, present, and reasonably foreseeable future actions, regardless of which agency (federal or non-federal) or person undertakes such other actions (40 CFR 1508.7).

Cumulative impacts are the overall, net effects on a resource that arise from multiple actions. Impacts can accumulate spatially when different actions affect different areas of the same resource. They can also accumulate over the course of time. Occasionally, different actions counterbalance one another, partially canceling out each other's effects. More typically, multiple effects add up, with each additional action contributing an incremental impact on the resource. Sometimes the overall effect is greater than the sum of the individual effects, such as when one more impact causes a reduction in a population that crosses a threshold of reproductive sustainability and threatens to extinguish the population.

A thorough analysis of impacts always considers their cumulative aspects. Because actions do not take place in a vacuum, there almost always are other actions that have affected the resource in the past, are affecting it in the present, or would affect it in the reasonably foreseeable future. Any assessment of a specific action's effects must consider what else has happened to that resource, what else is happening, or what else would likely happen to it.

The refuge is not aware of any past, present or future planned actions that would result in a significant cumulative impact when added to the actions outlined in the proposed alternative.

DIRECT AND INDIRECT EFFECTS OR IMPACTS

Direct effects are caused by an action and occur at the same time as the action. Indirect effects are caused by an action but are manifested later in time or further removed in distance, but still are reasonably foreseeable.

The actions proposed in the proposed alternative include wildlife and population management, resource protection, public use and facility development, and administrative programs. These would result in both direct and indirect effects. Facility development, for example, would lead to increased public use, a direct effect; it also would lead to indirect effects, such as increased littering, noise, and vehicular traffic.

Other indirect effects that could result from implementing the proposed alternative include minor impacts from siltation due to disturbance of soils and vegetation, while expanding or creating new trails, constructing new facilities, and restoring water control structures; and due to increased public use.

SHORT-TERM IMPACTS VERSUS LONG-TERM PRODUCTIVITY

The key to protecting and ensuring the refuge's long-term productivity is to find a threshold where public uses do not degrade or interfere with the refuge's natural resources. The plans for habitat protection and management described in the proposed alternative have been carefully conceived to achieve that threshold. While there would be some short-term adverse impacts of the individual recommendations, implementing the proposed alternative as a comprehensive plan would produce long-term wildlife protection and land conservation benefits for the refuge's entire Lower Mississippi River Ecosystem that would far outweigh short-term adverse impacts of the individual actions.

V. Consultation and Coordination

OVERVIEW

This chapter summarizes the consultation and coordination that resulted in the issues, alternatives, and proposed alternative presented in this Draft CCP/EA. It lists the meetings that have been held with the various agencies, organizations, and individuals who were consulted in the preparation of the Draft CCP/EA.

Preplanning activities for the Draft CCP/EA development began in early 2007. Preplanning activities included the formation of a Core Planning Team, review of biological and visitor services currently offered on the refuge and public involvement in the scoping process.

CORE PLANNING TEAM
The core planning team primarily involved staff from Bayou Sauvage NWR. This team was the primary decision-making team for this Draft CCP/EA. The fundamental tasks of the team involved defining and refining the vision; identifying, reviewing, and filtering issues; defining the goals; and outlining the alternatives. The team members included:

- Kenneth Litzenberger, Project Leader, Southeast Louisiana National Wildlife Refuge Complex
- Pon Dixson, Deputy Project Leader, Southeast Louisiana National Wildlife Refuge Complex
- Jack Bohannan, Manager, Southeast Louisiana National Wildlife Refuge Complex
- Charlotte Parker, Former Natural Resource Planner, Southeast Louisiana NWR Complex
- James Harris, Supervisory Wildlife Biologist, Southeast Louisiana NWR Complex
- Shelley Stiaes, Refuge Operations Specialist, Southeast Louisiana NWR Complex
- Byron Fortier, Supervisory Park Ranger, Southeast Louisiana NWR Complex
- Diane Barth, Park Ranger, Southeast Louisiana NWR Complex
- Chevales Williams, Environmental Engineer, TVA

BIOLOGICAL AND HABITAT REVIEW TEAM
The Biological and Habitat Review Team consisted of Service staff and invited participants. The invited participants included local and regional experts, researchers, and individuals with intimate knowledge of and expertise in the biological resources of the refuge. This review took place on February 27, 2008. Members of the review team included:

- Todd Baker, Area Manager Pass a Loutre, LDWF
- Diane Barth, Park Ranger, Southeast Louisiana NWR Complex
- Jack Bohannan, Manager, Southeast Louisiana NWR Complex
- Jennifer Coulson, President, New Orleans Audubon Society
- Pon Dixson, Deputy Project Leader, Southeast Louisiana NWR Complex
- Byron Fortier, Supervisory Park Ranger, Southeast Louisiana NWR Complex
- Sue Grace, Fire Ecologist, Southeast Regional Office, Division of Fire Management
- James Harris, Supervisory Wildlife Biologist, Southeast Louisiana NWR Complex
- Brian Lezina, Marine Fisheries Division, LDWF
- Ken Litzenberger, Project Leader, Southeast Louisiana NWR Complex
- David Muth, Chief of Resource Management, Jean Lafitte National Historical Park and Preserve
- Charlotte Parker, Former Natural Resource Planner, Southeast Louisiana NWR Complex

- Shelley Stiaes, Refuge Operations Specialist, Southeast Louisiana NWR Complex
- Bob Strader, Migratory Bird Biologist, Jackson, Mississippi
- Chevales Williams, Environmental Engineer, TVA

VISITOR SERVICES REVIEW TEAM

The Visitor Services Review Team consisted of staff from the Service's Regional Office and the Southeast Louisiana NWR Complex. Additional members of the team included local and regional educators, members of volunteer and friends groups, and individuals with intimate knowledge of the refuge. This review took place the week of March 5-8, 2007. Members of the review team included:

- Diane Barth, Park Ranger, Southeast Louisiana NWR Complex
- Heather Egger, Research Associate I, UNO Pontchartrain Institute for Environmental Sciences, New Orleans, Louisiana
- Byron Fortier, Supervisory Park Ranger, Southeast Louisiana NWR Complex
- Michele Hubert, Friends of Louisiana Refuges, Inc.
- Amy LeGaux, former Education Curator, Audubon Louisiana Nature Center, New Orleans, Louisiana
- Dinah Maygarden, Coastal Wetlands Education Program Manager, UNO Pontchartrain Institute for Environmental Sciences, New Orleans, Louisiana
- Charlotte Parker, Former Natural Resource Planner, Southeast Louisiana NWR Complex
- Marie Tizzard, Biology and Environmental Science Teacher, Grace King High School, Metairie, Louisiana
- Garry Tucker, Chief, Visitor Services and Outreach, FWS, Atlanta, Georgia

Appendix A. Glossary

Adaptive Management:	Refers to a process in which policy decisions are implemented within a framework of scientifically driven experiments to test predictions and assumptions inherent in a management plan. Analysis of results helps managers determine whether current management should continue as is or whether it should be modified to achieve desired conditions.
Alluvial:	Sediment transported and deposited in a delta or riverbed by flowing water.
Alternative:	1. A reasonable way to fix the identified problem or satisfy the stated need (40 CFR 1500.2). 2. Alternatives are different sets of objectives and strategies or means of achieving refuge purposes and goals, helping fulfill the Refuge System mission, and resolving issues (Service Manual 602 FW 1.6B).
Anadromous:	Migratory fishes that spend most of their lives in the sea and migrate to fresh water to breed.
Approved Acquisition Boundary:	A project boundary which the Director of the Fish and Wildlife Service approves upon completion of a detailed planning and environmental compliance process.
Biological Diversity:	The variety of life and its processes, including the variety of living organisms, the genetic differences among them, and the communities and ecosystems in which they occur (Service Manual 052 FW 1. 12B). The System's focus is on indigenous species, biotic communities, and ecological processes. Also referred to as biodiversity.
Biological Integrity:	The biotic composition, structure, and functioning at genetic, organism, and community levels comparable with historic conditions including the natural biological processes that shape genomes, organisms, and communities.
Brackish Marsh:	Marshes occurring where salinity ranges from 3-15 parts per thousand (ppt); dominated by wiregrass.
Categorical Exclusion:	A category of actions that does not individually or cumulatively have a significant effect on the human environment and have been found to have no such effect in procedures adopted by a federal agency pursuant to the National Environmental Policy Act (40 CFR 1508.4).
CFR:	Code of Federal Regulations.

Compatible Use: A proposed or existing wildlife-dependent recreational use or any other use of a national wildlife refuge that, based on sound professional judgment, will not materially interfere with or detract from the fulfillment of the National Wildlife Refuge System mission or the purpose(s) of the national wildlife refuge [50 CFR 25.12 (a)]. A compatibility determination supports the selection of compatible uses and identifies stipulations or limits necessary to ensure compatibility.

Comprehensive Conservation Plan: A document that describes the desired future conditions of a refuge or planning unit and provides long-range guidance and management direction to achieve the purposes of the refuge; helps fulfill the mission of the Refuge System; maintains and, where appropriate, restores the ecological integrity of each refuge and the Refuge System; helps achieve the goals of the National Wilderness Preservation System; and meets other mandates (Service Manual 602 FW 1.6 E).

Concern: See Issue

Cover Type: The present vegetation of an area.

Cultural Resource Inventory: A professionally conducted study designed to locate and evaluate evidence of cultural resources present within a defined geographic area. Inventories may involve various levels, including background literature search, comprehensive field examination to identify all exposed physical manifestations of cultural resources, or sample inventory to project site distribution and density over a larger area. Evaluation of identified cultural resources to determine eligibility for the National Register follows the criteria found in 36 CFR 60.4 (Service Manual 614 FW 1.7).

Cultural Resource Overview: A comprehensive document prepared for a field office that discusses, among other things, its prehistory and cultural history, the nature and extent of known cultural resources, previous research, management objectives, resource management conflicts or issues, and a general statement on how program objectives should be met and conflicts resolved. An overview should reference or incorporate information from a field office's background or literature search described in Section VIII of the Cultural Resource Management Handbook (Service Manual 614 FW 1.7).

Cultural Resources: The remains of sites, structures, or objects used by people in the past.

Designated Wilderness Area: An area designated by the U.S. Congress to be managed as part of the National Wilderness Preservation System (Draft Service Manual 610 FW 1.5).

Disturbance: Significant alteration of habitat structure or composition. May be natural (e.g., fire) or human-caused events (e.g., aircraft overflight).

Diurnal Range:	The difference in height between mean higher high water and mean lower low water.
Dredging:	The removal of sediment (spoil) from a channel to produce sufficient depths for navigation.
Ecosystem:	A dynamic and interrelating complex of plant and animal communities and their associated non-living environment.
Ecosystem Management:	Management of natural resources using system-wide concepts to ensure that all plants and animals in ecosystems are maintained at viable levels in native habitats and basic ecosystem processes are perpetuated indefinitely.
Endangered Species (Federal):	A plant or animal species listed under the Endangered Species Act that is in danger of extinction throughout all or a significant portion of its range.
Endangered Species (State):	A plant or animal species in danger of becoming extinct or extirpated in the state within the near future if factors contributing to its decline continue. Populations of these species are at critically low levels or their habitats have been degraded or depleted to a significant degree.
Endemic	An organism being exclusively native to a place or biota.
Environmental Assessment (EA):	A concise public document, prepared in compliance with the National Environmental Policy Act, that briefly discusses the purpose and need for an action, alternatives to such action, and provides sufficient evidence and analysis of impacts to determine whether to prepare an environmental impact statement or finding of no significant impact (40 CFR 1508.9).
Environmental Impact Statement (EIS):	A detailed written statement required by section 102(2)(C) of the National Environmental Policy Act, analyzing the environmental impacts of a proposed action, adverse effects of the project that cannot be avoided, alternative courses of action, short-term uses of the environment versus the maintenance and enhancement of long-term productivity, and any irreversible and irretrievable commitment of resources (40 CFR 1508.11).
Estuary:	The wide lower course of a river into which the tides flow. The area where the tide meets a river current.
Fast Lands:	Land which is above the mean or ordinary high tide line; also called uplands.
Finding of No Significant Impact (FONSI):	A document prepared in compliance with the National Environmental Policy Act, supported by an environmental assessment, that briefly presents why a federal action will have no significant effect on the human environment and for which an environmental impact statement, therefore, will not be prepared (40 CFR 1508.13).
Forest	A form of habitat fragmentation, occurring when forests are cut down in a

Fragmentation:	manner that leaves relatively small, isolated patches of forest know as fragments or remnants.
Goal:	Descriptive, open-ended, and often broad statement of desired future conditions that conveys a purpose but does not define measurable units (Service Manual 620 FW 1.6J).
Habitat:	Suite of existing environmental conditions required by an organism for survival and reproduction. The place where an organism typically lives.
Habitat Restoration:	Management emphasis designed to move ecosystems to desired conditions and processes, and/or to healthy ecosystems.
Habitat Type:	See Vegetation Type.
Hypoxic Zone:	An area located along the Louisiana-Texas coast in which water near the bottom of the Gulf contains less than 2 parts per million of dissolved oxygen, causing stress or even death to bottom dwelling organisms.
Improvement Act:	The National Wildlife Refuge System Improvement Act of 1997.
Informed Consent:	The grudging willingness of opponents to "go along" with a course of action that they actually oppose (Bleiker).
Issue:	Any unsettled matter that requires a management decision [e.g., an initiative, opportunity, resource management problem, threat to the resources of the unit, conflict in uses, public concern, or other presence of an undesirable resource condition (Service Manual 602 FW 1.6K)].
Management Alternative:	See Alternative
Management Concern:	See Issue
Management Opportunity:	See Issue
Migration:	The seasonal movement from one area to another and back.
Mission Statement:	Succinct statement of the unit's purpose and reason for being.
Monitoring:	The process of collecting information to track changes of selected parameters over time.
National Environmental Policy Act of	Requires all agencies, including the Service, to examine the environmental impacts of their actions, incorporate environmental information, and use public participation in the planning and implementation of all actions. Federal

| **1969 (NEPA):** | agencies must integrate NEPA with other planning requirements, and prepare appropriate NEPA documents to facilitate better environmental decision-making (40 CFR 1500). |

National Wildlife Refuge System Improvement Act of 1997 (Public Law 105-57): Under the Improvement Act, the Fish and Wildlife Service is required to develop 15-year comprehensive conservation plans for all national wildlife refuges outside Alaska. The Act also describes the six public uses given priority status within the Refuge System (i.e., hunting, fishing, wildlife observation, wildlife photography, and environmental education and interpretation).

National Wildlife Refuge System Mission: The mission is to administer a national network of lands and waters for the conservation, management, and where appropriate, restoration of the fish, wildlife, and plant resources and their habitats within the United States for the benefit of present and future generations of Americans.

National Wildlife Refuge System: Various categories of areas administered by the Secretary of the Interior for the conservation of fish and wildlife, including species threatened with extinction; all lands, waters, and interests therein administered by the Secretary as wildlife refuges; areas for the protection and conservation of fish and wildlife that are threatened with extinction; wildlife ranges; game ranges; wildlife management areas; or waterfowl production areas.

National Wildlife Refuge: A designated area of land, water, or an interest in land or water within the Refuge System.

Native Species: Species that normally live and thrive in a particular ecosystem.

Noxious Weed: A plant species designated by federal or state law as generally possessing one or more of the following characteristics: aggressive or difficult to manage; parasitic; a carrier or host of serious insect or disease; or non-native, new, or not common to the United States. According to the Federal Noxious Weed Act (P.L. 93-639), a noxious weed is one that causes disease or had adverse effects on man or his environment and therefore is detrimental to the agriculture and commerce of the Untied States and to the public health.

Objective: A concise statement of what we want to achieve, how much we want to achieve, when and where we want to achieve it, and who is responsible for the work. Objectives derive from goals and provide the basis for determining strategies, monitoring refuge accomplishments, and evaluating the success of strategies. Making objectives attainable, time-specific, and measurable (Service Manual 602 FW 1.6N).

Plant Association: A classification of plant communities based on the similarity in dominants of all layers of vascular species in a climax community.

Plant Community:	An assemblage of plant species unique in its composition; occurs in particular locations under particular influences; a reflection or integration of the environmental influences on the site such as soils, temperature, elevation, solar radiation, slope, aspect, and rainfall; denotes a general kind of climax plant community.
Preferred Alternative:	This is the alternative determined (by the decision-maker) to best achieve the refuge purpose, vision, and goals; contributes to the Refuge System mission, addresses the significant issues; and is consistent with principles of sound fish and wildlife management.
Prescribed Fire:	The application of fire to wildland fuels to achieve identified land use objectives (Service Manual 621 FW 1.7). May occur from natural ignition or intentional ignition.
Priority Species:	Fish and wildlife species that require protective measures and/or management guidelines to ensure their perpetuation. Priority species include the following: (1) State-listed and candidate species; (2) species or groups of animals susceptible to significant population declines within a specific area or statewide by virtue of their inclination to aggregate (e.g., seabird colonies); and (3) species of recreation, commercial, and/or tribal importance.
Public Involvement Plan:	Broad long-term guidance for involving the public in the comprehensive conservation planning process.
Public Involvement:	A process that offers impacted and interested individuals and organizations an opportunity to become informed about, and to express their opinions on Service actions and policies. In the process, these views are studied thoroughly and thoughtful consideration of public views is given in shaping decisions for refuge management.
Public:	Individuals, organizations, and groups; officials of federal, state, and local government agencies; Indian tribes; and foreign nations. It may include anyone outside the core planning team. It includes those who may or may not have indicated an interest in service issues and those who do or do not realize that Service decisions may affect them.
Purposes of the Refuge:	"The purposes specified in or derived from the law, proclamation, executive order, agreement, public land order, donation document, or administrative memorandum establishing, authorizing, or expanding a refuge, refuge unit, or refuge sub-unit." For refuges that encompass congressionally designated wilderness, the purposes of the Wilderness Act are additional purposes of the refuge (Service Manual 602 FW 106 S).

Recommended Wilderness:	Areas studied and found suitable for wilderness designation by both the Director of the Fish and Wildlife Service and the Secretary of the Department of the Interior, and recommended for designation by the President to Congress. These areas await only legislative action by Congress in order to become part of the Wilderness System. Such areas are also referred to as "pending in Congress" (Draft Service Manual 610 FW 1.5).
Record of Decision (ROD):	A concise public record of decision prepared by the federal agency, pursuant to NEPA, that contains a statement of the decision, identification of all alternatives considered, identification of the environmentally preferable alternative, a statement as to whether all practical means to avoid or minimize environmental harm from the alternative selected have been adopted (and if not, why they were not), and a summary of monitoring and enforcement where applicable for any mitigation (40 CFR 1505.2).
Refuge Goal:	See Goal
Refuge Purposes:	See Purposes of the Refuge
Saltwater Intrusion:	The invasion of freshwater bodies by denser salt water.
Sea-level Rise:	A rise in the surface of the sea due to increased water volume of the ocean and/or sinking of the land.
Shoreline Progradation:	A shoreline that is being built seaward by accumulation of deposition.
Songbirds: (Also Passerines)	A category of birds that is medium to small, perching landbirds. Most are territorial singers and migratory.
Step-down Management Plan:	A plan that provides specific guidance on management subjects (e.g., habitat, public use, fire, and safety) or groups of related subjects. It describes strategies and implementation schedules for meeting CCP goals and objectives (Service Manual 602 FW 1.6 U).
Strategy:	A specific action, tool, technique, or combination of actions, tools, and techniques used to meet unit objectives (Service Manual 602 FW 1.6 U).
Study Area:	The area reviewed in detail for wildlife, habitat, and public use potential. For purposes of this CCP, the study area includes the lands within the currently approved refuge boundary and potential refuge expansion areas.
Subsidence:	A gradual sinking of land with respect to its previous level.
Threatened Species	Species listed under the Endangered Species Act that are likely to become endangered within the foreseeable future throughout all or a significant portion

(Federal):	of their range.
Threatened Species (State):	A plant or animal species likely to become endangered in the state within the near future if factors contributing to population decline or habitat degradation or loss continue.
Tiering:	The coverage of general matters in broader environmental impact statements with subsequent narrower statements of environmental analysis, incorporating by reference, the general discussions and concentrating on specific issues (40 CFR 1508.28).
U.S. Fish and Wildlife Service Mission:	The mission of the Fish and Wildlife Service is working with others to conserve, protect, and enhance fish and wildlife and their habitats for the continuing benefit of the American people.
Unit Objective:	See Objective
Vegetation Type, Habitat Type, Forest Cover Type:	A land classification system based upon the concept of distinct plant associations.
Vision Statement:	A concise statement of what the planning unit should be, or what we hope to do, based primarily upon the Refuge System mission and specific refuge purposes, and other mandates. We will tie the vision statement for the refuge to the mission of the Refuge System; the purpose(s) of the refuge; the maintenance or restoration of the ecological integrity of each refuge and the Refuge System; and other mandates (Service Manual 602 FW 1.6 Z).
Wilderness Study Areas:	Lands and waters identified through inventory as meeting the definition of wilderness and undergoing evaluation for recommendation for inclusion in the Wilderness System. A study area must meet the following criteria:

- Generally appears to have been affected primarily by the forces of nature, with the imprint of man's work substantially unnoticeable;

- Has outstanding opportunities for solitude or a primitive and unconfined type of recreation; and

- Has at least 5,000 contiguous roadless acres or is sufficient in size as to make practicable its preservation and use in an unimpaired condition (Draft Service Manual 610 FW 1.5).

Wilderness:	See Designated Wilderness
Wildfire:	A free-burning fire requiring a suppression response; all fire other than prescribed fire that occurs on wildlands (Service Manual 621 FW 1.7).
Wildland Fire:	Every wildland fire is either a wildfire or a prescribed fire (Service Manual 621 FW 1.3

ACRONYMS AND ABBREVIATIONS

BCC	Birds of Conservation Concern
CCP	Comprehensive Conservation Plan
CFR	Code of Federal Regulations
cfs	cubic feet per second
CPRA	Coastal Protection and Restoration Authority of Louisiana
CWCS	Comprehensive Wildlife Conservation Strategy
CWFCU	Coastal Wetland Forest Conservation and Use Science
CWPPRA	Coastal Wetlands Planning, Protection and Restoration Act
DU	Ducks Unlimited
EA	Environmental Assessment
EIS	Environmental Impact Statement
EPA	U.S. Environmental Protection Agency
ESA	Endangered Species Act
FTE	full-time equivalent
FY	Fiscal Year
GCPM	Gulf Coast Prairies and Marshes
GIS	Global Information System
GIWW	Gulf Intracoastal Waterway
GWV	Gulf Coast Joint Venture
IPCC	Intergovernmental Panel on Climate Change
LDEQ	Louisiana Department of Environmental Quality
LMRE	Lower Mississippi River Ecosystem
LRA	Louisiana Recovery Authority
MLG	Mean Low Gulf
MSA	Metropolitan Statistical Area
NAAQS	National Ambient Air Quality Standards
NAMS	National Ambient Monitoring Stations
NAWMP	North American Waterfowl Management Plan
NEPA	National Environmental Policy Act
NOAA	National Oceanic and Atmospheric Administration
NRHP	National Register of Historic Places
NWRS	National Wildlife Refuge System
PFT	Permanent Full Time
SAV	Submerged Aquatic Vegetation
SLAMM	Sea Level Rise Affects Marshes Model
SLAMS	State and Local Ambient Monitoring Stations
RM	Refuge Manual
RNA	Research Natural Area
ROD	Record of Decision
RONS	Refuge Operating Needs System
RRP	Refuge Roads Program
FWS	U.S. Fish and Wildlife Service (also Service)
TFT	Temporary Full Time
TVA	Tennessee Valley Authority
UNO	University of New Orleans
USC	United States Code
USDA	United States Department of Agriculture
USGS	United States Geological Survey
WCRP	Wildlife Conservation and Restoration Program

Appendix B. References and Literature Citations

Answers.com. (Definition of "prograding shoreline.") http://www.answers.com/topic/prograding-shoreline?cat=technology (accessed July 8, 2008).

Barataria Terrebonne National Estuary Program. http://btnep.org/home.asp

"City's Population Up 14 Percent Since July 2006." *The Times-Picayne.* May 3, 2007.

Coastal Protection and Restoration Authority of Louisiana. "Integrated Ecosystem Restoration and Hurricane Protection: Louisiana's Comprehensive Master Plan for a Sustainable Coast." 2007. http://www.lacpra.org

Coastal Wetland Forest Conservation and Use Science Working Group. "Conservation, Protection, and Mitigation of Louisiana's Coastal Wetland Forests." Final Report to the Governor of Louisiana. April 30, 2005. http://www.coastalforestswg.lsu.edu/THEFinalReport.pdf

"Coastal Wetlands Planning, Protection, and Restoration Act (CWPPRA): A Response to Louisiana's Land Loss." 2006. http://www.lacoast.gov

"Coastal Wetland Planning, Protection, and Restoration Act (CWPPRA) Restoration Projects." http://www.lacoast.gov/projects/list.asp

"Coastal Wetlands Planning, Protection, and Restoration Act (CWPPRA) Restoration Projects: PO-16 and PO-18." http://www.lacoast.gov/projects/overview.asp?statenumber=PO%2D16; and http://www.lacoast.gov/projects/overview.asp?statenumber=PO%2D18

Conservation Commission of Missouri. "Managing Wetlands: Moist-Soil Management (Seasonally Flooded Impoundments)." 2007. http://mdc.mo.gov/landown/wetland/wetmng/8.htm (accessed August 13, 2007)

Dupree, A. Hunter. 1957. Science in the Federal Government: A History of Policies and Activities to 1940. Harvard University Press, Cambridge, Massachusetts. 460 pp.

Ecology and Environment, Inc. April 2007. "Hurricane Katrina Habitat Damage Assessment – Big Branch Marsh and Bayou Sauvage National Wildlife Refuges." Prepared for U.S. Fish and Wildlife Service, Southeastern Louisiana Refuge Complex, St. Tammany and Orleans Parishes, Louisiana.

Environmental Defense. "Hurricanes Stronger Due to Warming." May 29, 2007. http://www.environmentaldefense.org/article.cfm?contentid=6452 (accessed July 30, 2007).

Environmental Defense. "Summaries of Recent Storm Research." 2007. http://www.environmentaldefense.org/page.cfm?tagid=654 (accessed July 30, 2007).

Gabrielson, Ira N. 1943. Wildlife Conservation. The Macmillan Company, New York, New York. 250 pp.

Galle, Julie. "Vulnerable Cities: New Orleans, LA."
http://www.weather.com/newscenter/specialreports/hurricanes/vulnerablecities/neworleans.ht
ml (accessed August 3, 2007).

Hoffman, John S. 1984. "Chapter 3—Estimates of Future Sea Level Rise." *Greenhouse Effect and Sea Level Rise: A Challenge for this Generation.* Van Nostrand Reinhold Company, Inc.

Krabill, W., W. Abdalati, E. Frederick, S. Manizade, C. Martin, J. Sonntag, R. Swift, R. Thomas, W. Wright, and J. Yungel. "Greenland Ice Sheet: High-elevation Balance and Peripheral Thinning." *Science.* July 21, 2000: pp. 428-430.

Lake Pontchartrain Basin Foundation. "Comprehensive Habitat Management Plan for the Lake Pontchartrain Basin." February 28,2006
http://www.saveourlake.org/pdfs/JL/CHMP_final_%2022706.pdf

Laycock, George. 1965. The Sign of the Flying Goose: A Guide to the National Wildlife Refuges. The Natural History Press, Garden City, New York. 299 pp.

Lester, Gary D., S.G. Sorensen, P.L. Faulkner, C.S. Reid, and I.E. Maxit. 2005. Louisiana Comprehensive Wildlife Conservation Strategy. Louisiana Department of Wildlife and Fisheries. Baton Rouge, LA. 455 pp.

Louisiana Department of Natural Resources, Baton Rouge. Louisiana Coastal Wetlands Conservation and Restoration Task Force and the Wetlands Conservation and Restoration Authority. 1998. "Coast 2050: Toward a Sustainable Coastal Louisiana."
http://www.lacoast.gov/Programs/2050/MainReport/report1.pdf

Louisiana Department of Wildlife & Fisheries. "Louisiana Comprehensive Wildlife Conservation Strategy (Wildlife Action Plan)." December 2005.
http://www.wlf.state.la.us/experience/wildlifeactionplan/

Matthews, S., R. O'Connor, L.R. Iverson, and A.M. Prasad. 2004. *Atlas of Climate Change Effects in 150 Bird Species of the Eastern United States.* Newton Square, PA: U.S. Fish and Wildlife Service, General Technical Report NE-GTR-318. http://www.usgcrp.gov/usgcrp/Library/ocp2006/ocp2006-hi-eco.htm

National Oceanic and Atmospheric Administration (NOAA). (Definition of "diurnal range (GT).") http://tidesandcurrents.noaa.gov/gt.html (accessed July 8, 2008).

"National Watersheds: Lower Mississippi." *Watersheds—Where the Atmosphere Meets the Earth.* http://wrc.iewatershed.com/index.php?pagename=ow_regionalWatersheds_08 (accessed August 6, 2007).

Nieves, Delissa Padilla, April 2008. "*SLAMM Analysis for Bayou Sauvage National Wildlife Refuge.*" (pages 3-7)

Penland, S., A. Beall, and J. Kindinger (editors). "Environmental Atlas of the Lake Pontchartrain Basin." U.S. USGS Open File Report 02-206. Lake Pontchartrain Basin Foundation, New Orleans, LA.
http://pubs.usgs.gov/of/2002/of02-206/index.html

State of Mississippi. "Public Lands – Glossary." Definition of "dryland." http://lands.sos.state.ms.us/tfl/glossary.asp (accessed July 7, 2008).

Strader, Robert W. and Pat H. Stinson. July 2005. Moist-Soil Management Guidelines for the U.S. Fish and Wildlife Service Southeast Region. Migratory Bird Field Office. Division of Migratory Birds. Southeast Region. U.S. Fish and Wildlife Service.

U.S. Department of Agriculture. Natural Resources Conservation Service. "Emergency Watershed Protection Program." http://www.la.nrcs.usda.gov/

U.S. Department of Agriculture. Natural Resources Conservation Service. "Louisiana Native Plant Initiative." http://www.la.nrcs.usda.gov/

U.S. Department of the Interior. U.S. Geological Survey. "Physiographic Regions." *A Tapestry of Time and Terrain: The Union of Two Maps—Geology and Topography.* April 17, 2003. http://tapestry.usgs.gov/physiogr/physio.html (accessed April 12, 2007).

U.S. Department of the Interior. U.S. Geological Survey. "Environmental Atlas of the Lake Pontchartrain Basin." December 2005. http://pubs.usgs.gov/of/2002/of02-206/env-overview/water-quality.html (accessed August 6, 2007).

U.S.. Department of the Interior, U.S. Geological Survey. "Geologic Framework and Processes of the Lake Pontchartrain Basin." December 2002. http://coastal.er.usgs.gov/pontchartrain/ (accessed August 6, 2007).

U.S. Department of the Interior, U.S. Geological Survey. "The Fragile Fringe – A Guide for Teaching About Coastal Wetlands, Glossary." (Definition of "brackish marsh," "dredging," "saltwater intrusion," and "subsidence.") June 6, 2008. http://www.nwrc.usgs.gov/fringe/glossary.html (accessed July 7, 2008).

U.S. Department of the Interior, U.S. Geological Survey. "The Gulf of Mexico Hypoxic Zone." (Definition of "hypoxia.") April 9, 2008. http://toxics.usgs.gov/hypoxia/hypoxic_zone.html (accessed July 7, 2008).

U.S. Environmental Protection Agency. "Climate Change." http://www.epa.gov/climatechange/

U.S. Environmental Protection Agency. "Global Warming—Publications." July 24,2000. http://yosemite.epa.gov/oar/globalwarming.nsf/content/ResourceCenterPublicationsSLRChallenge.html (accessed July 30, 2007).

U.S. Environmental Protection Agency. "305(b) Lists/Assessment Unit." http://iaspub.epa.gov/tmdl/enviro_v2.wcontrol?p_id305b=LA041702_00

U.S. Environmental Protection Agency. "National Estuary Program Coastal Condition Report." Publication #EPA-842-B-06-001. June 2007. http://www.epa.gov/owow/oceans/nepccr/

U.S. Environmental Protection Agency. Office of Wetlands, Oceans, and Watersheds. Mississippi River/Gulf of Mexico Watershed Nutrient Task Force. "Action Plan for Reducing, Mitigating, and Controlling Hypoxia in the Northern Gulf of Mexico." 2001. http://www.epa.gov/msbasin/taskforce/pdf/actionplan.pdf

U.S. Fish and Wildlife Service. April 2007. Bayou Sauvage National Wildlife Refuge, Biological Review Report, Southeast Louisiana National Wildlife Refuge Complex. Lacombe, LA.

U. S. Fish and Wildlife Service. "Bayou Sauvage National Wildlife Refuge (Map & Info Sheet)." http://www.fws.gov/southeast/pubs/BSauvage-tear.pdf

U. S. Fish and Wildlife Service, Southeast Region. April 2007. Draft Comprehensive Conservation Plan and Environmental Assessment for Big Branch Marsh National Wildlife Refuge, St. Tammany Parish, Louisiana. Atlanta, GA.

U. S. Fish and Wildlife Service. March 2007. Draft – ver. 3/14/2007 Visitor Services Review Report—Bayou Sauvage National Wildlife Refuge.

U.S. Fish and Wildlife Service. "Ecosystem Conservation." http://www.fws.gov/ecosystems/

U.S. Fish and Wildlife Service. Final Environmental Impact Statement (FEIS)—Bayou Sauvage National Wildlife Refuge Master Plan—Orleans Parish, Louisiana. August 1994. Atlanta, GA.

U. S. Fish and Wildlife Service. September 2002. Lower Mississippi River Ecosystem Plan (Final Draft) Version 2.5.

U.S. Fish and Wildlife Service. New Employee Handbook.

U. S. Fish and Wildlife Service. (prepared by Cashio Cochran Torre/Design Consortium, Ltd., Coastal Environments, Inc., N-Y Associates, Inc.). October 1994. Bayou Sauvage National Wildlife Refuge Master Plan Report. Orleans Parish, Louisiana. 98 pp.

U.S. Fish and Wildlife Service. "Southeast Louisiana National Wildlife Refuges, Bayou Sauvage National Wildlife Refuge (Map and Info. Sheet). http://www.fws.gov/bayousauvage/

Wikipedia. "Endemic." http://en.wikipedia.org/wiki/Endemic (accessed July 8, 2008).

Wikipedia. "Forest fragmentation." http://en.wikipedia.org/wiki/Forest_fragmentation (accessed July 7, 2008.)

Wikipedia. "Water hyacinth." http://en.wikipedia.org/wiki/Water_hyacinth (accessed August 8, 2007)

Wilson, Glynn. "Bayou Sauvage National Wildlife Refuge at Risk from Landfill." *The Locust Fork Journal.* May 21, 2007. http://www.locustfork.net/blog/new_orleans_environment/bayou_sauvage_national_wildlif_1.html (accessed July 13, 2007).

Appendix C. Relevant Legal Mandates and Executive Orders

STATUE	DESCRIPTION
Administrative Procedures Act (1946)	Outlines administrative procedures to be followed by federal agencies with respect to identification of information to be made public; publication of material in the *Federal Register*; maintenance of records; attendance and notification requirements for specific meetings and hearings; issuance of licenses; and review of agency actions.
American Antiquities Act of 1906	Provides penalties for unauthorized collection, excavation, or destruction of historic or prehistoric ruins, monuments, or objects of antiquity on lands owned or controlled by the United States. The Act authorizes the President to designate as national monuments objects or areas of historic or scientific interest on lands owned or controlled by the Unites States.
American Indian Religious Freedom Act of 1978	Protects the inherent right of Native Americans to believe, express, and exercise their traditional religions, including access to important sites, use and possession of sacred objects, and the freedom to worship through ceremonial and traditional rites.
Americans With Disabilities Act of 1990	Intended to prevent discrimination of and make American society more accessible to people with disabilities. The Act requires reasonable accommodations to be made in employment, public services, public accommodations, and telecommunications for persons with disabilities.
Anadromous Fish Conservation Act of 1965, as amended	Authorizes the Secretaries of Interior and Commerce to enter into cooperative agreements with states and other non-federal interests for conservation, development, and enhancement of anadromous fish and contribute up to 50 percent as the federal share of the cost of carrying out such agreements. Reclamation construction programs for water resource projects needed solely for such fish are also authorized.
Archaeological Resources Protection Act of 1979, as amended.	This Act strengthens and expands the protective provisions of the Antiquities Act of 1906 regarding archaeological resources. It also revised the permitting process for archaeological research.
Architectural Barriers Act of 1968	Requires that buildings and facilities designed, constructed, or altered with federal funds, or leased by a federal agency, must comply with standards for physical accessibility.
Bald and Golden Eagle Protection Act of 1940, as amended	Prohibits the possession, sale or transport of any bald or golden eagle, alive or dead, or part, nest, or egg except as permitted by the Secretary of the Interior for scientific or exhibition purposes, or for the religious purposes of Indians.

STATUE	DESCRIPTION
Bankhead-Jones Farm Tenant Act of 1937	Directs the Secretary of Agriculture to develop a program of land conservation and utilization in order to correct maladjustments in land use and thus assist in such things as control of soil erosion, reforestation, conservation of natural resources and protection of fish and wildlife. Some early refuges and hatcheries were established under authority of this Act.
Cave Resources Protection Act of 1988	Established requirements for the management and protection of caves and their resources on federal lands, including allowing the land managing agencies to withhold the location of caves from the public, and requiring permits for any removal or collecting activities in caves on federal lands.
Clean Air Act of 1970	Regulates air emissions from area, stationary, and mobile sources. This Act and its amendments charge federal land managers with direct responsibility to protect the "air quality and related values" of land under their control. These values include fish, wildlife, and their habitats.
Clean Water Act of 1974, as amended	This Act and its amendments have as its objective the restoration and maintenance of the chemical, physical, and biological integrity of the nation's waters. Section 401 of the Act requires that federally permitted activities comply with the Clean Water Act standards, state water quality laws, and any other appropriate state laws. Section 404 charges the U.S. Army Corps of Engineers with regulating discharge of dredge or fill materials into waters of the United States, including wetlands.
Coastal Barrier Resources Act of 1982 (CBRA)	Identifies undeveloped coastal barriers along the Atlantic and Gulf Coasts and included them in the John H. Chafee Coastal Barrier Resources System (CBRS). The objectives of the act are to minimize loss of human life, reduce wasteful federal expenditures, and minimize the damage to natural resources by restricting most federal expenditures that encourage development within the CBRS.
Coastal Barrier Improvement Act of 1990	Reauthorized the Coastal Barrier Resources Act (CBRA), expanded the CBRS to include undeveloped coastal barriers along the Great Lakes and in the Caribbean, and established "Otherwise Protected Areas (OPAs)." The Service is responsible for maintaining official maps, consulting with federal agencies that propose spending federal funds within the CBRS and OPAs, and making recommendations to Congress about proposed boundary revisions.
Coastal Wetlands Planning, Protection, and Restoration (1990)	Authorizes the Director of the Fish and Wildlife Service to participate in the development of a Louisiana coastal wetlands restoration program, participate in the development and oversight of a coastal wetlands conservation program, and lead in the implementation and administration of a national coastal wetlands grant program.

STATUE	DESCRIPTION
Coastal Zone Management Act of 1972, as amended	Established a voluntary national program within the Department of Commerce to encourage coastal states to develop and implement coastal zone management plans and requires that "any federal activity within or outside of the coastal zone that affects any land or water use or natural resource of the coastal zone" shall be "consistent to the maximum extent practicable with the enforceable policies" of a state's coastal zone management plan. The law includes an Enhancement Grants Program for protecting, restoring, or enhancing existing coastal wetlands or creating new coastal wetlands. It also established the National Estuarine Research Reserve System, guidelines for estuarine research, and financial assistance for land acquisition.
Emergency Wetlands Resources Act of 1986	This Act authorized the purchase of wetlands from Land and Water Conservation Fund moneys, removing a prior prohibition on such acquisitions. The Act requires the Secretary to establish a National Wetlands Priority Conservation Plan, required the states to include wetlands in their Comprehensive Outdoor Recreation Plans, and transfers to the Migratory Bird Conservation Fund amounts equal to import duties on arms and ammunition. It also established entrance fees at national wildlife refuges.
Endangered Species Act of 1973, as amended	Provides for the conservation of threatened and endangered species of fish, wildlife, and plants by federal action and by encouraging the establishment of state programs. It provides for the determination and listing of threatened and endangered species and the designation of critical habitats. Section 7 requires refuge managers to perform internal consultation before initiating projects that affect or may affect endangered species.
Environmental Education Act of 1990	This Act established the Office of Environmental Education within the U.S. Environmental Protection Agency to develop and administer a federal environmental education program in consultation with other federal natural resource management agencies, including the Fish and Wildlife Service.
Estuary Protection Act of 1968	Authorized the Secretary of the Interior, in cooperation with other federal agencies and the states, to study and inventory estuaries of the United States, including land and water of the Great Lakes, and to determine whether such areas should be acquired for protection. The Secretary is also required to encourage state and local governments to consider the importance of estuaries in their planning activities relative to federal natural resource grants. In approving any state grants for acquisition of estuaries, the Secretary was required to establish conditions to ensure the permanent protection of estuaries.

STATUE	DESCRIPTION
Estuaries and Clean Waters Act of 2000	This law creates a federal interagency council that includes the Director of the Fish and Wildlife Service, the Secretary of the Army for Civil Works, the Secretary of Agriculture, the Administrator of the Environmental Protection Agency and the Administrator for the National Oceanic and Atmospheric Administration. The council is charged with developing a national estuary habitat restoration strategy and providing grants to entities to restore and protect estuary habitat to promote the strategy.
Food Security Act of 1985, as amended (Farm Bill)	The Act contains several provisions that contribute to wetland conservation. The Swampbuster provisions state that farmers who convert wetlands for the purpose of planting after enactment of the law are ineligible for most farmer program subsidies. It also established the Wetland Reserve Program to restore and protect wetlands through easements and restoration of the functions and values of wetlands on such easement areas.
Farmland Protection Policy Act of 1981, as amended	The purpose of this law is to minimize the extent to which federal programs contribute to the unnecessary conversion of farmland to nonagricultural uses. Federal programs include construction projects and the management of federal lands.
Federal Advisory Committee Act (1972), as amended	Governs the establishment of and procedures for committees that provide advice to the federal government. Advisory committees may be established only if they will serve a necessary, nonduplicative function. Committees must be strictly advisory unless otherwise specified and meetings must be open to the public.
Federal Coal Leasing Amendment Act of 1976	Provided that nothing in the Mining Act, the Mineral Leasing Act, or the Mineral Leasing Act for Acquired Lands authorized mining coal on refuges.
Federal-Aid Highways Act of 1968	Established requirements for approval of federal highways through national wildlife refuges and other designated areas to preserve the natural beauty of such areas. The Secretary of Transportation is directed to consult with the Secretary of the Interior and other federal agencies before approving any program or project requiring the use of land under their jurisdiction.
Federal Noxious Weed Act of 1990, as amended	The Secretary of Agriculture was given the authority to designate plants as noxious weeds and to cooperate with other federal, state, and local agencies, farmers' associations, and private individuals in measures to control, eradicate, prevent, or retard the spread of such weeds. The Act requires each federal land-managing agency, including the Fish and Wildlife Service, to designate an office or person to coordinate a program to control such plants on the agency's land and implement cooperative agreements with the states, including integrated management systems to control undesirable plants.

STATUE	DESCRIPTION
Fish and Wildlife Act of 1956	Establishes a comprehensive national fish, shellfish, and wildlife resources policy with emphasis on the commercial fishing industry but also includes the inherent right of every citizen and resident to fish for pleasure, enjoyment, and betterment and to maintain and increase public opportunities for recreational use of fish and wildlife resources. Among other things, it authorizes the Secretary of the Interior to take such steps as may be required for the development, advancement, management, conservation, and protection of fish and wildlife resources including, but not limited to, research, development of existing facilities, and acquisition by purchase or exchange of land and water or interests therein.
Fish and Wildlife Conservation Act of 1980, as amended	Requires the Service to monitor non-gamebird species, identify species of management concern, and implement conservation measures to preclude the need for listing under the Endangered Species Act.
Fish and Wildlife Coordination Act of 1958	Promotes equal consideration and coordination of wildlife conservation with other water resource development programs by requiring consultation with the Fish and Wildlife Service and the state fish and wildlife agencies where the "waters of a stream or other body of water are proposed or authorized, permitted or licensed to be impounded, diverted…or otherwise controlled or modified" by any agency under federal permit or license.
Improvement Act of 1978	This Act was passed to improve the administration of fish and wildlife programs and amends several earlier laws, including the Refuge Recreation Act, the National Wildlife Refuge System Administration Act, and the Fish and Wildlife Act of 1956. It authorizes the Secretary to accept gifts and bequests of real and personal property on behalf of the United States. It also authorizes the use of volunteers on Service projects and appropriations to carry out volunteer programs.
Fishery (Magnuson) Conservation and Management Act of 1976	Established Regional Fishery Management Councils comprised of federal and state officials, including the Fish and Wildlife Service. It provides for regulation of foreign fishing and vessel fishing permits.
Freedom of Information Act, 1966	Requires all federal agencies to make available to the public for inspection and copying administrative staff manuals and staff instructions; official, published and unpublished policy statements; final orders deciding case adjudication; and other documents. Special exemptions have been reserved for nine categories of privileged material. The Act requires the party seeking the information to pay reasonable search and duplication costs.
Geothermal Steam Act of 1970, as amended	Authorizes and governs the lease of geothermal steam and related resources on public lands. Section 15 c of the Act prohibits issuing geothermal leases on virtually all Service-administrative lands.

STATUE	DESCRIPTION
Lacey Act of 1900, as amended	Originally designed to help states protect their native game animals and to safeguard U.S. crop production from harmful foreign species, this Act prohibits interstate and international transport and commerce of fish, wildlife or plants taken in violation of domestic or foreign laws. It regulates the introduction to America of foreign species.
Land and Water Conservation Fund Act of 1948	This Act provides funding through receipts from the sale of surplus federal land, appropriations from oil and gas receipts from the outer continental shelf, and other sources for land acquisition under several authorities. Appropriations from the fund may be used for matching grants to states for outdoor recreation projects and for land acquisition by various federal agencies, including the Fish and Wildlife Service.
Marine Mammal Protection Act of 1972, as amended	The 1972 Marine Mammal Protection Act established a federal responsibility to conserve marine mammals with management vested in the Department of the Interior for sea otter, walrus, polar bear, dugong, and manatee. The Department of Commerce is responsible for cetaceans and pinnipeds, other than the walrus. With certain specified exceptions, the Act establishes a moratorium on the taking and importation of marine mammals, as well as products taken from them.
Migratory Bird Conservation Act of 1929	Established a Migratory Bird Conservation Commission to approve areas recommended by the Secretary of the Interior for acquisition with Migratory Bird Conservation Funds. The role of the commission was expanded by the North American Wetland Conservation Act to include approving wetlands acquisition, restoration, and enhancement proposals recommended by the North American Wetlands Conservation Council.
Migratory Bird Hunting and Conservation Stamp Act of 1934	Also commonly referred to as the "Duck Stamp Act," requires waterfowl hunters 16 years of age or older to possess a valid federal hunting stamp. Receipts from the sale of the stamp are deposited into the Migratory Bird Conservation Fund for the acquisition of migratory bird refuges.
Migratory Bird Treaty Act of 1918, as amended	This Act implements various treaties and conventions between the United States and Canada, Japan, Mexico, and the former Soviet Union for the protection of migratory birds. Except as allowed by special regulations, this Act makes it unlawful to pursue, hunt, kill, capture, possess, buy, sell, purchase, barter, export or import any migratory bird, part, nest, egg, or product.
Mineral Leasing Act for Acquired Lands (1947), as amended	Authorizes and governs mineral leasing on acquired public lands.

STATUE	DESCRIPTION
Minerals Leasing Act of 1920, as amended	Authorizes and governs leasing of public lands for development of deposits of coal, oil, gas, and other hydrocarbons; sulphur; phosphate; potassium; and sodium. Section 185 of this title contains provisions relating to granting rights-of-way over federal lands for pipelines.
Mining Act of 1872, as amended	Authorizes and governs prospecting and mining for the so-called "hardrock" minerals (i.e., gold and silver) on public lands.
National and Community Service Act of 1990	Authorizes several programs to engage citizens of the U.S. in full- and/or part-time projects designed to combat illiteracy and poverty, provide job skills, enhance educational skills, and fulfill environmental needs. Among other things, this law establishes the American Conservation and Youth Service Corps to engage young adults in approved human and natural resource projects, which will benefit the public or are carried out on federal or Indian lands.
National Environmental Policy Act of 1969	Requires analysis, public comment, and reporting for environmental impacts of federal actions. It stipulates the factors to be considered in environmental impact statements, and requires that federal agencies employ an interdisciplinary approach in related decision-making and develop means to ensure that unqualified environmental values are given appropriate consideration, along with economic and technical considerations.
National Historic Preservation Act of 1966, as amended	It establishes a National Register of Historic Places and a program of matching grants for preservation of significant historical features. Federal agencies are directed to take into account the effects of their actions on items or sites listed or eligible for listing in the National Register.
National Trails System Act (1968), as amended	Established the National Trails System to protect the recreational, scenic, and historic values of some important trails. National recreation trails may be established by the Secretaries of Interior or Agriculture on land wholly or partly within their jurisdiction, with the consent of the involved state(s), and other land managing agencies, if any. National scenic and national historic trails may only be designated by Congress. Several national trails cross units of the National Wildlife Refuge System.
National Wildlife Refuge System Administration Act of 1966	Prior to 1966, there was no single federal law that governed the administration of the various national wildlife refuges that had been established. This Act defines the National Wildlife Refuge System and authorizes the Secretary of the Interior to permit any use of a refuge provided such use is compatible with the major purposes(s) for which the refuge was established.

STATUE	DESCRIPTION
National Wildlife Refuge System Improvement Act of 1997	This Act amends the National Wildlife Refuge System Administration Act of 1966. This Act defines the mission of the National Wildlife Refuge System, establishes the legitimacy and appropriateness of six priority wildlife-dependent public uses, establishes a formal process for determining compatible uses of Refuge System lands, identifies the Secretary of the Interior as responsible for managing and protecting the Refuge System, and requires the development of a comprehensive conservation plan for all refuges outside of Alaska.
Native American Graves Protection and Repatriation Act of 1990	Requires federal agencies and museums to inventory, determine ownership of, and repatriate certain cultural items and human remains under their control or possession. The Act also addresses the repatriation of cultural items inadvertently discovered by construction activities on lands managed by the agency.
Neotropical Migratory Bird Conservation Act of 2000	Establishes a matching grant program to fund projects that promote the conservation of neotropical migratory birds in the united States, Latin America, and the Caribbean.
North American Wetlands Conservation Act of 1989	Provides funding and administrative direction for implementation of the North American Waterfowl Management Plan and the Tripartite Agreement on wetlands between Canada, the United States, and Mexico. The North American Wetlands Conservation Council was created to recommend projects to be funded under the Act to the Migratory Bird Conservation Commission. Available funds may be expended for up to 50 percent of the United States' share cost of wetlands conservation projects in Canada, Mexico, or the United States (or 100 percent of the cost of projects on federal lands).
Refuge Recreation Act of 1962, as amended	This Act authorizes the Secretary of the Interior to administer refuges, hatcheries, and other conservation areas for recreational use, when such uses do not interfere with the area's primary purposes. It authorizes construction and maintenance of recreational facilities and the acquisition of land for incidental fish and wildlife-dependent recreational development or protection of natural resources. It also authorizes the charging of fees for public uses.
Partnerships for Wildlife Act of 1992	Establishes a Wildlife Conservation and Appreciation Fund to receive appropriated funds and donations from the National Fish and Wildlife Foundation and other private sources to assist the state fish and game agencies in carrying out their responsibilities for conservation of non-game species. The funding formula is no more that 1/3 federal funds, at least 1/3 foundation funds, and at least 1/3 state funds.

STATUE	DESCRIPTION
Refuge Revenue Sharing Act of 1935, as amended	Provided for payments to counties in lieu of taxes from areas administered by the Fish and Wildlife Service. Counties are required to pass payments along to other units of local government within the county, which suffer losses in tax revenues due to the establishment of Service areas.
Rehabilitation Act of 1973	Requires nondiscrimination in the employment practices of federal agencies of the executive branch and contractors. It also requires all federally assisted programs, services, and activities to be available to people with disabilities.
Rivers and Harbors Appropriations Act of 1899, as amended	Requires the authorization by the U.S. Army Corps of Engineers prior to any work in, on, over, or under a navigable water of the United States. The Fish and Wildlife Coordination Act provides authority for the Service to review and comment on the effects on fish and wildlife activities proposed to be undertaken or permitted by the Corps of Engineers. Service concerns include contaminated sediments associated with dredge or fill projects in navigable waters.
Sikes Act (1960), as amended	Provides for the cooperation by the Departments of Interior and Defense with state agencies in planning, development, and maintenance of fish and wildlife resources and outdoor recreation facilities on military reservations throughout the United States. It requires the Secretary of each military department to use trained professionals to manage the wildlife and fishery resources under his jurisdiction, and requires that federal and state fish and wildlife agencies be given priority in management of fish and wildlife activities on military reservations.
Transfer of Certain Real Property for Wildlife Conservation Purposes Act of 1948	This Act provides that upon determination by the Administrator of the General Services Administration, real property no longer needed by a federal agency can be transferred, without reimbursement, to the Secretary of the Interior if the land has particular value for migratory birds, or to a state agency for other wildlife conservation purposes.
Transportation Equity Act for the 21st Century (1998)	Established the Refuge Roads Program, requires transportation planning that includes public involvement, and provides funding for approved public use roads and trails and associated parking lots, comfort stations, and bicycle/pedestrian facilities.
Uniform Relocation and Assistance and Real Property Acquisition Policies Act (1970), as amended	Provides for uniform and equitable treatment of persons who sell their homes, businesses, or farms to the Service. The Act requires that any purchase offer be no less than the fair market value of the property.

STATUE	DESCRIPTION
Water Resources Planning Act of 1965	Established Water Resources Council to be composed of Cabinet representatives including the Secretary of the Interior. The Council reviews river basin plans with respect to agricultural, urban, energy, industrial, recreational and fish and wildlife needs. The act also established a grant program to assist States in participating in the development of related comprehensive water and land use plans.
Wild and Scenic Rivers Act of 1968, as amended	This Act selects certain rivers of the nation possessing remarkable scenic, recreational, geologic, fish and wildlife, historic, cultural, or other similar values; preserves them in a free-flowing condition; and protects their local environments.
Wilderness Act of 1964, as amended	This Act directs the Secretary of the Interior to review every roadless area of 5,000 acres or more and every roadless island regardless of size within the National Wildlife Refuge System and to recommend suitability of each such area. The Act permits certain activities within designated wilderness areas that do not alter natural processes. Wilderness values are preserved through a "minimum tool" management approach, which requires refuge managers to use the least intrusive methods, equipment, and facilities necessary for administering the areas.
Youth Conservation Corps Act of 1970	Established a permanent Youth Conservation Corps (YCC) program within the Departments of Interior and Agriculture. Within the Service, YCC participants perform many tasks on refuges, fish hatcheries, and research stations.

EXECUTIVE ORDERS	DESCRIPTIONS
EO 11593, Protection and Enhancement of the Cultural Environment (1971)	States that if the Service proposes any development activities that may affect the archaeological or historic sites, the Service will consult with Federal and State Historic Preservation Officers to comply with Section 106 of the National Historic Preservation Act of 1966, as amended.
EO 11644, Use of Off-road Vehicles on Public Land (1972)	Established policies and procedures to ensure that the use of off-road vehicles on public lands will be controlled and directed so as to protect the resources of those lands, to promote the safety of all users of those lands, and to minimize conflicts among the various uses of those lands.
EO 11988, Floodplain Management (1977)	The purpose of this Executive Order is to prevent federal agencies from contributing to the "adverse impacts associated with occupancy and modification of floodplains" and the "direct or indirect support of floodplain development." In the course of fulfilling their respective authorities, federal agencies "shall take action to reduce the risk of flood loss, to minimize the impact of floods on human safety, health and welfare, and to restore and preserve the natural and beneficial values served by floodplains."
EO 11989 (1977), Amends Section 2 of EO 11644	Directs agencies to close areas negatively impacted by off-road vehicles.
EO 11990, Protection of Wetlands (1977)	Federal agencies are directed to provide leadership and take action to minimize the destruction, loss of degradation of wetlands, and to preserve and enhance the natural and beneficial values of wetlands.
EO 12372, Intergovernmental Review of Federal Programs (1982)	Seeks to foster intergovernmental partnerships by requiring federal agencies to use the state process to determine and address concerns of state and local elected officials with proposed federal assistance and development programs.
EO 12898, Environmental Justice (1994)	Requires federal agencies to identify and address disproportionately high and adverse effects of its programs, policies, and activities on minority and low-income populations.

EXECUTIVE ORDERS	DESCRIPTIONS
EO 12906, Coordinating Geographical Data Acquisition and Access (1994), Amended by EO 13286 (2003). Amendment of EOs and other actions in connection with transfer of certain functions to Secretary of DHS.	Recommended that the executive branch develop, in cooperation with state, local, and tribal governments, and the private sector, a coordinated National Spatial Data Infrastructure to support public and private sector applications of geospatial data. Of particular importance to comprehensive conservation planning is the National Vegetation Classification System (NVCS), which is the adopted standard for vegetation mapping. Using NVCS facilitates the compilation of regional and national summaries, which in turn, can provide an ecosystem context for individual refuges.
EO 12962, Recreational Fisheries (1995)	Federal agencies are directed to improve the quantity, function, sustainable productivity, and distribution of U.S. aquatic resources for increased recreational fishing opportunities in cooperation with states and tribes.
EO 13007, Native American Religious Practices (1996)	Provides for access to, and ceremonial use of, Indian sacred sites on federal lands used by Indian religious practitioners and direction to avoid adversely affecting the physical integrity of such sites.
EO 13061, Federal Support of Community Efforts Along American Heritage Rivers (1997)	Established the American Heritage Rivers initiative for the purpose of natural resource and environmental protection, economic revitalization, and historic and cultural preservation. The Act directs federal agencies to preserve, protect, and restore rivers and their associated resources important to our history, culture, and natural heritage.
EO 13084, Consultation and Coordination With Indian Tribal Governments (2000)	Provides a mechanism for establishing regular and meaningful consultation and collaboration with tribal officials in the development of federal policies that have tribal implications.
EO 13112, Invasive Species (1999)	Federal agencies are directed to prevent the introduction of invasive species, detect and respond rapidly to and control populations of such species in a cost effective and environmentally sound manner, accurately monitor invasive species, provide for restoration of native species and habitat conditions, conduct research to prevent introductions, and to control invasive species, and promote public education on invasive species and the means to address them. This EO replaces and rescinds EO 11987, Exotic Organisms (1977).

EXECUTIVE ORDERS	DESCRIPTIONS
EO 13186, Responsibilities of Federal Agencies to Protect Migratory Birds. (2001)	Instructs federal agencies to conserve migratory birds by several means, including the incorporation of strategies and recommendations found in Partners in Flight Bird Conservation plans, the North American Waterfowl Plan, the North American Waterbird Conservation Plan, and the United States Shorebird Conservation Plan, into agency management plans and guidance documents.

Appendix D. Public Involvement

SUMMARY OF PUBLIC SCOPING COMMENTS

Public involvement and input into the development of the Draft CCP/EA was initiated by the submission of a notice of intent (NOI). The NOI summarizing the intent of the refuge to begin the CCP process was published in the *Federal Register* on May 16, 2007 (72 FR 27585). A public scoping meeting was held June 18, 2007, to allow stakeholders the opportunity for their concerns to be considered in the refuge's future management.

The team directed the process of obtaining public input through a June 18, 2007 public scoping meeting at the Resurrection of Our Lord Church conference room in New Orleans East, Louisiana. The meeting was announced in the Times Picayune newspaper, New Orleans edition. Flyers were also distributed in the area surrounding the meeting location. This meeting gave interested stakeholders the ability to ask questions and register their concerns. The 13 attendees submitted 16 different questions or public comments. Three additional comment letters were sent to the refuge during this process. The following comments were made during the public scoping phase of this plan:

Fish and Wildlife Habitat Management	• Better control of invasive species of plants to reduce clogging of canals and waterways. • Disguise City Recovery landfill. • Flush out salt water to encourage good emergent vegetation back. • Ban prescribed burning. • Control invasive and nuisance animals by trapping. • Do not build any additional roads. • Do not allow widening of the Maxent Canal.
Habitat Conservation	• Maintain and restore diverse habitats greatly compromised by Hurricane Katrina; especially focus on the restoration of the freshwater marsh and hardwood forest ridge. • When planting marsh grasses, expand to also include trees. • Do not use toxic chemicals on the refuge.
Visitor and Education Services	• Additional signage is needed to better navigate and provide public awareness of the refuge. Signage along Chef Highway, Highway 11 and I-10 as needed. • Provide a welcome center.

Visitor and Education Services (Cont'd)	• Allow hunting. • No hunting or trapping. • Develop a "pioneer swamp village" in the area of the boardwalk to demonstrate swamp life and for use as an educational tool.
Refuge Administration	• Additional law enforcement presence is needed to provide better security. • Litter and dumping are significant problems and need to be better addressed. • Expand the refuge to include Brazillier/St. Catherine's Island. • Cut back the bushes next to public access areas to deter theft. • Acquire a strip of land adjacent to the Maxent Canal as a buffer zone from the more industrialized surrounding area.

Appendix E. Appropriate Use Determinations

Bayou Sauvage National Wildlife Refuge Appropriate Use Determinations

An appropriate use determination is the initial decision process a refuge manager follows when first considering whether or not to allow a proposed use on a refuge. The refuge manager must find that a use is appropriate before undertaking a compatibility review of the use. This process clarifies and expands on the compatibility determination process by describing when refuge managers should deny a proposed use without determining compatibility. If a proposed use is not appropriate, it will not be allowed and a compatibility determination will not be undertaken.

Except for the uses noted below, the refuge manager must decide if a new or existing use is an appropriate refuge use. If an existing use is not appropriate, the refuge manager will eliminate or modify the use as expeditiously as practicable. If a new use is not appropriate, the refuge manager will deny the use without determining compatibility. Uses that have been administratively determined to be appropriate are:

- Six wildlife-dependent recreational uses - As defined by the National Wildlife Refuge System Improvement Act of 1997, the six wildlife-dependent recreational uses (hunting, fishing, wildlife observation, wildlife photography, and environmental education and interpretation) are determined to be appropriate. However, the refuge manager must still determine if these uses are compatible.

- Take of fish and wildlife under state regulations - States have regulations concerning take of wildlife that includes hunting, fishing, and trapping. The Service considers take of wildlife under such regulations appropriate. However, the refuge manager must determine if the activity is compatible before allowing it on a refuge.

Statutory Authorities for this policy:

National Wildlife Refuge System Administration Act of 1966, as amended by the National Wildlife Refuge System Improvement Act of 1997, 16 U.S.C. §668dd-668ee. This law provides the authority for establishing policies and regulations governing refuge uses, including the authority to prohibit certain harmful activities. The Act does not authorize any particular use, but rather authorizes the Secretary of the Interior to allow uses only when they are compatible and "under such regulations as he may prescribe." This law specifically identifies certain public uses that, when compatible, are legitimate and appropriate uses within the Refuge System. The law states ". . . it is the policy of the United States that . . .compatible wildlife-dependent recreation is a legitimate and appropriate general public use of the System . . .compatible wildlife-dependent recreational uses are the priority general public uses of the System and shall receive priority consideration in refuge planning and management; and . . . when the Secretary determines that a proposed wildlife-dependent recreational use is a compatible use within a refuge, that activity should be facilitated . . . the Secretary shall . . . ensure that priority general public uses of the System receive enhanced consideration over other general public uses in planning and management within the System . . . ." The law also states "in administering the System, the Secretary is authorized to take the following actions: . . . issue regulations to carry out this Act." This policy implements the standards set in the Act by providing enhanced consideration of priority general public uses and ensuring other public uses do not interfere with our ability to provide quality, wildlife-dependent recreational uses.

Refuge Recreation Act of 1962, 16 U.S.C. 460k. The Act authorizes the Secretary of the Interior to administer refuges, hatcheries, and other conservation areas for recreational use, when such uses do not interfere with the area's primary purposes. It authorizes construction and maintenance of recreational facilities and the acquisition of land for incidental fish and wildlife oriented recreational development or protection of natural resources. It also authorizes the charging of fees for public uses.

Other Statutes that Establish Refuges, including the Alaska National Interest Lands Conservation Act of 1980 (ANILCA) (16 U.S.C. §410hh - 410hh-5, 460 mm - 460mm-4, 539-539e, and 3101 - 3233; 43 U.S.C. 1631 et seq.).

Executive Orders. The Service must comply with Executive Order 11644 when allowing use of off-highway vehicles on refuges. This order requires the Service to designate areas as open or closed to off-highway vehicles in order to protect refuge resources, promote safety, and minimize conflict among the various refuge users; monitor the effects of these uses once they are allowed; and amend or rescind any area designation as necessary based on the information gathered. Furthermore, Executive Order 11989 requires the Service to close areas to off-highway vehicles when it is determined that the use causes or will cause considerable adverse effects on the soil, vegetation, wildlife, habitat, or cultural or historic resources. Statutes, such as ANILCA, take precedence over executive orders.

Definitions:

Appropriate Use
A proposed or existing use on a refuge that meets at least one of the following four conditions.

1) The use is a wildlife-dependent recreational use as identified in the Improvement Act.
2) The use contributes to fulfilling the refuge purpose(s), the Refuge System mission, or goals or objectives described in a refuge management plan approved after October 9, 1997, the date the Improvement Act was signed into law.
3) The use involves the take of fish and wildlife under state regulations.
4) The use has been found to be appropriate as specified in section 1.11.

Native American. American Indians in the conterminous United States and Alaska Natives (including Aleuts, Eskimos, and Indians) who are members of federally recognized tribes.

Priority General Public Use. A compatible wildlife-dependent recreational use of a refuge involving hunting, fishing, wildlife observation, wildlife photography, and environmental education and interpretation.

Quality. The criteria used to determine a quality recreational experience include:

- Promotes safety of participants, other visitors, and facilities.
- Promotes compliance with applicable laws and regulations and responsible behavior.
- Minimizes or eliminates conflicts with fish and wildlife population or habitat goals or objectives in a plan approved after 1997.
- Minimizes or eliminates conflicts with other compatible wildlife-dependent recreation.
- Minimizes conflicts with neighboring landowners.
- Promotes accessibility and availability to a broad spectrum of the American people.
- Promotes resource stewardship and conservation.

- Promotes public understanding and increases public appreciation of America's natural resources and the Service's role in managing and protecting these resources.
- Provides reliable/reasonable opportunities to experience wildlife.
- Uses facilities that are accessible and blend into the natural setting.
- Uses visitor satisfaction to help define and evaluate programs.

Wildlife-Dependent Recreational Use. As defined by the Improvement Act, a use of a refuge involving hunting, fishing, wildlife observation, wildlife photography, and environmental education and interpretation.

FINDING OF APPROPRIATENESS OF A REFUGE USE

Refuge Name: <u>Bayou Sauvage National Wildlife Refuge</u>

Use: <u>Bicycling</u>

This form is not required for wildlife-dependent recreational uses, take regulated by the State, or uses already described in a refuge CCP or step-down management plan approved after October 9, 1997.

Decision Criteria:	YES	NO
(a) Do we have jurisdiction over the use?	X	
(b) Does the use comply with applicable laws and regulations (Federal, State, tribal, and local)?	X	
(c) Is the use consistent with applicable executive orders and Department and Service policies?	X	
(d) Is the use consistent with public safety?	X	
(e) Is the use consistent with goals and objectives in an approved management plan or other document?	X	
(f) Has an earlier documented analysis not denied the use or is this the first time the use has been proposed?		X
(g) Is the use manageable within available budget and staff?	X	
(h) Will this be manageable in the future within existing resources?	X	
(i) Does the use contribute to the public's understanding and appreciation of the refuge's natural or cultural resources, or is the use beneficial to the refuge's natural or cultural resources?	X	
(j) Can the use be accommodated without impairing existing wildlife-dependent recreational uses or reducing the potential to provide quality (see section 1.6D, 603 FW 1, for description), compatible, wildlife-dependent recreation into the future?	X	

Where we do not have jurisdiction over the use ["no" to (a)], there is no need to evaluate it further as we cannot control the use. Uses that are illegal, inconsistent with existing policy, or unsafe ["no" to (b), (c), or (d)] may not be found appropriate. If the answer is "no" to any of the other questions above, we will **generally** not allow the use.

If indicated, the refuge manager has consulted with State fish and wildlife agencies.   Yes ___ No _X_

When the refuge manager finds the use appropriate based on sound professional judgment, the refuge manager must justify the use in writing on an attached sheet and obtain the refuge supervisor's concurrence.

Based on an overall assessment of these factors, my summary conclusion is that the proposed use is:

Not Appropriate____   Appropriate_X___

Refuge Manager:_____   Date:_____

If found to be **Not Appropriate**, the refuge supervisor does not need to sign concurrence if the use is a new use.
If an existing use is found **Not Appropriate** outside the CCP process, the refuge supervisor must sign concurrence.
If found to be **Appropriate**, the refuge supervisor must sign concurrence.

Refuge Supervisor:_____   Date:_____

A compatibility determination is required before the use may be allowed.

FINDING OF APPROPRIATENESS OF A REFUGE USE

Refuge Name: <u>Bayou Sauvage National Wildlife Refuge</u>

Use: <u>Camping</u>

This form is not required for wildlife-dependent recreational uses, take regulated by the State, or uses already described in a refuge CCP or step-down management plan approved after October 9, 1997.

Decision Criteria:	YES	NO
(a) Do we have jurisdiction over the use?	X	
(b) Does the use comply with applicable laws and regulations (Federal, State, tribal, and local)?	X	
(c) Is the use consistent with applicable executive orders and Department and Service policies?	X	
(d) Is the use consistent with public safety?	X	
(e) Is the use consistent with goals and objectives in an approved management plan or other document?		X
(f) Has an earlier documented analysis not denied the use or is this the first time the use has been proposed?		X
(g) Is the use manageable within available budget and staff?		X
(h) Will this be manageable in the future within existing resources?		X
(i) Does the use contribute to the public's understanding and appreciation of the refuge's natural or cultural resources, or is the use beneficial to the refuge's natural or cultural resources?		X
(j) Can the use be accommodated without impairing existing wildlife-dependent recreational uses or reducing the potential to provide quality (see section 1.6D, 603 FW 1, for description), compatible, wildlife-dependent recreation into the future?		X

Where we do not have jurisdiction over the use ["no" to (a)], there is no need to evaluate it further as we cannot control the use. Uses that are illegal, inconsistent with existing policy, or unsafe ["no" to (b), (c), or (d)] may not be found appropriate. If the answer is "no" to any of the other questions above, we will **generally** not allow the use.

If indicated, the refuge manager has consulted with State fish and wildlife agencies.   Yes ____ No _X_

When the refuge manager finds the use appropriate based on sound professional judgment, the refuge manager must justify the use in writing on an attached sheet and obtain the refuge supervisor's concurrence.

Based on an overall assessment of these factors, my summary conclusion is that the proposed use is:

Not Appropriate _X_   Appropriate ____

Refuge Manager:_____   Date:_____

If found to be **Not Appropriate**, the refuge supervisor does not need to sign concurrence if the use is a new use.
If an existing use is found **Not Appropriate** outside the CCP process, the refuge supervisor must sign concurrence.
If found to be **Appropriate**, the refuge supervisor must sign concurrence.

Refuge Supervisor:_____   Date:_____

A compatibility determination is required before the use may be allowed.

FINDING OF APPROPRIATENESS OF A REFUGE USE

Refuge Name: <u>Bayou Sauvage National Wildlife Refuge</u>

Use: <u>Forest Management</u>

This form is not required for wildlife-dependent recreational uses, take regulated by the State, or uses already described in a refuge CCP or step-down management plan approved after October 9, 1997.

Decision Criteria:	YES	NO
(a) Do we have jurisdiction over the use?	X	
(b) Does the use comply with applicable laws and regulations (Federal, State, tribal, and local)?	X	
(c) Is the use consistent with applicable executive orders and Department and Service policies?	X	
(d) Is the use consistent with public safety?	X	
(e) Is the use consistent with goals and objectives in an approved management plan or other document?	X	
(f) Has an earlier documented analysis not denied the use or is this the first time the use has been proposed?	X	
(g) Is the use manageable within available budget and staff?	X	
(h) Will this be manageable in the future within existing resources?	X	
(i) Does the use contribute to the public's understanding and appreciation of the refuge's natural or cultural resources, or is the use beneficial to the refuge's natural or cultural resources?	X	
(j) Can the use be accommodated without impairing existing wildlife-dependent recreational uses or reducing the potential to provide quality (see section 1.6D, 603 FW 1, for description), compatible, wildlife-dependent recreation into the future?	X	

Where we do not have jurisdiction over the use ["no" to (a)], there is no need to evaluate it further as we cannot control the use. Uses that are illegal, inconsistent with existing policy, or unsafe ["no" to (b), (c), or (d)] may not be found appropriate. If the answer is "no" to any of the other questions above, we will **generally** not allow the use.

If indicated, the refuge manager has consulted with State fish and wildlife agencies.   Yes ___ No _X_

When the refuge manager finds the use appropriate based on sound professional judgment, the refuge manager must justify the use in writing on an attached sheet and obtain the refuge supervisor's concurrence.

Based on an overall assessment of these factors, my summary conclusion is that the proposed use is:

    Not Appropriate____   **Appropriate** _X_

Refuge Manager:_____   Date:_____

If found to be **Not Appropriate**, the refuge supervisor does not need to sign concurrence if the use is a new use.
If an existing use is found **Not Appropriate** outside the CCP process, the refuge supervisor must sign concurrence.
If found to be **Appropriate**, the refuge supervisor must sign concurrence.

Refuge Supervisor:_____   Date:_____

A compatibility determination is required before the use may be allowed.

FINDING OF APPROPRIATENESS OF A REFUGE USE

Refuge Name: Bayou Sauvage National Wildlife Refuge

Use: Hunting

This form is not required for wildlife-dependent recreational uses, take regulated by the State, or uses already described in a refuge CCP or step-down management plan approved after October 9, 1997.

Decision Criteria:	YES	NO
(a) Do we have jurisdiction over the use?	X	
(b) Does the use comply with applicable laws and regulations (Federal, State, tribal, and local)?	X	
(c) Is the use consistent with applicable executive orders and Department and Service policies?	X	
(d) Is the use consistent with public safety?		X
(e) Is the use consistent with goals and objectives in an approved management plan or other document?		X
(f) Has an earlier documented analysis not denied the use or is this the first time the use has been proposed?		X
(g) Is the use manageable within available budget and staff?	X	
(h) Will this be manageable in the future within existing resources?	X	
(i) Does the use contribute to the public's understanding and appreciation of the refuge's natural or cultural resources, or is the use beneficial to the refuge's natural or cultural resources?		X
(j) Can the use be accommodated without impairing existing wildlife-dependent recreational uses or reducing the potential to provide quality (see section 1.6D, 603 FW 1, for description), compatible, wildlife-dependent recreation into the future?	X	

Where we do not have jurisdiction over the use ["no" to (a)], there is no need to evaluate it further as we cannot control the use. Uses that are illegal, inconsistent with existing policy, or unsafe ["no" to (b), (c), or (d)] may not be found appropriate. If the answer is "no" to any of the other questions above, we will **generally** not allow the use.

If indicated, the refuge manager has consulted with State fish and wildlife agencies.   Yes ___ No _X_

When the refuge manager finds the use appropriate based on sound professional judgment, the refuge manager must justify the use in writing on an attached sheet and obtain the refuge supervisor's concurrence.

Based on an overall assessment of these factors, my summary conclusion is that the proposed use is:

                Not Appropriate____   **Appropriate_X___**

Refuge Manager:_____   Date:_____

If found to be **Not Appropriate**, the refuge supervisor does not need to sign concurrence if the use is a new use.
If an existing use is found **Not Appropriate** outside the CCP process, the refuge supervisor must sign concurrence.
If found to be **Appropriate**, the refuge supervisor must sign concurrence.

Refuge Supervisor:_____   Date:_____

A compatibility determination is required before the use may be allowed.

FINDING OF APPROPRIATENESS OF A REFUGE USE

Refuge Name: Bayou Sauvage National Wildlife Refuge

Use: Mosquito Control

This form is not required for wildlife-dependent recreational uses, take regulated by the State, or uses already described in a refuge CCP or step-down management plan approved after October 9, 1997.

Decision Criteria:	YES	NO
(a) Do we have jurisdiction over the use?	X	
(b) Does the use comply with applicable laws and regulations (Federal, State, tribal, and local)?	X	
(c) Is the use consistent with applicable executive orders and Department and Service policies?	X	
(d) Is the use consistent with public safety?	X	
(e) Is the use consistent with goals and objectives in an approved management plan or other document?	X	
(f) Has an earlier documented analysis not denied the use or is this the first time the use has been proposed?	X	
(g) Is the use manageable within available budget and staff?	X	
(h) Will this be manageable in the future within existing resources?	X	
(i) Does the use contribute to the public's understanding and appreciation of the refuge's natural or cultural resources, or is the use beneficial to the refuge's natural or cultural resources?	X	
(j) Can the use be accommodated without impairing existing wildlife-dependent recreational uses or reducing the potential to provide quality (see section 1.6D, 603 FW 1, for description), compatible, wildlife-dependent recreation into the future?	X	

Where we do not have jurisdiction over the use ["no" to (a)], there is no need to evaluate it further as we cannot control the use. Uses that are illegal, inconsistent with existing policy, or unsafe ["no" to (b), (c), or (d)] may not be found appropriate. If the answer is "no" to any of the other questions above, we will **generally** not allow the use.

If indicated, the refuge manager has consulted with State fish and wildlife agencies.   **Yes** ___ **No** __X__

When the refuge manager finds the use appropriate based on sound professional judgment, the refuge manager must justify the use in writing on an attached sheet and obtain the refuge supervisor's concurrence.

Based on an overall assessment of these factors, my summary conclusion is that the proposed use is:

Not Appropriate____   **Appropriate** _X___

Refuge Manager:_____   Date:_____

If found to be **Not Appropriate**, the refuge supervisor does not need to sign concurrence if the use is a new use.
If an existing use is found **Not Appropriate** outside the CCP process, the refuge supervisor must sign concurrence.
If found to be **Appropriate**, the refuge supervisor must sign concurrence.

Refuge Supervisor:_____   Date:_____

A compatibility determination is required before the use may be allowed.

FINDING OF APPROPRIATENESS OF A REFUGE USE

Refuge Name: <u>Bayou Sauvage National Wildlife Refuge</u>

Use: <u>Trapping (feral hogs)</u>

This form is not required for wildlife-dependent recreational uses, take regulated by the State, or uses already described in a refuge CCP or step-down management plan approved after October 9, 1997.

Decision Criteria:	YES	NO
(a) Do we have jurisdiction over the use?	X	
(b) Does the use comply with applicable laws and regulations (Federal, State, tribal, and local)?	X	
(c) Is the use consistent with applicable executive orders and Department and Service policies?	X	
(d) Is the use consistent with public safety?	X	
(e) Is the use consistent with goals and objectives in an approved management plan or other document?	X	
(f) Has an earlier documented analysis not denied the use or is this the first time the use has been proposed?		X
(g) Is the use manageable within available budget and staff?	X	
(h) Will this be manageable in the future within existing resources?	X	
(i) Does the use contribute to the public's understanding and appreciation of the refuge's natural or cultural resources, or is the use beneficial to the refuge's natural or cultural resources?	X	
(j) Can the use be accommodated without impairing existing wildlife-dependent recreational uses or reducing the potential to provide quality (see section 1.6D, 603 FW 1, for description), compatible, wildlife-dependent recreation into the future?	X	

Where we do not have jurisdiction over the use ["no" to (a)], there is no need to evaluate it further as we cannot control the use. Uses that are illegal, inconsistent with existing policy, or unsafe ["no" to (b), (c), or (d)] may not be found appropriate. If the answer is "no" to any of the other questions above, we will **generally** not allow the use.

If indicated, the refuge manager has consulted with State fish and wildlife agencies.   Yes ___ No _X_

When the refuge manager finds the use appropriate based on sound professional judgment, the refuge manager must justify the use in writing on an attached sheet and obtain the refuge supervisor's concurrence.

Based on an overall assessment of these factors, my summary conclusion is that the proposed use is:

Not Appropriate____   **Appropriate _X___**

Refuge Manager:_____   Date:_____

If found to be **Not Appropriate**, the refuge supervisor does not need to sign concurrence if the use is a new use.
If an existing use is found **Not Appropriate** outside the CCP process, the refuge supervisor must sign concurrence.
If found to be **Appropriate**, the refuge supervisor must sign concurrence.

Refuge Supervisor:_____   Date:_____

A compatibility determination is required before the use may be allowed.

FINDING OF APPROPRIATENESS OF A REFUGE USE

Refuge Name: <u>Bayou Sauvage National Wildlife Refuge</u>

Use: <u>Trapping (nutria)</u>

This form is not required for wildlife-dependent recreational uses, take regulated by the State, or uses already described in a refuge CCP or step-down management plan approved after October 9, 1997.

Decision Criteria:	YES	NO
(a) Do we have jurisdiction over the use?	X	
(b) Does the use comply with applicable laws and regulations (Federal, State, tribal, and local)?	X	
(c) Is the use consistent with applicable executive orders and Department and Service policies?	X	
(d) Is the use consistent with public safety?	X	
(e) Is the use consistent with goals and objectives in an approved management plan or other document?	X	
(f) Has an earlier documented analysis not denied the use or is this the first time the use has been proposed?	X	
(g) Is the use manageable within available budget and staff?	X	
(h) Will this be manageable in the future within existing resources?	X	
(i) Does the use contribute to the public's understanding and appreciation of the refuge's natural or cultural resources, or is the use beneficial to the refuge's natural or cultural resources?	X	
(j) Can the use be accommodated without impairing existing wildlife-dependent recreational uses or reducing the potential to provide quality (see section 1.6D, 603 FW 1, for description), compatible, wildlife-dependent recreation into the future?	X	

Where we do not have jurisdiction over the use ["no" to (a)], there is no need to evaluate it further as we cannot control the use. Uses that are illegal, inconsistent with existing policy, or unsafe ["no" to (b), (c), or (d)] may not be found appropriate. If the answer is "no" to any of the other questions above, we will **generally** not allow the use.

If indicated, the refuge manager has consulted with State fish and wildlife agencies.   Yes ___ No _X_

When the refuge manager finds the use appropriate based on sound professional judgment, the refuge manager must justify the use in writing on an attached sheet and obtain the refuge supervisor's concurrence.

Based on an overall assessment of these factors, my summary conclusion is that the proposed use is:

        Not Appropriate____   **Appropriate** _X_

Refuge Manager:_____   Date:_____

If found to be **Not Appropriate**, the refuge supervisor does not need to sign concurrence if the use is a new use.
If an existing use is found **Not Appropriate** outside the CCP process, the refuge supervisor must sign concurrence.
If found to be **Appropriate**, the refuge supervisor must sign concurrence.

Refuge Supervisor:_____   Date:_____

A compatibility determination is required before the use may be allowed.

Appendix F. Compatibility Determinations

Bayou Sauvage National Wildlife Refuge Compatibility Determination

Uses: The following uses were considered for compatibility determination.

1. Wildlife observation/photography
2. Recreational fishing
3. Recreational hunting
4. Environmental education and interpretation
5. Bicycling
6. Trapping (nutria)
7. Trapping (feral hogs)
8. Forest management
9. Mosquito control

Refuge Name: Bayou Sauvage National Wildlife Refuge

Date Established: November 10, 1986

Establishing and Acquisition Authorites: Emergency Wetland Resources Act of 1986 (Public Law 99-645); North American Wetlands Conservation Act, 16 U.S.C. 4401 2(b):

Refuge Purpose:

- To enhance the populations of migratory, shore, and wading birds within the refuge.
- To encourage natural diversity of fish and wildlife species within the refuge.
- To protect the endangered and threatened species and otherwise to provide for the conservation and management of fish and wildlife within the refuge.
- To fulfill the international treaty obligations of the United States respecting fish and wildlife.
- To protect the archaeological resources of the refuge.
- To provide opportunities for fish and wildlife-dependent public uses and recreation in an urban setting.

National Wildlife Refuge System Mission:

The mission of the Refuge System, as defined by the National Wildlife Refuge System Improvement Act of 1997, is:

> *... to administer a national network of lands and waters for the conservation, management, and where appropriate, restoration of the fish, wildlife and plant resources and their habitats within the United States for the benefit of present and future generations of Americans.*

Other Applicable Laws, Regulations, and Policies:

Antiquities Act of 1906 (34 Stat. 225)
Migratory Bird Treaty Act of 1918 (15 U.S.C. 703-711; 40 Stat. 755)
Migratory Bird Conservation Act of 1929 (16 U.S.C. 715r; 45 Stat. 1222)
Migratory Bird Hunting Stamp Act of 1934 (16 U.S.C. 718-178h; 48 Stat. 451)
Criminal Code Provisions of 1940 (18 U.S.C. 41)
Bald and Golden Eagle Protection Act (16 U.S.C. 668-668d; 54 Stat. 250)
Refuge Trespass Act of June 25, 1948 (18 U.S.C. 41; 62 Stat. 686)
Fish and Wildlife Act of 1956 (16 U.S.C. 742a-742j; 70 Stat.1119)
Refuge Recreation Act of 1962 (16 U.S.C. 460k-460k-4; 76 Stat. 653)
Wilderness Act (16 U.S.C. 1131; 78 Stat. 890)
Land and Water Conservation Fund Act of 1965
National Historic Preservation Act of 1966, as amended (16 U.S.C. 470, et seq.; 80 Stat. 915)
National Wildlife Refuge System Administration Act of 1966 (16 U.S.C. 668dd, 668ee; 80 Stat. 927)
National Environmental Policy Act of 1969, NEPA (42 U.S.C. 4321, et seq; 83 Stat. 852)
Use of Off-Road Vehicles on Public Lands (Executive Order 11644, as amended by Executive Order 10989)
Endangered Species Act of 1973 (16 U.S.C. 1531 et seq; 87 Stat. 884)
Refuge Revenue Sharing Act of 1935, as amended in 1978 (16 U.S.C. 715s; 92 Stat. 1319)
National Wildlife Refuge Regulations for the Most Recent Fiscal Year (50 CFR Subchapter C; 43 CFR 3101.3-3)
Emergency Wetlands Resources Act of 1986 (S.B. 740)
North American Wetlands Conservation Act of 1990
Food Security Act (Farm Bill) of 1990 as amended (HR 2100)
The Property Clause of the U.S. Constitution Article IV 3, Clause 2
The Commerce Clause of the U.S. Constitution Article 1, Section 8
The National Wildlife Refuge System Improvement Act of 1997 (Public Law 105-57, USC668dd)
Executive Order 12996, Management and General Public Use of the National Wildlife Refuge System. March 25, 1996
Title 50, Code of Federal Regulations, Parts 25-33
Archaeological Resources Protection Act of 1979
Native American Graves Protection and Repatriation Act of 1990

Compatibility determinations for each description listed were considered separately. Although for brevity, the preceding sections from "Uses" through "Other Applicable Laws, Regulations and Policies" and the succeeding sections, "Literature Cited," "Public Review," and the "Approval of Compatibility Determinations" are only written once within the CCP, they are part of each descriptive use and become part of that compatibility determination if considered outside of the CCP.

Description of Use: Wildlife observation/photography

Wildlife observation and photography have been identified in the National Wildlife Refuge System Improvement Act of 1997 as priority wildlife-dependent recreational uses provided they are compatible with the purpose for which the refuge was established.

Wildlife photography, including other image-capturing activities, such as videography, has occurred on the refuge. There are no blinds or platforms on the refuge specifically for photography and none are proposed at this time. However, opportunities exist for photography on the refuge. Commercial photography or videography, if allowed, would require a special use permit by the refuge and would include specific restrictions. Often, the public offers copies of exceptional pictures for refuge use in publications and reports.

The general public could participate in wildlife observation and photography year-round from sunrise to sunset on the refuge. Wildlife observation and photography could be accomplished while driving or walking on refuge roads open to public vehicular traffic. Also, these public uses could be enjoyed while walking on trails or by boating.

Availability of Resources: The refuge would incur the cost of boardwalk and trail maintenance. Administrative costs would occur for issuance of a special use permit in the case of commercial photography or videography, and staff time to conduct compliance checks.

Anticipated Impacts of the Use: Activities associated with wildlife observation and both commercial and personal photography have shown no measurable environmental impacts to the refuge, its habitats, or wildlife species. The use can cause temporary minor disturbance to wildlife. However, use is expected to remain at levels causing only random, limited, and temporary disturbance. Any malicious or unreasonable harassment of wildlife would be grounds for the manager to restrict the uses.

Photography can increase visitors' knowledge and appreciation of fish and wildlife and their habitats on the refuge, and lead to greater understanding of the Refuge System's public stewardship mission. Quality photographs taken on refuge lands and provided to the staff can enhance the refuge's outreach and public use programs.

Public Review and Comment: This compatibility determination is provided for public review and comment during the Draft CCP/EA review process.

Determination (check one below):

_____ Use is Not Compatible

__X__ Use is Compatible with Following Stipulations

Stipulations Necessary to Ensure Compatibility:

- All wildlife observation and photography activities would be conducted with the refuge's primary objectives, habitat management requirements, and goals as the guiding principles.
- Modes and times of uses would be limited to legal means and times according to refuge regulations on access available to the general public.

- All commercial photographers must have a special use permit that specifies access stipulations to prevent excessive disturbance to wildlife, damage to habitat, or conflicts with other public uses or management activities. The special use permit would stipulate that imagery produced on refuge lands be made available to the refuge for use in outreach, interpretation, internal documents, or other suitable uses.
- The commercial photography use must demonstrate a means to extend public appreciation and understanding of wildlife, natural habitats, enhance education, appreciation and/or understating of the Refuge System, or further outreach and education goals of the refuge.
- Commercial products must include appropriate credits to the refuge and to the Fish and Wildlife Service.

Justification: Wildlife observation and photography are priority public uses on Refuge System lands as identified in the National Wildlife Refuge System Improvement Act of 1997. By facilitating these uses on the refuge, we will increase visitors' knowledge and appreciation of fish, wildlife, and their habitats, which will lead to increased public stewardship. Increased stewardship supports and complements the refuge's purposes and the mission of the Refuge System.

NEPA Compliance for Refuge Use Description: *Place an X in appropriate space.*

_____ Categorical Exclusion without Environmental Action Statement
_____ Categorical Exclusion and Environmental Action Statement
__X__ Environmental Assessment and Finding of No Significant Impact
_____ Environmental Impact Statement and Record of Decision

Mandatory 15-year Re-evaluation Date:

Description of Use: Recreational fishing

Fishing was a traditional recreational use of the land and waters prior to their inclusion in the Refuge System and continues to be a popular recreational pursuit. Fishing is a wildlife-dependent recreational pursuit and has been identified in the National Wildlife Refuge System Improvement Act of 1997 as a priority public use, provided it is compatible with the purpose for which the refuge was established. Fishing is permitted year-round in all refuge waters subject to regulations established by the Louisiana Department of Wildlife and Fisheries, the general regulations governing fishing on national wildlife refuges set forth in the Code of Federal Regulations and the refuge fishing permit. Fishing is permitted to provide fishable waters to the public and to utilize a sustainable natural resource.

Availability of Resources: Funding for the fishing program is borne by annual operation and maintenance funds. Costs include permit printing, administration, maintenance of boat ramps and docks, and monitoring the activity.

Anticipated Impacts of the Use: Minor, short-term impacts to the environment from recreational fishing include litter and the possible contamination of refuge waters from oil and gas leaking from boat motors. Because the fish population is a sustainable natural resource and local fish habitat is vast, no long-term impacts are expected.

Public Review and Comment: This compatibility determination is provided for public review and comment during the Draft CCP/EA review process.

Determination (check one below):

_____ Use is Not Compatible

__X__ Use is Compatible with Following Stipulations

Stipulations Necessary to Ensure Compatibility:

- All sport fishing activities, including permitted methods of take, limits, species, and open/closed seasons, would be consistent with applicable state and refuge regulations. Enforcement efforts would be conducted by refuge law enforcement officers and agents from the Louisiana Department of Wildlife and Fisheries.
- Commercial fishing, limb lines, trotlines, slat traps, nets, gar sets, and jug fishing are prohibited.
- Sport fishing, crawfishing, and crabbing are permitted only during daylight hours.
- Only outboard motors, 25 horsepower or less, are permitted in waterways inside the hurricane protection levee.

Justification: The National Wildlife Refuge System Improvement Act of 1997 identified fishing as one of the priority public uses on national wildlife refuges, where compatible with refuge purposes. This use is legitimate and appropriate, and is dependent upon healthy fish populations. Offering recreational fishing is in compliance with refuge goals, is a management objective for Bayou Sauvage NWR, and furthers the goals and missions of the Refuge System.

NEPA Compliance for Refuge Use Description: *Place an X in appropriate space.*

_____ Categorical Exclusion without Environmental Action Statement
_____ Categorical Exclusion and Environmental Action Statement
__X__ Environmental Assessment and Finding of No Significant Impact
_____ Environmental Impact Statement and Record of Decision

Mandatory 15-year Re-evaluation Date:

Description of Use: Recreational hunting

Recreational hunting, a wildlife-dependent activity, has been identified in the National Wildlife Refuge System Improvement Act of 1997 as a priority public use, provided it is compatible with the purpose for which the refuge was established. This management use is identified in the Comprehensive Conservation Plan under the Visitor Services Goal.

The refuge has never been opened to hunting but a youth waterfowl hunt on a portion of the refuge is recommended to provide needed recreational opportunities to local youth.

Availability of Resources: Funding for the hunt program is supported by annual operation and maintenance funds. Costs will include permit printing, administration, monitoring, law enforcement and maintaining safe access points.

Anticipated Impacts of the Use: While managed hunting opportunities result in both short- and long-term impacts to individual animals, effects at the population level are usually negligible. Migratory bird regulations are established at the national level each year and harvest guidelines are based on population surveys and habitat conditions. The refuge hunting program will be within these regulations. As currently proposed the known and anticipated levels of disturbance by allowing waterfowl hunting are considered minimal and well within the tolerance of known populations present on the refuge. Monitoring activities will be utilized and public use programs will be adjusted as needed to maintain habitat, wildlife populations and quality public use programs.

Public Review and Comment: This compatibility determination is provided for public review and comment during the Draft CCP/EA review process.

Determination (check one below):

_____ Use is Not Compatible

___X__ Use is compatible with following Stipulations

Stipulations Necessary to Ensure Compatibility:
   a. A Station Hunt Plan and Environmental Assessment will be developed.
   b. Hunting seasons for the refuge are established annually.
   c. Hunters will be required to possess a signed refuge hunting permit.

Justification: The National Wildlife Refuge System Improvement Act of 1997 identified hunting as one of the priority public uses on national wildlife refuges, where compatible with refuge purposes. Offering recreational youth waterfowl hunting is appropriate and furthers the goals and mission of the National Wildlife Refuge System.

NEPA Compliance for Refuge Use Description: Place an X in appropriate space.
   _____ Categorical Exclusion without Environmental Action Statement
   _____ Categorical Exclusion and Environmental Action Statement
   __X_ Environmental Assessment and Finding of No Significant Impact
   _____ Environmental Impact Statement and Record of Decision

Mandatory 15-year Re-evaluation Date:

Description of Use: Environmental education and interpretation

Environmental education and interpretation have been identified in the National Wildlife Refuge System Improvement Act of 1997 as priority public uses, provided they are compatible with the purpose for which the refuge was established. Environmental education and interpretation consist of public outreach and onsite activities conducted by refuge staff, volunteers, teachers, Friends Group members, conservation partners, university professors, and others. Most activities occur during daylight hours, with exceptions for night events such as owl and bat viewing, and tours using light from a full moon. Activities include educational programs and teacher workshops carried out on nature trails, canoe trips, and at refuge observation towers, refuge areas of interest, and other areas suitable for teaching environmental science. Interpretation occurs when information is explained for the public by refuge staff or others using exhibits, displays, signs, kiosks, facilities, and brochures. Refuge facilities and lands may be used as outdoor classrooms by groups of students with a teacher and a formalized plan of environmental study, by members of organizations, or by other members of the public with approval of the refuge manager.

Environmental education and interpretation activities can occur throughout the year and are conducted with the refuge's primary goals, objectives, and habitat management requirements as the guiding principles. Activities conducted under these restrictions allow the refuge to accomplish its management goals and also provide for the safety of visitors.

Environmental education and interpretation are utilized to encourage understanding in citizens of all ages to develop land ethics, foster public support, increase visibility of the Refuge System, and improve the public's knowledge of the Service.

Availability of Resources: Funding for these activities is with annual operation and maintenance funds. Existing facilities exist at Bayou Sauvage Ridge Trail, Joe Madere Marsh Unit, Wayside Park and Highway 11 boat launch area.

Anticipated Impacts of the Use: Minimal impacts are expected, such as temporary disturbance to wildlife species and possibly some trampling of vegetation in the immediate vicinity of the activity. Most activities would take place on existing roads, trails, and facilities with no additional disturbance. Environmental education and interpretation activities are not expected to indirectly or cumulatively negatively impact refuge resources.

Public Review and Comment: This compatibility determination is provided for public review and comment during the Draft Comprehensive Conservation Plan comment period.

Determination (check one below):

_____ Use is Not Compatible

__X__ Use is Compatible with Following Stipulations

Stipulations Necessary to Ensure Compatibility:

- Adequate precautions would be taken to ensure that permanent facilities are sited an adequate distance from sensitive wildlife areas.
- Evaluations of sites and programs would be conducted periodically to assess if objectives are being met and that natural resources are not being degraded.

Justification: The National Wildlife Refuge System Improvement Act of 1997 identified environmental education and interpretation as priority public uses on national wildlife refuges, where compatible with refuge purposes. Offering environmental education and interpretation is in compliance with refuge goals, is a management objective for Bayou Sauvage NWR, and furthers the goals and missions of the Refuge

System. Environmental education and interpretation encourage understanding of ecological and biological principles and refuge-specific issues, and develop support for refuges.

NEPA Compliance for Refuge Use Description: *Place an X in appropriate space.*

_____ Categorical Exclusion without Environmental Action Statement
_____ Categorical Exclusion and Environmental Action Statement
___X___ Environmental Assessment and Finding of No Significant Impact
_____ Environmental Impact Statement and Record of Decision

Mandatory 15-year Re-evaluation Date:

Description of Use: Bicycling

Bicycling is not a priority public use designated by the National Wildlife Refuge System Improvement Act of 1997; however, it can occur on the refuge provided it is compatible with the purpose for which the refuge was established. Requests to ride bicycles on refuge roads not open to public vehicular traffic have been made. These requests have been made associated with wildlife-dependent recreational uses, such as photography, and wildlife/wildland observation. The only areas available for bike riding are the Maxent Levee and the hurricane protection levee that encircles most of the refuge.

Availability of Resources: Funding for this program would be from annual operation and maintenance funds, but little to no cost is associated with this activity. No special equipment, facilities, or improvements are necessary to support the use.

Anticipated Impacts of the Use: Since only non-motorized bicycles would be allowed on two dirt and gravel refuge trails, little disturbance to wildlife and habitat would occur. As long as bike riders are courteous, no conflict should occur between hikers, who can also access these trails.

Public Review and Comment: This compatibility determination is provided for public review and comment during the Draft CCP/EA review process.

Determination (check one below):

____ Use is Not Compatible

__x__ Use is Compatible with Following Stipulations

Stipulation Necessary to Ensure Compatibility:

- Bicycling is only allowed on Maxent Levee and the Citrus Levee during daylight hours.

Justification: At the present level, few bicyclists use the designated biking areas. The trails are primarily used for photography, birding, and wildlife observation. Bicycling is not detrimental to the environment if only allowed on these two dirt and gravel trails that are closed to motorized vehicles, and requires no added expenses to regulate. This use is in compliance with the CCP and furthers the goals and missions of the Refuge System and Bayou Sauvage NWR.

NEPA Compliance for Refuge Use Description: *Place an X in appropriate space.*

_____ Categorical Exclusion without Environmental Action Statement
_____ Categorical Exclusion and Environmental Action Statement
__X__ Environmental Assessment and Finding of No Significant Impact
_____ Environmental Impact Statement and Record of Decision

Mandatory 10-year Re-evaluation Date:

Description of Use: Trapping (nutria)

Trapping is employed to prevent or reduce habitat damage and targets nutria, an exotic species native to South America, which was imported for fur farms in the early 1900s. When the fur farming industry collapsed after World War II, many were released or were not recaptured after escaping. The descendents established themselves in the marshes and have adapted well to the semi-aquatic environment. Since nutria are almost exclusively vegetarians, and can eat 2.5 to 3.5 pounds of food daily, they can be very detrimental to marsh vegetation. Their burrows can also damage levees and banks. They are in direct competition with the native muskrat for habitat and resources. Trapping nutria would be allowed under special use permits that designate locations and methods for their removal. Trappers are encouraged to participate in the Coastwide Nutria Control Program, which is administered by the Louisiana Department of Wildlife and Fisheries.

Availability of Resources: Funding for these activities would be with annual operation and maintenance funds and consists of administration. Equipment and maintenance costs associated with trapping activities would be carried out by the trapper.

Anticipated Impacts of the Use: The special use permit system allows the refuge manager to specifically regulate locations and methods for nutria removal. Areas would be well marked and traps would not be set in areas with high use by visitors. Disturbance to non-target wildlife would be occasional, temporary, and isolated to small geographic areas. Positive impacts would be the control of an exotic species and less damage to refuge resources.

Public Review and Comment: This compatibility determination is provided for public review and comment during the Draft CCP/EA review process.

Determination (check one below):

_____ Use is Not Compatible

__X__ Use is Compatible with Following Stipulations

Stipulations Necessary to Ensure Compatibility:

- Trapping would be conducted in compliance with a special use permit.
- Trapping would not be allowed in high-use public areas.
- Take of non-target animals would be minimized by trap set and locations.
- A trapping report would be required of the individual named in the special use permit.
- All traps must be well marked and checked daily.

Justification: Trapping is a valuable management tool that is used to prevent and reduce damage to refuge habitat by nutria. With the above stipulations, little to no adverse effects to other refuge programs or wildlife species would occur. This use is in compliance with the CCP and furthers the goals and missions of the Refuge System and the refuge.

NEPA Compliance for Refuge Use Description: *Place an X in appropriate space.*

_____ Categorical Exclusion without Environmental Action Statement
_____ Categorical Exclusion and Environmental Action Statement
__X__ Environmental Assessment and Finding of No Significant Impact
_____ Environmental Impact Statement and Record of Decision

Mandatory 10-year Re-evaluation Date:

Description of Use: Trapping (feral hog)

Trapping is employed to prevent or reduce habitat damage and targets feral hogs, an exotic species native to Europe. Boars (a type of wild pig) are not native to North America. They were brought here from Europe, first by the Spanish explorers in the 1500s (for food) and later in the 1900s by people who wanted to hunt the pigs for sport. The wild boars you see today are the great grandchildren which were imported in the 1960s. In the autumn, they eat forest foods like acorns, hickory nuts, and pecans. During the rest of the year, boars eat berries, carrion, roots, tubers, refuse, fruits, insects, mushrooms, bugs, eggs, small reptiles--even young deer or dead animals. If there is plenty of food, the boars will stay in a 10-square-mile territory. They really dig up the ground while looking for roots. Boars have tough noses, or snouts, which help them dig. They have an excellent sense of smell and can sniff out underground foods. When they dig up the ground for roots, they kill many native plants. When they wallow near the edge of a pond or canal, they tear up the water plants. This causes the soil to wash away (erosion) because the plant roots cannot hold onto the dirt anymore, they can be very detrimental to the levee system. Their burrows can damage levees and banks. Boars have very few natural predators. Trapping feral hogs would be allowed under special use permits that designate locations and methods for their removal.

Availability of Resources: Funding for these activities would be with annual operation and maintenance funds and consists of administration. Equipment and maintenance costs associated with trapping activities would be carried out by the trapper.

Anticipated Impacts of the Use: The special use permit system allows the refuge manager to specifically regulate locations and methods for feral hog removal. Areas would be well marked and traps would not be set in areas with high use by visitors. Disturbance to non-target wildlife would be occasional, temporary, and isolated to small geographic areas. Positive impacts would be the control of an exotic species and less damage to refuge resources.

Public Review and Comment: This compatibility determination is provided for public review and comment during the Draft CCP/EA review process.

Determination (check one below):

_____ Use is Not Compatible

__X__ Use is Compatible with Following Stipulations

Stipulations Necessary to Ensure Compatibility:

- Trapping would be conducted in compliance with a special use permit.
- Trapping would not be allowed in high-use public areas.
- Take of non-target animals would be minimized by trap set and locations.
- A trapping report would be required of the individual named in the special use permit.
- All traps must be well marked and checked daily.

Justification: Trapping is a valuable management tool that is used to prevent and reduce damage to refuge habitat by feral hogs. With the above stipulations, little to no adverse effects to other refuge programs or wildlife species would occur. This use is in compliance with the CCP and furthers the goals and missions of the Refuge System and the refuge.

NEPA Compliance for Refuge Use Description: *Place an X in appropriate space.*

_____ Categorical Exclusion without Environmental Action Statement
_____ Categorical Exclusion and Environmental Action Statement
__X__ Environmental Assessment and Finding of No Significant Impact
_____ Environmental Impact Statement and Record of Decision

Mandatory 10-year Re-evaluation Date:

Description of Use: Forest management

The proposed forest management for Bayou Sauvage NWR is to eradicate non-native species, such as Chinese tallow, and reforest with native species, such as live oak, red maple, sweetgum, red bay, green ashe and dwarf palmetto; to provide quality habitat and forage for native wildlife species in the hardwood stands; to compile information on the refuge hardwood forests, such as species, age, size, condition, and soil moisture; and to promote a refuge landscape more reminiscent of the historic forest complex by facilitating the regeneration of mixed hardwood forests on the higher elevations and cypress/hardwood forests on the lower elevations.

Availability of Resources: Funding for these activities would be through annual operation and maintenance funds and would consist predominantly of administration and monitoring. Equipment and maintenance costs associated contracted activities would be carried out through federal funds for invasive species control.

Anticipated Impacts of the Use: Forest management operations can cause adverse impacts on habitat values and water quality if not carefully controlled and supervised. Restrictions and conditions, such as only operating in dry conditions, creating buffers along waterways, and minimizing damage to residual trees, must be placed on operations to minimize adverse effects from equipment. Minor, short-term impacts from using equipment, such as disturbance to wildlife and trampling of understory vegetation, are expected to occur. In the long-term, forest conditions after management treatments would be more beneficial to wildlife by restoring the functions and values necessary to meet their needs.

Public Review and Comment: This compatibility determination is provided for public review and comment during the Draft CCP/EA review process.

Determination (check one below):

_____ Use is Not Compatible

__X__ Use is Compatible with Following Stipulations

Stipulations Necessary to Ensure Compatibility: Forest management operations may be conducted throughout the year, but only according to the guidelines detailed in a Habitat Management Plan or the special conditions section of the special use permit.

Justification: The forest management actions, proposed in the CCP, are in accordance with Service guidelines for the protection, management, and enhancement of habitats for wildlife populations on refuges. The Habitat Management Plan, a step-down plan, details how forest management actions promote the enhancement of habitats for threatened or endangered species, migratory birds, and resident wildlife species; promote habitat restoration; protect cultural resources; and provide opportunities for public recreation and environmental education. This use furthers the goals and missions of the Refuge System and Bayou Suavage NWR.

NEPA Compliance for Refuge Use Description: *Place an X in appropriate space.*

_____ Categorical Exclusion without Environmental Action Statement
_____ Categorical Exclusion and Environmental Action Statement
__X___ Environmental Assessment and Finding of No Significant Impact
_____ Environmental Impact Statement and Record of Decision

Mandatory 10-year Re-evaluation Date:

Description of Use: Mosquito control

The New Orleans Mosquito and Termite Control Board proposes the use of biological larvicides and chemical adulticides for the abatement and/or control of mosquito populations on Bayou Sauvage NWR.

The refuge encompasses a variety of habitats along the south shore of Lake Pontchartrain, which contains potential mosquito breeding sites. The marsh and forested wetland areas of the refuge are considered by the Board to be significant in both the potential production of mosquitoes and control of mosquito populations before they spread to adjacent urban areas. The species of mosquitoes found within the refuge include several species known or suspected to be important biological vectors of arthropod borne diseases, specifically St. Louis encephalitis, eastern equine encephalitis, West Nile virus, and LaCrosse encephalitis. Dengue fever, another mosquito transmitted disease, also poses a potential health threat. St. Louis, eastern equine, and LaCrosse encephalitis, and West Nile virus have been documented in Orleans Parish. In 2002, a major human outbreak of West Nile virus occurred in Louisiana, resulting in 329 cases and 29 deaths.

The location, habitats, and climate of the refuge all contribute to the potential need for control of mosquito populations. Factors contributing to this need include the sub-tropical location in southeast Louisiana, large amounts of rainfall throughout the year (an average of 63 inches), susceptibility to major rain events associated with hurricanes and other tropical storm systems, a long warm/hot growing season, abundant vegetation, and wetland habitats. Adding to this is the large number of mosquito species present, including known disease vector species.

The New Orleans Mosquito and Termite Control Board may propose a low volume application of pesticide, when warranted, for the control of adult mosquitoes. The application would be near or on the refuge and may be added to the refuge in the future. The Board would spray at night, which maximizes potential for exposure to mosquitoes by the insecticide since they are most active aerially at night. This also minimizes exposure by diurnal insects and wildlife. The Board would have to submit an environmental assessment before approval of these actions could take place.

Availability of Resources: Costs to the refuge for this use would include administrative overhead to issue and monitor pesticide use proposals, special use permits, and other requirements supported by annual operation and maintenance funds. This use would result in a need for refuge staff to periodically inspect spray operations, review and maintain records of treatment history, and conduct wildlife assessments and monitoring. The refuge would not supply equipment or facilities for these operations, but would expend funds for salaries dealing with administrative overhead. Unanticipated costs associated with the administration of this use could require a re-evaluation.

Anticipated Impacts of the Use: The New Orleans Mosquito and Termite Control Board has not conducted mosquito control activities in this location prior to acquisition by the refuge or for emergency control of mosquito populations after acquisition. According to EPA's risk assessment, the use of Naled for mosquito control does not exceed the Agency's level of concern for human health, mammals, and plants. If new labeling restrictions or additional risk assessment information become available, they would be incorporated into the re-evaluation of this use.

Public Review and Comment: This compatibility determination is provided for public review and comment during the Draft CCP/EA review process.

Determination (check one below):

_____ Use is Not Compatible

_X_ Use is Compatible with Following Stipulations

Stipulations Necessary to Ensure Compatibility: Use of any pesticide must be approved by the Fish and Wildlife Service's Division of Environmental Contaminants in the Washington Office, and any special conditions would be made a part of a special use permit and pesticide use permit.

Justification: Given the refuge's proximity to an urban area, the human health threat demonstrated in the Board's area of operation, and the dense mosquito populations of southeast Louisiana, the Service recognizes the need of mosquito population control on Bayou Sauvage NWR. The treatment would be permitted in order to reduce the occurrences of mosquito borne diseases in proximity to the refuge.

NEPA Compliance for Refuge Use Description: *Place an X in appropriate space.*

_____ Categorical Exclusion without Environmental Action Statement
_____ Categorical Exclusion and Environmental Action Statement
_X_ Environmental Assessment and Finding of No Significant Impact
_____ Environmental Impact Statement and Record of Decision

Mandatory 10-year Re-evaluation Date:

Approval of Compatibility Determinations

The signature of approval is for all compatibility determinations considered within the Comprehensive Conservation Plan for Bayou Sauvage National Wildlife Refuge. If one of the descriptive uses is considered for compatibility outside of the comprehensive conservation plan, the approval signature becomes part of that determination.

Refuge Manager: _____
                                              (Signature/Date)

Regional Compatibility
Coordinator: _____
                                              (Signature/Date)

Refuge Supervisor: _____
                                              (Signature/Date)

Regional Chief, National
Wildlife Refuge System,
Southeast Region: _____
                                              (Signature/Date)

Appendix G. Intra-Service Section 7 Biological Evaluation

Originating Person: Ken Litzenberger, Project Leader
Telephone Number: 985-882-2000
E-Mail: Kenneth_Litzenberger@FWS.GOV
Date: March 5, 2007

Project Name: Bayou Sauvage National Wildlife Refuge Comprehensive Conservation Plan

I.   **Service Program:**
_____ **Ecological Services**
_____ **Federal Aid**
_____ **Clean Vessel Act**
_____ **Coastal Wetlands**
_____ **Endangered Species Section 6**
_____ **Partners for Fish and Wildlife**
_____ **Sport Fish Restoration**
_____ **Wildlife Restoration**
_____ **Fisheries**
__X__ **Refuges/Wildlife**

II.   **State/Agency:** Louisiana/U.S. Fish and Wildlife Service

III.   **Station Name:** Bayou Sauvage National Wildlife Refuge

IV.   **Description of Proposed Action (attach additional pages as needed):** Implementation of the Comprehensive Conservation Plan for Bayou Sauvage National Wildlife Refuge by adopting the proposed alternative, which provides guidance, management direction, and operation plans for 15 years.

V.   **Pertinent Species and Habitat:**

   A.   **Include species/habitat occurrence map**

Bald eagles occur adjacent to the refuge from fall until early summer, and usually nest within adjacent lands. The nest is constructed in tall tallow trees along the tree line, which abruptly changes to marsh surrounding Lake Pontchartrain, their feeding grounds.

Waters of the refuge are within the designated critical habitat for the Gulf sturgeon. Research has shown that juveniles and subadults use Lake Pontchartrain as wintering habitat.

Although none of the species breeds in the area, brown pelicans are commonly seen feeding in refuge waters and an occasional West Indian manatee is sighted during the summer.

B: Complete the following table:

SPECIES/CRITICAL HABITAT	STATUS[1]
Bald eagle	T (now de-listed)
Gulf sturgeon	T
Brown pelican	E
West Indian manatee	E

[1]STATUS: E=endangered, T=threatened, PE=proposed endangered, PT=proposed threatened, CH=critical habitat, PCH=proposed critical habitat, C=candidate species, S/A=Similar Appearance

VI.   **Location (attach map):** Map Attached

A.   **Ecoregion Number and Name:** No. 27, Lower Mississippi River

B.   **County and State:** Orleans Parish, LA

Section, township, and range (or latitude and longitude): The area is located in section 37, township 11 south, ranges 13 and 14 east.

Distance (miles) and direction to nearest town: Inside the city limits of New Orleans

E.   **Species/habitat occurrence:**

Bald eagles occur on the refuge during winter months and nest in the tree line bordering the marshes of Lake Pontchartrain.

Gulf sturgeon winter in Lake Pontchartrain, brown pelicans use the refuge waters year-round as a feeding area, and West Indian manatees are occasionally sighted in Lake Pontchartrain and canals in the summer.

VII.   **Determination of Effects:**

Explanation of effects of the action on species and critical habitats in item V. B:

SPECIES/ CRITICAL HABITAT	IMPACTS TO SPECIES/CRITICAL HABITAT
Bald eagle	No negative impacts; provide habitat protection
Gulf sturgeon	No negative impacts; provide habitat protection
Brown pelican	No negative impacts; provide habitat protection
West Indian manatee	No negative impacts; provide habitat protection

B. Explanation of actions to be implemented to reduce adverse effects:

SPECIES/ CRITICAL HABITAT	ACTIONS TO MITIGATE/MINIMIZE IMPACTS
Bald eagle	Monitor nesting, provide protection, and provide more suitable habitat in growing urban environment.
Gulf sturgeon	Continue to monitor for occurrence and any problems.
Brown pelican	Continue to monitor.
West Indian manatee	Monitor and report any problems.

VIII. Effect Determination and Response Requested:

SPECIES/CRITICAL HABITAT	DETERMINATION[1]			REQUESTED
	NE	NA	AA	
Bald eagle		X		Concurrence
Gulf sturgeon		X		Concurrence
Brown pelican		X		Concurrence
West Indian manatee		X		Concurrence

[1]DETERMINATION/ RESPONSE REQUESTED:

NE = no effect. This determination is appropriate when the proposed action will not directly, indirectly, or cumulatively impact, either positively or negatively, any listed, proposed, candidate species or designated/proposed critical habitat. Response Requested is optional but a "Concurrence" is recommended for a complete Administrative Record.

NA = not likely to adversely affect. This determination is appropriate when the proposed action is not likely to adversely impact any listed, proposed, candidate species or designated/proposed critical habitat or there may be beneficial effects to these resources. Response Requested is a" Concurrence".

AA = likely to adversely affect. This determination is appropriate when the proposed action is likely to adversely impact any listed, proposed, candidate species or designated/proposed critical habitat. Response Requested for listed species is "Formal Consultation". Response requested for proposed and candidate species is "Conference".

_____   _____
Signature (originating station)   **Date**

_____
Title

IX.   Reviewing Ecological Services Office Evaluation:

A. Concurrence _____   Nonconcurrence _____

B. Formal consultation required _____

C. Conference required _____

D. Informal conference required _____

    E. Remarks (attach additional pages as needed):

_____   _____
Signature   Date

_____   _____
      Title   Office

Appendix H. Wilderness Review

The Wilderness Act of 1964 defines a wilderness area as an area of federal land that retains its primeval character and influence, without permanent improvements or human inhabitation, and is managed so as to preserve its natural conditions and which:

1. generally appears to have been influenced primarily by the forces of nature, with the imprint of man's work substantially unnoticeable;

2. has outstanding opportunities for solitude or primitive and unconfined types of recreation;

3. has at least 5,000 contiguous roadless acres or is of sufficient size to make practicable its preservation and use in an unimpeded condition; or is a roadless island, regardless of size;

4. does not substantially exhibit the effects of logging, farming, grazing, or other extensive development or alteration of the landscape, or its wilderness character could be restored through appropriate management at the time of review; and

5. may contain ecological, geological, or other features of scientific, educational, scenic, or historic value.

The lands within Bayou Sauvage National Wildlife Refuge were reviewed for their suitability in meeting the criteria for wilderness, as defined by the Wilderness Act of 1964. No lands in the refuge were found to meet these criteria. Therefore, the suitability of refuge lands for wilderness designation is not further analyzed in this plan.

Appendix I. Refuge Biota

Species of concern and/or significance for management purposes occurring Bayou Sauvage National Wildlife Refuge are listed below. For a complete list of birds found on the refuge, contact refuge headquarters for a bird list.

<u>Common Name</u>	<u>Scientific Name</u>
Birds	
Bald Eagle	*Haliaeetus leucocephalus*
Eastern Brown Pelican	*Pelecanus occidentalis carolinensis*
Wood Duck	*Aix sponsa*
Mottled Duck	*Anas fulvigula*
Blue-winged Teal	*Anas discors*
Northern Pintail	*Anas acuta*
Black-bellied Whistling Duck	*Dendrocygna autumnalis*
King Rail	*Rallus elegans*
Clapper Rail	*Rallus longirostris*
Purple Gallinule	*Porphyrio porphyrio*
Common Moorhen	*Porphyrio martinica*
Great Blue Heron	*Ardea herodias*
Great Egret	*Ardea alba*
Green Heron	*Butorides virescens*
Louisiana or Tricolored Heron	*Egretta tricolor*
Black-necked Stilt	*Himantopus mexicanus*
Least Bittern	*Ixobrychus exilis*
Sora Rail	*Ortygometra carolinus*
Virginia Rail	*Rallus virginianus*
Little Blue Heron	*Egretta caerulea*
White Ibis	*Eudocimus albus*
Yellow-billed Cuckoo	*Coccyzus americanus*
Acadian Flycatcher	*Empidonax virescens*
Prothonotary Warbler	*Protonotaria citrea*
Glossy Ibis	*Plegadis falcinellus*
White-faced Ibis	*Plegadis chihi*
Common Yellowthroat	*Geothlypis trichas*
Mammals	
Nutria	*Myocastor coypus*
Feral Hogs	*Sus scrofa*
Reptiles and Amphibians	
American Alligator	*Alligator missisippiensis*
Alligator Snapping Turtle	*Macrochelys temminckii*
Canebrake Rattlesnake	*Crotalus horridus*
Gulf Coast Box Turtle	*Terrapene carolina major*

Fish and Shellfish

Alligator Gar	*Atractosteus spatula*
Largemouth Bass	*Micropterus salmoides*
Bream sp.	*Lepomis spp.*
Crawfish sp.	*Procambarus spp.*
Blue Crab	*Callinectes sapidus*

Plant Communities

Fresh Marsh
Intermediate Marsh
Submergent Vascular Vegetation
Bottomland Hardwoods

Appendix J. Budget Requests

REFUGE OPERATING NEEDS SYSTEM (RONS)

RONS PROJECT NAME	PROJECT NUMBER	AMOUNT
Enhance Preventive Law Enforcement Program (Law Enforcement Officer)	97016	$139,000
Restore Wading Bird Rookery	99027	$302,000
Control Invasive Tree Species	97024	$103,000
Acquisition Of Digital Aerial Photography	00020	$50,000
Develop and Monitor Habitat Restoration and Wildlife Programs (Wildlife Biologist)	00010	$133,000
Provide Student Intern	97031	$33,000
Production of Bayou Sauvage NWR Video	98021	$25,000
Conduct Waterfowl Surveys of Populations and Habitat Use	00017	$25,000
Effects of Feral Hogs on Vegetation, Reptile and Amphibian Communities	03001	$25,000
Develop Curriculum Based Education Programs for 7[h] and 8th Graders	03006	$44,000
Use Coir Logs for Shoreline Stabilization	04003	$176,000
Placement of Cribbing for Marsh Protection/Restoration	04001	$56,000
Terracing and Vegetative Planting	04002	$176,000
Vegetation Planting of Emergent Marsh	04004	$167,000

MAINTENANCE MANAGEMENT SYSTEM NEEDS

SAMMS PROJECT NAME	WORK ORDER NUMBER	COST
Replace Worn Verticle Pump In Unit Three	00102355	$428,991.00
Replace Worn Verticle Pump Unit Four	00102357	$428,991.00
Replace Worn Diesel Engine For Pumps Three and Four	04136735	$428,991.00
Repair Water Control Structure In Unit Five	2006473301	$35,355.00
Replace Failed Water Control Structure For Units Two And Three	2007716225	$33,744.00
Rehabilitate Gravel Road To Pump Station Five	04136901	$127,217.00

Appendix K. List of Preparers

PLANNING TEAM

Kenneth Litzenberger, Project Leader, Fish and Wildlife Service, Southeast Louisiana National Wildlife Refuge Complex – Editor; provided overall guidance and oversight

Pon Dixson, Deputy Project Leader, Fish and Wildlife Service, Southeast Louisiana National Wildlife Refuge Complex – Editor; Provided guidance

Jack Bohannan, Refuge Manager, Fish and Wildlife Service, Southeast Louisiana National Wildlife Refuge Complex – Writer and Editor

Charlotte Parker, Former Natural Resource Planner, Fish and Wildlife Service, Southeast Louisiana National Wildlife Refuge Complex – Planning Team Leader, Writer and Editor

James Harris, Supervisory Wildlife Biologist, Fish and Wildlife Service, Southeast Louisiana National Wildlife Refuge Complex – Writer and Editor

Shelley Stiaes, Refuge Operations Specialist, Fish and Wildlife Service, Southeast Louisiana National Wildlife Refuge Complex – Writer and Editor

Byron Fortier, Supervisory Park Ranger, Fish and Wildlife Service, Southeast Louisiana National Wildlife Refuge Complex – Writer and Editor

Diane Barth, Park Ranger, Fish and Wildlife Service, Southeast Louisiana National Wildlife Refuge Complex – Editor

Chevales Williams, Environmental Engineer, Tennessee Valley Authority – Contracting Writer, Editor, Plan and NEPA Coordinator

CONTRIBUTORS

Pre-planning for this Draft CCP/EA began in 2007, with a review of the biological and visitor services programs for Bayou Sauvage NWR by several state and federal biologists, university researchers, and personnel from other refuges. Recommendations from these meetings were used during the development of this Draft CCP/EA. Contributors included:

Todd Baker, Area Manager, Pass a Loutre, LDWF, Baton Rouge, LA

Jennifer Coulson, President, New Orleans Audubon Society, New Orleans, LA

Heather Egger, Research Associate I, UNO Pontchartrain Institute for Environmental Sciences, New Orleans, LA

Sue Grace, Fire Ecologist, Fish and Wildlife Service, Southeast Louisiana National Wildlife Refuge Complex

Michele Hubert, Friends of Louisiana Refuges, Inc.

Amy LeGaux, former Education Curator, Audubon Louisiana Nature Center, New Orleans, LA

Brian Lezina, Marine Fisheries Division, LDWF, Baton Rouge, LA

Shawn Markus, Geographic Analyst, Geographic Information and Engineering, TVA, Chattanooga, TN

Dinah Maygarden, Coastal Wetlands Education Program Manager, UNO Pontchartrain Institute for Environmental Sciences, New Orleans, LA

David Muth, Chief of Resource Management, National Park Service

Bob Strader, Migratory Bird Biologist, Fish and Wildlife Service, Jackson, MS

Marie Tizzard, Biology and Environmental Science Teacher, Grace King High School, Metairie, LA

Garry Tucker, Chief, Visitor Services and Outreach, Fish and Wildlife Service, Atlanta, GA